FROM APHRA BEHN TO
FUN HOME

FROM APHRA BEHN TO *FUN HOME*

A Cultural History of Feminist Theater

Carey Purcell

ROWMAN & LITTLEFIELD
Lanham • Boulder • New York • London

Published by Rowman & Littlefield
An imprint of The Rowman & Littlefield Publishing Group, Inc.
4501 Forbes Boulevard, Suite 200, Lanham, Maryland 20706
www.rowman.com

86-90 Paul Street, London EC2A 4NE

British Library Cataloguing in Publication Information Available

Library of Congress Control Number: 2019949308

ISBN: 978-1-5381-1525-1 (cloth : alk. paper)
ISBN: 978-1-5381-9885-8 (pbk : alk. paper)
ISBN: 978-1-5381-1526-8 (ebook)

∞™ The paper used in this publication meets the minimum requirements of
American National Standard for Information Sciences—Permanence of Paper
for Printed Library Materials, ANSI/NISO Z39.48-1992.

CONTENTS

Introduction   vii

1 Off Stage   1
2 Fighting the Female Wit   15
3 The Groundbreaking Work of Hellman and Hansberry   33
4 Revolting Women   51
5 Voices, New and NOW   81
6 Winning Awards for Doing a "Man's Job"   107
7 A Wicked Wave of Feminist Theater   137
8 Broadway Comes to the *Fun Home*   171
9 Revivals Eclipsed by Milestones   199
10 Critical Progress?   227

Notes   241
Index   287
About the Author   291

INTRODUCTION

I wrote my first play, *Uncommon Women and Others*, in the hopes of seeing an all-female curtain call in the basement of the Yale School of Drama. A man in the audience stood up during a postshow discussion and announced, "I can't get into this, it's all about girls." I thought to myself, "Well, I've been getting into *Hamlet* and *Laurence of Arabia* my whole life, so you better start trying."—Wendy Wasserstein[1]

The relationship between feminism and theater is complicated, to say the least. The performing arts has long been considered a feminine interest for which women consistently purchase the majority of theater tickets while the shows they are seeing typically are written and brought to the stage by men. Not only are these shows overwhelmingly by men, the stories they tell are often about men and the complex leading roles in these shows are written for and performed by male actors.

The definition of feminism itself, and feminist theater, differs from person to person and has evolved throughout the years. Is a work of theater feminist simply if it is written by a woman? Or if it features strong female characters who pass the Bechdel test—the shockingly simple evaluation that asks whether a work of fiction features at least two women who talk to one another about something other than a man? Is it feminist if the story and cast are all white, or does feminism automatically include intersectionality? How much inherent privilege should be taken into account when considering what stories to tell and who should tell them?

I will not attempt to answer these questions. To do so would be impossible, nor should it be attempted by one single, privileged person. But I will explore how and why feminism has or has not been represented by the theater by examining the roles women have played onstage and behind the scenes and the political, economic, and cultural conditions that have shaped these representations. I will also celebrate the remarkable accomplishments feminism has brought about throughout the years and how cultural attitudes are and are not changing. Lastly, I will attempt to illustrate how the arts have suffered from a lack of parity and explain why women, female-identifying, trans, and nonbinary artists, need to be seen and heard.

Merriam-Webster defines feminism as the "theory of the political, economic, and social equality of the sexes." It sounds so simple. While the dictionary doesn't include a definition for feminist theater, newspapers, magazines, and websites regularly feature articles about the subject. One could thus infer that feminist theater is theater that promotes and supports "political, economic, and social equality of the sexes."

But what supports equality? Do only new, original works by women fit the bill? Or can revivals that educate the audience in the suppression of women throughout history also be considered feminist? Sophie Treadwell's play *Machinal* candidly portrays a woman so desperate to escape the confines of her life that she murders her husband—who she married only because she was expected to and foresaw no other options. Inspired by the life of Ruth Snyder, who was executed for her crime, the drama was first produced in 1928, but it was seen on Broadway again until 2014. Directed by Lindsey Turner and starring Rebecca Hall, the revival provided a stark depiction of how miserable the young woman's life was and how fiercely she longed for and needed more fulfillment—an intimate and unfiltered look at a time period in which contemporary audiences may not have otherwise been educated.

Telling stories onstage has long been a form of activism, but for centuries those stories were told only by men. To the ancient Greeks and Romans, public speaking was considered an exclusively masculine skill. Even Penelope, a strategic and calculating female character in *The Odyssey*, is ordered by her son to "go back up into your quarters, and take up your own work, the loom and the distaff . . . speech will be the business of men, all men, and of me most of all; for mine is the power in this household."

While writing this book, I spoke with many people in the industry, listening to their thoughts on feminism in theater and their personal involvement in the industry. The more people I spoke with, the clearer it became that there is no one, or even few, definitions or meanings of feminist theater.

While looking forward, feminist theater involves an examination of the past. Jennifer Ashley Tepper, a Broadway producer and author of *The Untold Stories of Broadway*, said,

> Feminist theater is any show that asserts women deserve an equal amount of space at the table. As a theater historian, I have come to discover that so many of our most prolific and successful female writers never receive revivals the way their male counterparts do. Rachel Crothers had twenty-eight Broadway productions as a writer produced in her lifetime, but where are her revivals? At the same time as we look to produce more new work by female writers, we have to ask: Why aren't we elevating what women of the past had to say? Is it because they are not given ample space in the history books so that their legacy becomes apparent? Is it because the world these women experienced and thus present in their work has changed, so we feel their words are now irrelevant or outdated? Feminist theater is partially dependent on a more careful examination of what our foremothers had to say.[2]

It has to be a supportive movement. Said Wendy Goldberg, director and artistic director of the Eugene O'Neill Theater Center's National Playwright Conference,

> As a woman coming up in the field, the only support I received early on was from other fearless women who knew how difficult this path would be. Once established, slightly more men stepped up in my life as allies and supporters. I did learn early on that in order to facilitate change I would have to achieve status to hire women, to mentor women, and to effect change. I think if we all do our part to move the needle toward more equitable practices, we'd be in a much better place—but it takes egoless leadership, accountability, and a true awareness and desire to change.[3]

Feminist theater should be as expansive as possible. According to Pooya Mohseni, actor, writer, filmmaker, and activist:

> I see it as a modern, fresh point of view. It's from women's point of view. A lot of stories are written by women, so I think it has a different point of view than stories that have for the most part have been written

by men and how they're directed and put together. I personally am never a fan of things that exclude other people. . . . I'm more interested in stories that bring different people from different walks of life and experiences and backgrounds *together*. This creates threads of connection between people who otherwise wouldn't cross paths. I personally think that is the kind of theater that I like. . . . While I hold true to the fact that everyone has the right to express themselves as they wish, especially any form of performance and entertainment—I'm not a fan of preaching just to the choir. Because I think the value of theater, entertainment in general—one part of it is to hold up a mirror to society, on the other side is showing possibilities of what society can be like. So if what people mean by feminist theater that it is only exclusive to not just women, but a particular category of women, then that goes into what I consider to be exclusionary theater, and that is not what I gravitate towards.[4]

Inclusivity is imperative. Said writer and composer Teresa Lotz,

One time I found out that I was not given an opportunity because my work was "too feminist." Since it was "too feminist," the judges thought it wouldn't resonate with a larger audience. I beg to differ—women make up *more* than half of theater audiences. We define the trends of theater. We make the majority of ticketing decisions. These are statistical facts—and yet there is still this stigma against work that appeals to women and trans/GNC folk.

In recent years I have become very passionate about intersectionality and forwarding opportunities for not just cis-gender women, but also trans and gender nonconforming people. To fight the patriarchy and change the landscape of theater, we need *all* of us. . . . In my own work, I seek to break down stereotypes and stigmas. I want to introduce audiences to cis-gender and trans/gender-nonconforming characters that challenge the tropes we always see. I want to create female antiheroes (where are these???). I want to capture complex and full queer relationships on stage—lesbians that aren't just "the token lesbian couple." It's crucial that we humanize women's perspectives, and through theater I believe we can change the world.[5]

Activism has to extend beyond the stage. According to Rachel Spencer-Hewitt, actress and founder of the Parent-Artist Advocacy League,

We must recognize parenting and elder care as significant obstacles to many individuals' path to career sustainability and leadership trajectory. We do not make theater in a vacuum. Our craft and the contributors who are available to participate are both product of and response to socio-economic realities of our communities. Statistics around the world, including those gathered in the United States, continue to show that the majority of individuals providing for the majority of caregiving responsibilities are women. These statistics directly impact multiple factors, including delayed parity, the gender wage gap, workforce retention, and upward mobility in employment. We cannot have intersectional parity, feminist spaces, or progressive theater without recognizing childcare as a point of access and shaping our spaces and infrastructures to accommodate pregnant bodies, caregiver lifestyles, and the reality of major life events—such as birth, miscarriage, adoption, foster care, and IVF needs and benefits, to name a few. The future of our craft is accessible inclusion of all people, and that includes access for those who care for others.[6]

Intersectionality and representation are integral. Playwright Winter Miller said,

Feminist theater is, like any other art or intellectual pursuit or behavior, not feminist because its creator considers themself a feminist, but because the work itself holds as a value that the sexes are equal in stature, that women have been denied our rightful places based on patriarchal assumptions about what is women's and men's work. Audiences are unlikely to encounter truly feminist work that uplifts, celebrates, critiques, and discusses powerful women *not* made by a feminist, but to try to rate a play based on its level of feminism is probably in the mind of the beholder. Feminism is contextual—it's related to historical eras and those customs, and it's also intersectional, we're looking at how does a feminist work relate to race, sexuality, gender, ethnicity, class, ability, etc. Something that is perceived as feminist that doesn't take into account the experiences of a wide swath of women and centralizes the narrative or experiences of white, cis-gender female, heterosexual experience, and ignores the rest of us, is not, in my mind feminist—or rather, it may be intentioned to be feminist but doesn't go far enough in being inclusive.

Since feminism was coined, it has been a euphemism for the goals and triumphs of straight white women, so until we scrub the word of that narrow association, it's important to remind audiences that feminism is for anyone who believes that we all deserve equal rights, equal access to opportunities, equal pay for equal work, and control over our own bodies and intellectual property. It's never occurred to me to hold feminist theater as a category, in place of, say, theater for everyone, but I certainly would take pride in being considered a writer or an artist who makes feminist work.[7]

Feminist theater involves breaking free from traditional structures. Mfoniso Udofia, playwright, said the following:

> For me, for theater to become more feminist, we must not only produce theater written from a woman's gaze, we must also teach and stage theater structured by a feminine energy. Most of the theater we laud in the West is written on a traditional bell curve: exposition, rising action, climax, falling action, denouement. That structure is inherently masculine. There are, however, structures where characters do not race towards a culmination. There is an infinite amount of ways one can structure a play. Theater could potentially become more feminist the moment we hold different frameworks of storytelling.[8]

Advocacy has to translate into new opportunities. Said actress Donna Lynne Champlin,

> Feminist theater means equal opportunities for all genders to create new works and to participate across the board. As actors, playwrights, directors, conductors, musical directors, choreographers, producers, stage managers, artistic directors, etc., who are not white males, it's not enough that we create our own content and stories from our points of view. We also deserve to have equal opportunities to be funded, supported, and given viable platforms to showcase that content and tell our stories. I believe that the more we amplify underrepresented voices in theater, the more we will be able to define our own generation of creatives instead of the (bewildering) tendency to keep reviving old shows that had their time and reflected their own (less progressive) societal norms.
>
> Besides most revivals being written and conceived by men in a very nonfeminist time period, modern actresses are given a much more difficult task of trying to soften or skew misogynistic material that we just don't find quaint anymore. Why do we choose to retread and reenergize these old *Mad Men*–esque chestnuts when that money and that theater could be used to amplify a new feminist voice that is

speaking to things happening now. . . . I would like to see theaters and producers make conscious choices to produce (and, if they have to, revive) productions that are at least equal between genders. Maybe instead of reviving *1776* for the millionth time, you choose to do *Nine*. Or *Quilters*. Or do *1776* but with nineteen women and two men. There has to be a conscious choice with the people *behind* the table to even things up a bit. . . .

That's really the crux of it for me. Feminism, in any aspect, implies equality (with a positive byproduct of favoring new voices instead of retreading old outdated, mostly white male, ones). An equal ratio of parts, shows, stories, scores, productions, grants, etc., that's the goal. And as a woman in theater I really don't ask for more than that. But when you start really looking at the bigger picture of theater in regards to being feminist or "equal"? We have a shockingly long way to go.[9]

Representation has to be universal. Playwright Gina Gionfriddo once said,

When I was coming up as a young playwright, there really was this problem of how plays with female protagonists were perceived. In general, a play about a male protagonist was recognized (by critics, by theaters) as a universally human journey, whereas plays with female protagonists were considered stories about women, which is to say not universal. I do feel that this is changing, and I am heartened to see many, many more women's plays being produced. . . . I would like to think that our greater opportunity is correlated to evolving consciousness. . . . But let's focus on the good news, which is that I've seen major leaps forward over the last twenty years.[10]

It's about changing the status quo and supporting the next generation. Georgia Stitt, composer/lyricist and founding director of Maestra Music, said the following:

My way into theater has always been through music. I knew I was a musician before I knew I was a theater artist. I was one of the many young girls who took piano lessons, and I grew up to be one of the few women who composes and conducts music for the theater. Almost every time I've music directed a show, someone from the audience has found me afterwards and said, "We've never seen a female conductor before!" As a writer and a vocal coach, I found myself telling young actresses over and over again to try to find their power within a song, especially when a song seemed to be *about* the very act of giving away one's power. I recall working with one actress who told me she was having a hard time claiming agency because she'd never been asked to do it. Further, she told me that as a singing-dancing woman of the theater, she'd never been on stage wearing more than a bikini. I vowed then to make sure the women characters I write have substantial character arcs, meaty content in their songs, and ample coverage in their costumes. In fact, I recently turned down a project about a madam and her slew of prostitutes, "feminist" though perhaps it was, because the world doesn't need me to create another role where a woman has to play a prostitute.

Two years ago I founded Maestra Music, Inc., a not-for-profit organization that provides community, visibility, and opportunity for the women who work as musicians in the theater. It's amazing how many of us there are in this business, and through Maestra, I'm trying to shine a spotlight on the work these women do. Giving these female composers, conductors, arrangers, orchestrators, copyists, and pit musicians visibility to the world was my first goal, but it turns out that giving them visibility to each other is just as important. When Jeanine Tesori and Lisa Kron won the Tony Award in 2014 for *Fun Home*—the first female writing team *ever* to win for Best Original Score—Jeanine said, "For girls, you have to see it to be it." At Maestra, that's our goal.[11]

Feminist theater presents women as people, not archetypes or ideals. As Diep Tran, journalist and critic, once said,

I want to clarify that I don't think a feminist play is the same as a play about a woman. There are plenty of plays about women that I find misogynist. But that golden unicorn of feminist theater is something more specific. I define it for myself as a play where a woman (or preferably women) are treated as multifaceted human beings with both beauty and flaws, and motivations that don't just include men, romance, or children.

At the same time, I am reminded of this Maisie Williams quote: "We should stop calling feminists 'feminists' and just start calling people who aren't feminist 'sexist'—and then everyone else is just a human. You are either a normal person or a sexist." I prickle at the term feminist theater, because I don't think of plays like that. I think of them in terms of being bad or good. Does the work treat women like

> human beings? Then it's a good play. Does it treat women like props
> or stereotypes? Then it's bad or at least lacks something important.
>   I don't want feminist theater to be an aberration that you need a
> label for. I just want it to be the norm. [12]

So what is keeping theater from becoming a feminist art form and industry? Both society and religion have long served as ways to silence women. It is ironic that poet and writer Hrotsvitha of Gandersheim, a German nun, is credited with being the first female playwright, having written comedies in Latin that contained Christian themes between 935 and 1005. Christian dogma, which dictated that exhibiting oneself in public was indecent and immoral for women, forbade women from performing onstage. More than six hundred years passed before women were permitted to perform publicly, and it wasn't until 1613 that an English woman published an original play under her own name, when Elizabeth Cary, Viscountess Falkland, wrote *The Tragedy of Mariam the Fair Queen of Jewry*, a revenge tragedy in iambic pentameter.

Religion was a popular topic for female playwrights at first—a subject that was appropriately feminine and pure for them to address. But they soon began bringing their own stories to the stage, writing comedies and dramas about domesticity, motherhood, and romance, and the ways in which these societal norms restricted and confined them. These stories often covertly addressed politics and civil rights through the mask of soft, feminine subjects, and as time passed, women were harbingers of social and political justice onstage.

Despite their voices being stifled, women have continued to write for the stage, recently taking on every subject, ranging from sexual abuse and torture (*Ruined*), to economic despair (*Sweat*), to immigration (*Miss You Like Hell*), to gun violence (*Office Hour*), to feminism itself (*The Heidi Chronicles*)—stories to which men can and should bear witness.

But these successful, acclaimed productions are few and far between. When bringing women's works to mainstream stages, the numbers remain consistently low, and women are grossly underrepresented both on Broadway and Off-Broadway—a fact many activist groups and organizations are striving to change. It's a change that is desperately needed· Studies have proven that seeing theater increases one's empathy, as well as education and literacy, and by seeing these stories being told onstage, audiences will cultivate a more compassionate view of this underserved and often-silenced half of the population.

It's crucial to view these historic texts with a critical eye when evaluating equality and examine more than just the character's gender. Race and historic and current prejudices must also be considered with regards to what was written, by whom it was written, and what was presented to the public, establishing a long history of whitewashing, usurping, and appropriating the stories of marginalized communities and limiting the access of historic perspectives.

The limits of theater's context and content with regards to gender, race, and economic privilege was never more apparent than when researching theatrical history and finding works whose influence is cited decades or centuries later. As a result, this book is an overview rather than an exhaustive evaluation of the subject, and in no way is it as inclusive as I wish it could be. Fulfillment of that wish would constitute a series of books authored by many different authors with different backgrounds.

What this book will do is offer a look into the history of why women were kept silent for so long, how they finally found platforms for their voices, and what still needs to change so that the glass curtain can finally be lifted.

I

OFF STAGE

It's no surprise that women have been underrepresented onstage throughout history. Excluded and silenced, women were prevented from participating in the performing arts, in one way or another, starting with Western theater's origins. Beginning in Greece in about 532 BC, with tragic plays exploring the grand themes of love and loss, as well as the relationships between men and gods, acting or writing for the stage was a strictly male profession.[1] Female roles in theater were written and performed by men.

This forbiddance came at a cost, but one that was seemingly incomprehensible to citizens at the time. With women seen, performed, and voiced through and by men, the true stories of their lives were invisible. Their thoughts and emotions were excised from public knowledge. This singular focus removed the consideration of women from the creation of the governments that inspired politics for centuries to come, creating a system that only represented half the population.

The roots of theater, in both activity and literature, can be traced to the Athenian state festivals, held in celebration of Dionysus, the god of wine, merriment, and theater, in the sixth and fifth centuries BC. While both men and women participated in sixth-century theater, as the ceremonies evolved into what is now known as theater, women were no longer present.[2]

ATTIC MORALITY, OFFSTAGE

No single event, politically or socially, explains women's disappearance from the stage. Instead, their relegation to domestic life can be credited to a series of social, economic, and political standards established through-out time and still visible in society today. The evolution of the single-family unit and its impact on Greece's economy, along with the increas-ing "attic morality"—cultural codes rather than political or even theatrical ones—removed women from public life, firmly rooting them in individu-al households. [3]

Even the name of Greece's family unit belittled women, viewing them as a form of property. The word for marriage, *ekdosis*, translates to "loan"—of women from their fathers to their husbands. In situations of divorce, women were returned to their fathers, moving from living as possessions of their fathers to possessions of their husbands, and if they were freed from one, they were returned to the other. At no point in their lives were they autonomous beings. [4] If widowed, women were expected to maintain property ownership within their family by remarrying a close relative. [5]

The single-family unit in Greece confined Athenian women to the house, where, if she performed her duties in a proper manner, her hus-band would not have to worry himself with matters of the family and could devote his energy to his public life. Depicted in Aristophanes' dramas, women were only permitted to appear in public on special occa-sions and associate with men in the close proximity of relatives. [6]

Enforced by the Laws of Solon, which dictated both public and private life, the orderly conduct of women was defined by many, notably Aristo-tle, as remaining indoors with a singular focus on domestic life, child-bearing, and parenthood. [7] Women were ostracized from an existence away from home, and men were established as figures of authority in both public and private life. [8]

Nancy Rabinowitz wrote in "Politics of Inclusion/Exclusion in Attic Tragedy,"

> The geographical city of Athens was inhabited by men and women, free and slave, Greek and foreigner, but it was also the ideological democratic *polis* of free, Athenian citizen men. Athens was a culture based on democracy, but it was also an elite men's club. We cannot minimize the novelty of the democracy that gave unprecedented direct

power to the common man, nor can we forget that it also excluded women and foreigners from citizenship and was a slave-holding culture.[9]

The confinement of women to society's domestic sphere was evident even in Greece's economic practices, as the single-family unit established itself as the venue for transactions of personal wealth. The structure of traditional aristocracies was maneuvered toward individual control of assets but only for men. Women were limited in any ownership of or ability to exchange goods, and they were only permitted to barter for equal or less than one *medimnos* (bushel).[10]

This restriction was not merely economic: As new forms of religion, writing, architecture, and theater flourished, so did the restraints of gender. The establishment of the role "woman" oppressed the feminine gender, while benefiting the masculine. Theater reflected this attitude, as the perceived characteristics of the different genders were not only given a voice and a venue, but also an audience. Centuries later, these writings are often referred to as "classics"—works that throughout time have been judged to be of the highest quality and whose ideals are solidly established, enacting the expulsion of women from the stage as a standard of theatrical history.[11] Whether women were permitted to attend theatrical performances is unclear, but societal standards indicate that married women—seen as proper in the eyes of men—were not in the audience.

Such psychology is reflected in the Greek myths, stories of the gods that were spoken and written, and in the community's culture. Beginning in the Bronze Age and evolving through the spoken word, the myths were centered around the pantheon of gods and goddesses who resided on Mount Olympus, perpetuating the division between the genders.[12]

"Myth has two main functions," wrote poet and scholar Robert Graves.

> The first is to answer the sort of awkward questions that children ask, such as, "Who made the world? How will it end? Who was the first man? Where do souls go after death?" . . . The second function of myth is to justify an existing social system and account for traditional rites and customs.[13]

In these myths, and in society, women are often silent. They are also silenced, often by brutal physical pain, torture, or death. This subduing of women was part of everyday life, both in the home and outside of it, where politics were exclusively male. In the public sphere, women were only permitted to speak in defense of their homes, children, husbands, and other women's interests—topics that were appropriately feminine, humble, and modest.[14]

The very idea of women serving as voices of public authority was a source of comedy for writers. Playwright Aristophanes penned an entire comedy about the idea of women running the government, presenting them as unable to adapt from private communication to the elevated ideals of manly public speaking. *Assemblywomen* chronicles women taking over the city parliament—which they accomplish by disguising themselves as men—and instituting radical reforms, including communal property and sexual liberation, with the aged and unattractive having first choice of sexual partners.

The popular stories of the time illustrate this mentality. Women who strayed from their prescribed gender roles were faced with disempowerment, desexualization, and discipline. In the *Heracleidae*, Macaria states that "for a woman, silence and self-control are best."[15] Ovid's *Metamorphoses* frequently presents women being silenced during their transformations. Mythical character Arachne was transformed into a spider after falling prey to hubris. Pandora, the first woman created by the gods, is written as responsible for releasing all of the evils of humanity by opening a forbidden box. And Aristotle, the renowned philosopher and scientist, said women were incomplete males, deformed and created to be deferential and submissive to men.[16] In a starkly contrasting portrait of femininty, when Eurydice died a second death after Orpheus looked at her despite being forbidden, she "had no reproach to bring against her husband. What was there to complain of? One thing; only; He loved her."[17]

Strength and autonomy came at a cost. Athena, goddess of war, as well as courage, inspiration, civilization, law and justice, strategic warfare, mathematics, strength, strategy, the arts, crafts, and skill, held considerable power, but it denied her sexuality: A motherless virgin, Athena was not considered a woman. Her powers were only viewed concurrently with her lack of sexuality; the two were mutually exclusive.

The Greek myths were abundant with sex, as Paul Chrystal described in "A Brief History of Sex and Sexuality in Ancient Greece," but relations were tumultuous and inequitable, further establishing women in roles of maternity and men in roles of dominance and power.

> Greek myth was a theogony of incest, murder, polygamy, and inter-marriage in which eroticism and fertility were elemental; they were there right from the start, demonstrating woman's essential reproductive role in securing the cosmos, extending the human race and ensuring the fecundity of nature. . . . Zeus . . . set a precedent for centuries of mortal male domination and female subservience.[18]

WOMEN THROUGH THE EYES OF MEN

These convictions of male domination and female subservience were apparent in theater, where all the women of the stage had been created by men. And women were not only prevented from performing onstage, but also forbidden to write for it. The female characters still featured predominately in works from that period, offering piercing insight into women's lives through the male gaze.

Women in theater were developed solely from the male perspective—a perspective that was both narrow and finite due to society's segregation of the genders. This represented and reinforced the patriarchal values held by the men creating these characters and thus maintained and bolstered the representation of the gendered creation of "woman" created by the patriarchy.[19] A man dressing as a woman was distanced from the role, wrote Nancy Sorkin Rabinowitz in "The Male Actor of Greek Tragedy: Evidence of Misogyny or Gender-Bending?"

> And makes it clear that the role of the woman is an idealization, not a realization. In addition, the male playing female indicates a possible relevance of the form to Dionysus, a god associated with masks and characterized by softness, woman's curls, and dress (*Bacchae*), and worshipped with transvestite ceremonies at the Oschophoria.[20]

The title character in Euripides' *Alcestis* personifies such ideals of womanhood, offering her own life so her Admetos, her husband, can live. Rather than leave her children without a father or live without her husband, Alcestis gives herself, personifying the ideal of the noble, self-sacrificing wife, described by the chorus as "who all men would say the best of wives has been" and "noblest by far of women 'neath the Sun."[21]

The playwright presents a radically different portrayal of a wife and mother in *Medea*: Devastated by her husband's abandonment, Medea plans to avenge his wrongs through violent acts of murder. Imprisoned by her sex and the restrictions placed upon her by a society governed by men, the enraged woman declares to her fellow women of Corinth,

> Of all things which are living and can form a judgment, we women are the most unfortunate creatures. Firstly, with an excess of wealth it is required for us to buy a husband and take for our bodies a master; for not to take one is even worse. And now the question is serious whether we take a good or bad one; for there is no easy escape for a woman, nor can she say no to her marriage.[22]

Medea illustrates the entrapment women of the time faced, describing how women must learn to "best manage him who shares the bed with her" and how if a man grows weary of his marriage, he can seek companionship elsewhere but women are "forced to keep our eyes on one alone."

As the play begins, Medea is presented in a sympathetic manner. Following her speech, the chorus declares, "This I will promise. You are in the right, Medea, in paying your husband back. I am not surprised at

Medea (1870) by Anselm Feuerbach (1829–1880). *Peter Horree/Alamy Stock Photo*

you for being sad."[23] She proceeds to defy the conventions of femininity by which she had lived, avenging her husband's infidelity through the murder of their children, as well as his new wife. Commonly perceived as a "monster" or "crazy," ruled by her sexual jealousy, *Medea* presented a threat to the patriarchal establishments of Greece that dominated culture when the play was first produced in 431 BC, the title character seen as a cautionary tale of the enraged, impassioned women, while Glauce, the innocent, virginal victim, does not speak a single line.

One of the few notable portrayals of female sexual autonomy not punished by silence, torture, or death is seen in Aristophanes' *Lysistrata*, which narrates the title character's attempt to end the Peloponnesian War by convincing the women of Greece to deny their husbands and lovers sex until they negotiate peace—a strategy that ignites a ferocious battle of wills between the sexes. When asked if the men instigate sex through violence, Lysistrata advises passive resistance that appealed to men's desires to be wanted by their wives: "Yield then, but with a sluggish, cold indifference. There is no joy to them in sullen mating. Besides we have other ways to madden them: They cannot stand up long, and they've no delight unless we fit their aim with merry succor."[24]

Lysistrata was notable for its exposure of sexual relations in a male-dominated society, but its message was no doubt weakened by the inevitable comedy of the performance, with the sexually rebellious, politically driven women in the play performed by men dressed in drag. Sue-Allen Case wrote the following in "Classic Drag: The Greek Creation of Female Parts":

> Within theater practice, the clearest illustration of this division is in the tradition of the all-male stage. "Woman" was played by male actors in drag, while actual women were banned from the stage. The classical acting practice reveals the construction of the fictional gender created by the patriarchy. The classical plays and theatrical conventions can now be regarded as allies in the project of suppressing actual women and replacing them with the masks of patriarchal production.[25]

The portrayals of women in Greek dramas were often unflattering and frequently biased. Male-authored dialogue for women often had them speak disparagingly of themselves, a technique used to pander to the male audiences. Presented as subservient to their husbands, they were often disciplined through violence, and the marriages presented onstage were

Hrotsvitha (Roswitha von Gandersheim). *Sueddeutsche Zeitung Photo/Alamy Stock Photo*

far from equitable, with women forbidden to leave their homes without their husband's permission.

Aristophanes' depiction of men and women in *Lysistrata* clearly demonstrates how the male gaze shaped dramatic works of the time. When women dare to seize power, attempting to end a war by denying men sex until fighting is stopped, their efforts are viewed with skepticism and disbelief, and the men proclaim women the "most shameless beast of all the beasts that be."[26] The Magistrate personifies many of these prejudices, declaring, "If I should take orders from the one who wears veils, may my neck straightaway be deservedly wrung," encouraging the beating of women and refusing to believe they could manage the finances of war, despite their experience managing household finances for years.[27]

> Aristophanes was influenced by the fact that he was composing for a male audience. Women in real life would probably not have spoken so disparagingly of themselves. But surely he would not have used such language unless they were actually inclined to put a low estimate on their own sex. . . . [Aristophanes'] plays reflect the sentiments of the public for which he wrote, as well as his own personal tastes and feelings. He never would have treated women with such severity if he had not been sure that he would please his audience by so doing.[28]

"THE STRONG VOICE OF GANDERSHEIM"

There was one woman who was writing plays, and she could be found, of all places, in a convent. Hrotsvitha was the first of many: the first Saxon poet, the first known Christian playwright, and the first female historian of Europe. Born in approximately 935, her name in Saxon translates to "strong voice," a fitting description for the intelligent and prolific woman. After entering the Benedictine convent the Abbey of Gandersheim, Hrotsvitha penned six comedies illustrating themes of faith and female perseverance with writing so skilled that its authenticity has been questioned and its impact acknowledged as irrefutable.[29]

First published in 1501, Hrotsvitha serves as a connection between classical Greek and Roman drama and the religious theater of the medieval years of about 1100 and 1600 CE.[30] This connection inspires reexamination of accepted norms of theater, as well as the ways in which gender biases were established, Ellen J. Gainor wrote in the *Norton Anthology of Drama*: "The study of Hrotsvitha's plays from the mid-twentieth century onward has forced scholars to both carefully reexamine foundational as-

sumptions in theater history and to reconsider dismissive attitudes towards women's writing throughout the Western tradition."[31]

Hrotsvitha defied feminine societal conventions by authoring plays,
but her scripts were, at first glance, appropriately feminine. Written in
Latin and intended to be read rather than performed, the nun penned six
partially rhyming comedies in Latin that, by embodying themes of Chris-
tianity, attempted to serve as a rebuttal to the pagan philosophy seen in
popular classical dramas.

Of noble birth, Hrotsvitha was educated in the Scriptures and Christian theologians and philosophers, but also in Plautus, Terence, Horace,
Virgil, and Ovid.[32] Her works were drawn from the Latin and Greek
Patrologiae, a collection of writings by the Christian Church Fathers and
different secular writers, with which she took liberties by crafting characters beyond their previous development, as well as adding and enhancing
comedic situations.[33]

Hrotsvitha described her work as imitative of Roman comic Terence,
but in contrast to Terence, whose view of women was considered misogy-
nistic, she presented female characters with strength. Elevating women
beyond the stereotypes of courtesans and shrews was a notable shift from
male playwrights' portrayals in dramas since the times of Aeschylus and
Shakespeare. Women were typically presented as one of two stereotypes
of the time, with portrayals of strength and wisdom of virginal purity or
oversexed cruelty.[34]

The playwright herself stated the following in the preface to her dramas:

> Many Catholics one may find, and we are also guilty of charges of this
> kind, who for the beauty of their eloquent style, prefer the use of pagan
> guile to the usefulness of Sacred Scripture. There are also others who,
> devoted to sacred reading and scorning the works of other pagans, yet
> frequently read Terence's fiction, and as they delight in the sweetness
> of his style and diction, they are stained by learning of wicked things
> in his depiction. Therefore I, the strong voice of Gandersheim, have
> not refused to imitate him in writing whom others laud in reading, so
> that in the selfsame form of composition in which the shameless acts
> of lascivious women were phrased the laudable chastity of sacred vir-
> gins may be praised within the limits of my little talent.[35]

Two focal points characterize Hrotsvitha's dramatic work: the "prosti-tution plays" *Abraham* and *Paphnutius*, and the "martyrdom plays," which include *Sapientia* and *Dulcitius*. Described as "lost sheep" dramas, the prostitution plays feature a female sex worker being rescued and brought to grace by an angelic man. Howard McNaughton described them in *The International Dictionary of the Theatre: Playwrights* as fol-lows:

> Blatantly exemplary pieces which do little to question the pervasive tradition of medieval misogyny, and focus on a character trait that is the antecedent of late medieval obsession with Magdalene. The title characters are the male retrievers who are presented as showing con-siderable courage and self-sacrifice in venturing outside the sphere of asceticism, risking contamination from the larger world. [36]

Hrotsvitha's writing found humor in its piety, despite her devout Christian lifestyle, according to Christopher St. John, who described her approach as conveying the "impression that the dignity was mingled with impudence."[37] The "martyrdom plays" depicted the persecution of a woman by a ruthless emperor, and three of Hrotsvitha's works—*Gallica-nus*, *Dulcitius*, and *Sapientia*—addressed conflicts between early Chris-tianity and paganism.

Hrotsvitha's writing employed drama to promote the Christian ideals of chastity, poverty, and obedience—a unique combination of clashing ideals. Theater, an institution against which edicts had been issued during the conclusion of the Roman Empire, and the nun's spiritual approach to the art was unusual and unique.

Religion was the focus of each of her plays, and chastity was celebrat-ed among her female characters. But Hrotsvitha's writing went beyond the moral message. St. John wrote,

> In *Callimachus*, *Abraham*, and *Paphutias*, Roswitha sets out to de-scribe the war between the flesh and the spirit, and the long penance which must be done by those who have allowed the flesh to triumph. It is not enough for them to be converted and to realise their crime against the infinite beauty and goodness of God. They are called on to take practical measures to cleanse themselves. [38]

Lost for centuries, Hrotsvitha's works were rediscovered by humanist scholar Conradus Celtis in the Benedictine monastery of St. Emmeran,

Dancing Maenads: Illustration from Notor's *Lysistrata*, 1898 (litho), Roton, Gabriel de (1865–1964). *Private Collection/Prismatic Pictures/Bridgeman Images*

Ratisbon, in the late fifteenth century.[39] Long after her death, Hrotsvitha continued to foster discussion about gender bias in the arts. The sexist perception of female writers was never more clear than following its discovery, when the authenticity of Hrotsvitha's writing was questioned due to its high quality of writing and the fact that the playwright was a woman:

> Her sophisticated output has been a puzzle and anomaly for literary scholars and historians for centuries, and opinions about the works have often been shaped by an unwillingness to acknowledge that a medieval woman could possibly know as much or write with as much skill as Hrotsvit did.[40]

The skepticism Hrotsvitha's work underwent due to her gender continued long after her death. Women's voices were not seen or heard onstage in a significant way for centuries to come.[41]

2

FIGHTING THE FEMALE WIT

Society was so unaccustomed to the voices of women—offstage or on—that actions were taken against them, disrespecting, demeaning, and even disgracing them. In 1696, a group of female playwrights, including Delarivier Manley, Catharine Trotter, and Mary Pix, were parodied in a farce titled *The Female Wits*.[1] Women's voices were not only unwelcome, but also seen as a threat. The craft of playwriting was already extremely competitive, a state that was only heightened by women publicly sharing their voices and attempting to be financially self-sufficient.

"NOTORIOUS, IMPUDENT, PROSTITUTED STRUMPETS"

These satirized "wits" began writing shortly after the death of Aphra Behn. One of the most prominent female voices in the theater in the seventeenth century, she examined established cultural norms like marriage, widowhood, and even divorce, with a critical, questioning eye. These women attempted to draw attention to, and expand, women's places in society—an act that aroused such suspicion and anger that some were accused of licentiousness (lacking legal or moral restraints and disregarding rules of correctness and sexual restraints) and libertinage (practices of life that disregard authority and convention in matters of sex and religion).

While theater had already introduced characters like Cleopatra and Medea, who dared to defy gender norms, women were only officially permitted to be actresses on the English stage after a 1660 decree by Charles II.[2] Women appearing onstage and displaying their bodies to an audience only enhanced the discomfort regarding changing gender roles.

These shifts in society were hardly welcome but seemingly inevitable, as was the backlash and attempt to silence them. Daring to participate in the theater, by both writing and acting, defied the climate described in *Histrio-Mastix*, a critique written in 1633, by William Prynne, that declared actresses—women who dared to exhibit their bodies and voices in public—were "notorious, impudent, prostituted Strumpets."[3] This disdainful view of women considered them natural candidates for the theater, thanks to their "innate depravity": "She is seen as a dissembler, never revealing her true personality, always wearing a veil or mask. Thus, she is a born actress, a natural whore—someone who constantly plays a role, who play acts. This ideological construct ascribes to women in general a histrionic personality."[4]

Parallels were easily drawn, as the culture onstage and backstage mirrored life offstage. Roles that were available to women were finite and far from independent, always associated with their sexuality and relationships with men: courtesan, virgin, lover, wife, and prostitute. As Annette Kreis-Schnick wrote,

> The heroines of the "she-tragedies" from the late 1670s and well into the eighteenth century were structured according to two paradigms: either as the "beset and injured martyrs, whose plights and consequent sufferings make up the substance and the aim of their action"—a form that certainly creates female victims but fails to provide them with a space of desire for their own; or as an "erring lover who trusted the false vows of a vicious libertine"—somebody whose sexual transgression is immediately punished with repentance and death.[5]

The public sphere so strongly rejected women, many female playwrights wrote anonymously or using false names to facilitate and encourage greater acceptance of their work. As a result, much of their writing is mistakenly attributed to male authors or lost altogether, and little is known about these playwrights, for example, Mary Pix, the prolific author of one novel and seven plays, notably *The Beau Defeated* (now known as *The Fantastic Follies of Mrs. Rich*), *Ibrahim: The Thirteenth Emperor of the Turks*, and *The Spanish Wives*. Pix's comedies were so popular, they were performed in repertory by the royally chartered theater company Duke's, at Lincoln's Inn Fields and the Queens Theatre.[6] Women's writing embodied protofeminism, an "ancient or early author/thinker who, despite cultural and societal beliefs to the contrary, promoted or endorsed beliefs dealing with the equality of women to men in key aspects regarding social status and function."[7] It carried an air of mystery, as many of the "lost" female plays written then were considered obscene and kept under male supervision.[8]

But these women writers, who dared to live a life beyond the "triple concept" of chastity, silence, and obedience, were not only defying societal conventions, but also threatening the established norms of society—and, therefore, threatening the men who created and benefited from them.[9]

> Just as female subjecthood and female subjectivity become visible, thinkable, imaginable, and, therefore, speakable, the notions of subject and subjectivity are being seriously undermined, which confines women (living, historical beings) and Woman (universal womanhood) once again to theories that cheerfully disregard the concept of gender.[10]

"WHY THIS WRATH AGAINST THE WOMEN'S WORKS?"

Disregard of the concept of gender is what Susanna Centlivre desired: In the preface of her play *The Platonick Lady*, she expressed her frustration that her previous two plays had succeeded due to her concealing her identity, which led to audiences assuming they had been written by men.[11] Centlivre expressed her reasoning, and her dissatisfaction, asking, "Vulgar World . . . think it a proof of their Sense, to dislike everything that is writ by Women. . . . And why this Wrath against the Women's Works? Perhaps you'll answer, because they meddle with things out of their Sphere: But I say, no; for since the Poet is born, why not a Woman as well as a Man?"[12]

The author of nineteen plays, Centlivre penned political and social satires, many of which were in support of the Whig cause.[13] Her work often expressed resistance to patriarchal establishments and attitudes, with many of her female characters appearing in male disguises, and she strove to support fellow female writers. In a poem written for Sarah Fyge Egerton's *Poems on Several Occasions, Together with a Pastoral*, Centlivre began, "Thou Champion for our Sex go on and show/Ambitious Man what Womankind can do."[14]

MARRIAGE AS A GODLY PRISON

The very institutions that were confining women were presented, examined, and criticized in their work. Marriage, which had physically confined women to the house, was morally confining them as well, as the expectations and rules of polite society restricted women both physically and mentally. In theater, the street was a designated male area, while women were typically depicted inside a house or in a doorway. Theater offered a look inside someone's home, and much of what was seen onstage focused on how to escape it. In forced marriages, the most popular subject of comedies, homes were portrayed as prisons—especially when offering the female character's perspective.[15]

This new, broad perspective on society inspired conflict within the cultural discourse, which only provided more material for drama and comedy. Kreis-Schnick wrote,

> Thus, the drama of the period helped to shape and to resist, to contain and to transform, the dominant constructions of gender relations. It reflected, produced, and subverted the struggle to establish new gender boundaries. The theater of the time was awash with controversy, and right at the center, we find women's plays—plays that reflect all the frictions gender relations entail.[16]

Not only were these playwrights daring to question societal norms through their writing, but also having their work produced at all was an act of defiance. Women who independently earned money dared to achieve financial autonomy without a husband, endangering the institution of marriage, as well as economic structures. The backlash and disputes within the theater flourished, with female writers being accused of immorality, political bias, and "artistic deficiency." The women's morals were being attacked, as well as their work.[17]

Only two institutions were deemed appropriate for women to participate in, let alone write about. Those were marriage and widowhood, with both containing seemingly countless restrictions. But these playwrights dared to pen scripts that addressed extramarital sex, divorce, and education—institutions that established patriarchal authority and supervision over women and were, and continue to be, the fodder for scripts throughout history.[18]

One of the most, if not *the* most, popular subjects addressed onstage was marriage. The state of matrimony, in which both genders could be parodied, mocked, and satirized, provided ample fodder for both comedy and drama. Marriage's increased association with religion only escalated this state; following the dissolution of monasteries during the Reformation, Protestant clergymen worked to elevate marriage into a godly way of life that reinforced religious values, as well as patriarchal ones. Matrimony's doubling down on female obedience to both a monarch and a husband associated gender order with overall social order, referred to as the "state–family analogy" and leaving women powerless.[19]

> Locking his wife safely away and squandering her fortune was the legal right of every seventeenth-century husband. The familiar dichotomy between town and country frames this deprivation: A house in the country, almost a moral prison according to contemporary notions, with the drudgery of menial work—this is the way in which she envisions the inevitable consequence the match would have for the *wife*.[20]

FEMALE VOICES, DARING TO BE HEARD

The most prominent voice of these playwrights was Aphra Behn, a prolific playwright considered "unwomanly" by the male writers of the eighteenth century. The author of sixteen plays, Behn's writing provided a woman's perspective in a society that had been shaped by male voices and examines what, if any, options women had according to the law—a practice accessible only to men that shaped the dissolution of marriages and much of the interaction between the sexes.[21]

Behn's plays frequently focused on marriage, examining and unapologetically questioning both the societal and financial conditions of the institution in the comedies *Sir Patient Fancy*, *The Luckey Chance*, *The Town-Fopp*, and *The Feign'd Curtizans*. At times a daring and defiant voice, Behn's stories defied societal norms, depicting and celebrating women's rebellion and refusal to conform.[22]

A satire of seventeenth-century marriage, *The Luckey Chance* depicts a seduction taking place in the home of a married woman, ironically

Aphra Behn, dramatist. Art by Peter Lely (1618–1680). *Lebrecht Authors/Bridgeman Images*

emphasizing and then diminishing a woman's role as a natural actress and seductress. It also portrays the lengths to which a woman will go to subvert the restrictions within which she exists, seducing and arousing a man but also protecting her chastity by avoiding consummation. By demonstrating a woman using her sexuality to pursue her desires but preventing the act of sex to protect her reputation, Behn demonstrates the impasse in which women were trapped.[23] But Behn, unlike the male playwrights before her, provides a unique perspective on such a story:

> Behn, as a woman playwright writing at a later date, locates this struggle not over a kingdom, but over its proxy, woman's body, and its definition and appropriation. This body's most conspicuous characteristic is lack and absence, as patriarchal discourse offers nothing, or only overly little, that could represent it.[24]

Behn lost her husband in 1665, and his death and her subsequent poverty propelled her into writing as a career, but she authored little about widowhood, despite the lusty widow being a favorite character in comedic parody.[25] A widow's undefined status as a woman—no longer a virgin, having been married but now without a man by her side—was undefined and uncomfortable in a strictly and traditionally gendered society.

> While doubtless the greatest problem in any patriarchal context, female sexuality is nevertheless or perhaps, as a result, one of the most prominent structural devices of early modern comedy. Renaissance dramas abound with allusions to the "cuckold" and the male anxieties that term implies. The social, political, religious, and artistic transformations that followed in the wake of the English Revolution meant that the second half of the century featured much less indirect representations of female extramarital sexuality. Linking sex to power and tying the discourse on sex to political and social power relationships, the first chapter accounts for the simultaneous urge to present, analyze, and scrutinize, as well as to suppress, control, and contain, women's sexual activities.[26]

Widows were the most heavily satirized women in Renaissance, seventeenth-century, and world literature due to their socially and economically vulnerable state. A husband's death left his wife stripped of her economic, legal, and, according to society, moral provider. The only option for widows, who were sexually experienced, was to marry again, but remarriage was considered bigamy and a form of adultery—"an overlap of sexuality or posthumous cuckoldry."[27] Instead, women were told they should live quietly, forgo marriage, honor their late husband's reputation, and care for his children. But how they were to care for the children was a question left unanswered, given that the rights for widows to follow in their husbands' trades were tightly restricted, and unless she remarried after two years, those rights were lost. [28]

In her decades as a writer, Behn addressed widowhood only three times, once in her final play. Produced posthumously, *The Widow Ranker* was set in the United States, and it explored class, gender, and race. The title character thwarted gender conventions by drinking, smoking, swearing, cross-dressing, and fencing, and, perhaps even more daringly, she maintained control of her money. [29]

Behn was one of the first, and most prolific, female playwrights to evaluate the institution of marriage in her writing, but she was hardly the only one to do so. Elizabeth Baker also took on holy matrimony in her first full-length play, *Chains*, which scrutinized the motivations of both men and women regarding marriage. Years had passed between Behn and Baker, but the questions and problems remained constant. First produced in 1909, by the Play Actors at the Court Theatre, *Chains* examines the lives of the lower middle class working in clerical posts in Edwardian England, entrapped by marriage and unable to escape. In *Chains*, Baker correlates marriage and drudgery, with one character musing, "I can never understand why a man gets married. He's got so many chances to see the world and do things—but then he does and marries and settles down and is a family man before he's 24." [30]

A 2007 revival at the Orange Tree Theatre returned the play to the British stage for the first time in almost 100 years. The *Guardian* praised the show, saying it "evokes the seething discontent under the buoyant surface of Edwardian society. . . . The battle between enslavement and escape is dramatized with Ibsen-esque fervor." [31] That praise echoed the reviews of *Chains* from 1910, which described the real slavery as consisting "not in the work these city clerks do in the city, not in the routine of their occupations, not in their decent poverty, but in the narrowness, the ugliness, the vulgarity of the lives they lead at home." [32]

Before marrying at the age of thirty-nine, Baker wrote *The Price of Thomas Cook* (1910), *Miss Tassey* (1910), and *Miss Robinson* (1918). Both Baker and Githa Sowerby "employ stage realism as a means of indicting the societies they depict, exploiting what Austin Quigley has identified as 'the tension in naturalism between replicating the surfaces of the world and revealing underlying forces in the world,'" [33] and is now included in the repertoire of such late Victorian and Edwardian "condition of marriage" as *The Case of Rebellious Susan*, *The Liars*, *Getting Married*, *Mid-Channel*, and *The Fugitive*.

Baker's naturalistic style is further seen in *Miss Tassey*, which premiered at the Court Theatre in March 1910. Described in 1913 as painting a "grim little picture of the living-in system . . . with all its malignant conditions and abuses,"[34] the play juxtaposes one woman's physical transformation with another woman's suicide. A young shopgirl changes herself into a "Pierette" whose seduction of a man will expedite her ability to leave her job, while the title character loses her job because of her age and health, the latter of which is suffering because of the job. Forty-five years old and unmarried, she kills herself with a drug overdose. *Miss Tassey*'s unflinching portrayal of women living their lives in the service of men established Baker as a reputable realistic voice.[35]

Baker's writing drew on her own history. Born into a middle-class family, she began working as a cashier before progressing to jobs as a stenographer and a private secretary.[36] She worked for the suffragette movement, and her one-act play *Edith* was performed at the 1912 National Union of Women's Suffrage Societies fund-raiser. The play's title character is a single woman who, through self-employment, achieves financial independence—a marked contrast to the expected female roles of wife, widow, mother, or fiancé, defined by their relationships with men.[37] The play was powerful: "*Edith* provides a clear and positive alternative for women unhappy with a society that saw them as mere adjuncts to their husbands, confining them to the home to perform the suitably feminine labor of housework and childcare."[38]

Working-class social structures were also scrutinized by Githa Sowerby in *Rutherford and Son*. A smash hit after its 1912 opening, Sowerby's play placed capitalism and its faults center stage. Originally playing four matinee performances in 1912, the play tapped into the turbulent social discord of its time. *Rutherford and Son* was credited to playwright K. G. Sowerby, who people assumed was a man—including critics, who raved about the show. The reveal of playwright's identity and gender made headlines, and Sowerby performed the part of a young ingenue in interviews, resulting in news stories about a pretty woman who somehow happened to write a good, if uneducated, play. A slow writer, Sowerby could never repeat her success, but the popularity of *Rutherford and Son* was lasting; it was revived many times in the late 1990s and early 2000s.

Richard Beechman, who directed a 2009 revival, told the *Guardian*, "Githa has been airbrushed from history. It's been very important for me to celebrate and reinstate this forgotten voice . . . from our industrial past. It's also about remembering, honoring, and investigating Tyneside's past as the one of the world's leading glassmaking centers."[39]

SUFFRAGETTES ONSTAGE

Both Sowerby and Baker used stage realism to chronicle and condemn society, including the economic and political restraints that confined women. This lack of female representation was criticized and satirized by writer and activist Cicely Hamilton, who, along with Christopher St. John, wrote *How the Vote was Won*, a farcical comedy examining the notion that women are always protected by the male heads of their households. England's female workers go on strike, and, of course, seek financial support from their male relatives, motivating the men to march on Parliament in support of women's rights so they can return to their jobs. The play, which turns the tables on men's claim that women have no reason to vote because they have men to watch over them, concludes with the decidedly ironic line, "When you want a thing done, get a man to do it! Votes for Women!"[40]

Votes for Women! was also the title of another suffragette play written by Elizabeth Robins. The acclaimed actress sought strong female roles, even writing some herself. She extensively performed works by Norweigan playwright Henrik Ibsen, bringing Hedda Gabler to the English stage for the first time with Marion Lea. She frequently collaborated with Ibsen, who created female characters seeking independence, fulfillment, and sexual satisfaction—characters just as complex and complicated as those written for men.

"A woman cannot be herself in modern society," wrote Ibsen in the notes for *A Doll's House*. It was an "exclusively modern society with laws made by men and with prosecutors and judges who assess feminine conduct from a masculine standpoint."[41]

Robins's many collaborations with one of the founders of modernism and the creator of several notable female parts, known for his "New Woman" plays, contributed to the development of her own feminist voice. She began championing the cause after witnessing a politcal gathering, of which she said,

> A certain memorable afternoon in Trafalger Square when I first heard
> women talking politics in public. I went out of shamefaced curiosity,
> my head full of masculine criticism as to woman's limitations, her
> well-known inability to stick to the point, her poverty in logic and in
> humor, and the impossibility, in any case, of her coping with the mob.
>
> I had found in my own heart hitherto no firm assurance that these
> charges were not anchored in fact. But on that Sunday afternoon, in
> front of Nelson's monument, a new chapter was begun for me in the
> lesson of faith in the capacities of women.[42]

After joining the Women's Social and Political Union in 1906, of which she remained a member until 1912, Robins wrote *Votes for Women!* with the intention of raising women's voices in the theater, providing an unrestricted way to communicate with society. In Robins's eyes, supporting women to find and employ their individual voices was one of the purposes of the feminist movement, as she declared in a 1911 speech given to the Women Writers' Suffrage League:

> Critics have often said that women's men are badly drawn. Ladies,
> what shall we say of the many girls drawn by men? I think we shall be
> safer *not* to say. But there she stands—the Real Girl!—waiting for you
> to do her justice. No mere chocolate-box "type," but a creature of
> infinite variety, of curiosities and ambitions, of joy in physical action,
> of high dreams of love and service, sharer in her brother's . . . "exulta-
> tions, agonies/and man's unconquerable soul."[43]

Robins sought to demonstrate just that in *Votes for Women!*—presenting a female protagonist in defiance of the "chocolate-box type." The play could have been perceived as a domestic drama about a "tainted" woman but was actually an advocate for suffragettes and social justice. Vida Levering's past resurfaces when the upper-class woman encounters Geoffrey Stonor, an old lover who encouraged her to abort their unexpected pregnancy. A proud suffragette, Vida inspires her former lover's new fiancé, who, after learning of her past, orders that her fiancé reunite with his previous lover. When attempting to do so, he is drawn to the suffragette cause and by the play's conclusion has pledged his support of it.[44]

Votes for Women! daringly and deliberately defied theatrical convention. It placed female characters in a public space rather than confining
them to the domestic sphere, featured a woman with a past but did not
show her suffering from tragic consequences, and ensured her happy
ending through her devotion to public service rather than a marriage with
a respectable man. It even flouted the stereotype of suffragettes being
portrayed as unfeminine and unattractive: Levering is described as well-
attired and attractive. And after two acts in a domestic, drawing-room
setting, the play's third act features a gathering of forty-eight suffragettes,
which was described in the *Clarion* as follows:

> There never was anything like it. Here, on a stage little bigger than a
> suburban concert hall platform, we have a representation of a mass
> meeting in Trafalgar Square, and though the whole of an act is devoted
> to speeches of four agitators and the interruptions of the crowd, the
> outcome is an illusion of tumultuous excitement, and a scene more
> compact of laughs and dramatic thrills than any orthodox theater in
> London can now show.[45]

A commercial success, the play's run at the Court Theatre was extended, and its influence was widespread.[46] One year after *Votes for
Women!* premiered, the Women Writers' Suffrage League was formed,
along with the Actresses' Franchise League, which thanks to the success
of *Votes for Women!* saw the possibilities of bringing the work of suffragettes to the stage.[47]

One author of such plays was Cicely Hamilton, author of the suffrage
play *Pageant of Great Women*. Premiering in 1909, the play depicts a
female Justice hearing arguments from a woman who is presenting her
reasons for desiring enfranchisement to a female Justice, while Prejudice
argues against the woman's case. It was called the "finest practical piece
of political propaganda." The arguments presented by Prejudice, played
by the only man in the cast, are then answered by a parade of historical
female figures. The presence and accomplishments they represent defeat
his argument.[48] With the parade members largely silent, the play represents a suffragette cartoon.

Hamilton identified as a feminist, stating in her autobiography, *Life
Errant*,

> My personal revolt was feminist rather than suffragist; what I rebelled
> at chiefly was the dependence implied in the idea of "destined" mar-
> riage, "destined" motherhood—the identification of success with mar-
> riage, of failure with spinsterhood, the artificial concentration of the
> hopes of girlhood on sexual attraction and maternity. [49]

An active participant in the suffragette movement, Hamilton was also
a member of the Women's Social and Political Union, the Women's
Freedom League, and the Woman's Tax Resistance League, and she participated in the Open Door Council, which worked to improve women's
legal and economic conditions outside of dominant welfare feminism. [50]
These beliefs were inspired and supported by her work in the theater,
where she learned that women not only were paid less than men, but also
had to take on more financial burdens, because their costumes were not
always provided.

> Her professional circumstances thus encouraged feminist convictions.
> She made her first contribution to feminism, however, not by challeng-
> ing such unfair practices in the theatrical world, but simply by provid-
> ing roles, especially strong, unstereotyped roles, for women to play—a
> novelty for the Edwardian theater. [51]

Hamilton, who never married, wrote twenty plays containing a variety
of female roles. [52] Her first full-length play was *Diana of Dobson's*, a
comedy about a shopgirl who, after coming into an unexpected inheri-
tance, finds herself pursued by two different suitors. Along with the grim
living conditions of underpaid female employees, the play demonstrates
the "business-like aspect of love in woman, the social or commercial
necessity for sexual intercourse . . . usually ignored by an imitative feminine art—because it is lacking in man, and is, therefore, not really
grasped by him." [53] As Stowell wrote, "Although the play is conceived as
'romantic comedy,' Hamilton's depiction of the life of sweated female
shop-assistants is well-documented fact." [54]
Marriage was often a topic of Hamilton's writing, clearly demonstrated in *Marriage as a Trade* and *Just to Get Married*, which she adapted
into a novel the following year. Hamilton stated she was not opposed to
marriage as a whole—only enforced marriage. [55] In *Just to Get Married*,
Hamilton's protagonist is overcome with guilt about marrying someone

she doesn't love and breaks her engagement one day before her wedding, saying to her fiancé,

> I wanted to get married—because my people wanted me to get married—to you or to anyone. Because every woman is expected to get herself a husband somehow or another and is looked on as a miserable failure if she doesn't. I didn't want to be a miserable failure, so I said yes to the first man who asked me.[56]

Hamilton's own views on matrimony are expressed in *Marriage as a Trade*, in which she defines a woman as

> an individual human being whose life is her own concern; whose worth . . . is no way advanced or detracted from by the accident of marriage; who does not rise in my estimation by reason of a purely physical capacity for bearing children or sink in my estimation through a lack of that capacity . . . I never think of her either as a wife or as a mother—I separate the woman from her attributes. To me she is an entity in herself.[57]

While Hamilton lived as a single woman, her characters did not. Her plays often concluded with a socially acceptable ending, despite her characters defying convention throughout the show. *Just to Get Married* concludes with the runaway bride realizing she does love her fiancé and reuniting with him—with her proposing to him, in fact.

Hamilton was far from the only person questioning the role of marriage in society, but her questions were far from welcome. Any challenges to the established societal norms were feared, and women fighting for the right to vote represented even more than a demand for political representation. A writer—a woman writer—questioning the purpose and function of marriage was also questioning the social structure of church and government, as well as sexual principles and standards.[58] As Harriet Blodgett wrote in "Cicely Hamilton: Independent Feminist," "attacks on the institution of marriage formed part of Edwardian suffrage agitation only indirectly, insofar as a demand for sexual morality was linked with the demand for the vote, the argument being the vote would not only render women stronger and more self-respecting, but also enable them to introduce legislation to deal with male immorality."[59]

DIVORCE, SEX, AND MONEY

With marriage so deeply linked to morality, divorce was a contentious subject to publicly address. It's no surprise that Behn frequently wrote about the dissolution of marriages or that Baker exposed their grim realities. The circumstances surrounding the end of wedlock were complicated, difficult, and, at times, even comic.

Even during the seventeenth century, there were ways to end a marriage, but they were far from equitable. A woman could request a legal separation, but if it was rejected, she had no other options, often resulting in her leaving her home, abandoning her children, and forgoing her personal assets. This did not escape Behn's astute social criticism. Instead, she addressed the inequities: Almost one-third of her comedies conclude with the formal separation of a marriage.[60]

Behn addressed the financial problems that came with marriage, but money troubles regarding divorce also abounded. Women didn't risk losing their lives in a duel about love, but they did risk losing their financial well-being and faced the threat of being bought and sold as property themselves by being sold in a "wife sale," a publicly held acution that sold a divorced wife like a piece of livestock.[61]

Grounds for divorce were far from equitable, even regarding adultery.

> A single act of adultery by a wife was an unpardonable breach of the law of property and the idea of hereditary descent, since it presented a threat to the orderly transmission of property and status by the possible introduction of spurious offspring. It was also seen as a breach of the moral order, since it involved an invasion of a husband's property rights on the wife's body. Adultery by the husband, on the other hand, was generally regarded as a regrettable but understandable foible, rather than a serious threat to a marriage.[62]

Behn's first play, *The Forc'd Marriage*, was staged immediately following the famous "Roos case," which publicly dissolved a marriage on the grounds of a woman's adultery. She also examined the process of legal separation in *Sir Patient Fancy* (1678), an unrepentant denouncement of mercenary marriage that illustrates how few legal options were available to ex-wives.[63] *The False Count* (1683) and *The Luckey Chance* (1686) examined the difference between annulment with the right to marry and separation, and annulment was also included in the plots of *The Forc'd Marriage* (1670) and *The Town-Fopp* (1676).

Penning plays on marriage and divorce inevitably led to another subject, and one that was rarely discussed in public: sex. Empowerment through language was immediately correlated with empowerment in sexuality, both of which were deemed inappropriate for women. Women actors were condemned for displaying their bodies onstage, and women playwrights were equally judged, according to Kreis-Schnick:

> Fear of sexual license is always related to the fear of linguistic mastery. The commonplace identification of prostitution with female speaking and writing holds fast. . . . Women dramatists struggling into discourse were painfully unaware of the contemporary analogy between unbridled speech and unbridled sexuality. Behn frequently and self-consciously applied this metaphor herself when asserting, no matter how easily, her artistic endeavors.[64]

Female playwrights who dared to depict sexuality through their writing were doubly marginalized. Femininity's association with morality led to the increased restriction of women's desires and actions, and unrestrained female sexuality was seen as a threat to public order, with public speaking not far behind:

> As self-policing was recognized as a useful means of control, the concepts of female honor, female virtue, and female moral propriety, familiar from medieval times and earlier, were strengthened in an attempt to ward off any form of sexual self-determination. . . . Taming and civilizing both the sexual act and woman merged into one ideological construct, whose ultimate aim—the ideal family and state—was predicated upon female modesty, moderation, and submission.[65]

The disparity in the moral standards between men and women were clear in the rules regarding adultery, defined in 1650, by England's Rump Parliament, and establishing adultery a capital punishment offense "defined as sexual intercourse between a man and a married woman, intercourse between a married man and a single woman being *only* considered fornication."[66] Or, as literary critic Catherine Belsey wrote, "Love, which in men is a passion that cannot be constrained, is evidently in women the fruit of dutiful obedience to arrangements made on their behalf by others."[67]

That sentiment would continue to permeate politics and culture, and female playwrights would continue to oppose it, onstage and off.

3

THE GROUNDBREAKING WORK OF HELLMAN AND HANSBERRY

If theater was employed as a platform for women's voices in the 1700s and 1800s, the 1900s furthered this activism, as works by two of the most prominent female playwrights of the century demonstrate. Both Lillian Hellman and Lorraine Hansberry integrated gender politics and social justice issues into their writing both offstage and on—with the latter composing a groundbreaking, barrier-shattering drama that made and changed the history of American theater.

"THE KIND OF GIRL WHO CAN TAKE THE TOPS OFF BOTTLES WITH HER TEETH"

Playwright and screenwriter Lillian Hellman targeted sexism, gender politics, and slander throughout the decades. Described as a "tough broad . . . the kind of girl who can take the tops off bottles with her teeth,"[1] the rebellious and daring Hellman's work encompassed playwrighting, screenwriting, and writing several memoirs, and her debut dramatic work, *The Children's Hour*, addressed the controversial subjects of homophobia, slander, and deceit.

She was inspired by William Roughead's book *Bad Companions* and its story of two headmistresses accused of having an "inordinate affection" for one another in 1809.[2] One student's grandmother removed her from the school and advised her friends to do the same, and, within weeks, the headmistresses' work and livelihood were destroyed. After ten years of attempting to clear their names and reputations, the women eventually won a libel lawsuit and monetary damages.[3]

Hellman's script found its producer when, working as a reader for Herman Shumlin, she asked him to read her script. As the producer-director's obituary detailed, Shumlin read the first act and said, "Swell." He read the second act and remarked, "I hope it keeps up." And after he read the third, he said, "I'll produce it." He also directed.[4]

Opening in 1934, during a time when homosexuality was considered a mental illness and could result in imprisonment, *The Children's Hour* dramatized the story but clearly established Mary, the accuser, as a liar motivated by spite who blackmails other students who are being complicit. Hellman depicts the teachers as victims of slander. While Martha is in love with Karen, she never acts upon her desires and confesses her feelings in an outburst after the two women have lost their lawsuit and are resigned to their social and professional exile:

> I have loved you the way they said. . . . I've been telling myself that since the night we heard the child say it. I lie in bed night after night praying that it isn't true. But I know about it now. . . . I resented your marriage; maybe because I wanted you; maybe because I wanted you all these years; I couldn't call it by a name but maybe it's been there ever since I first knew you. . . . I've never loved a man—I never knew why before.[5]

Hellman's daring seemed to know no limits: She not only explored same-sex attraction in her play but also upended gender roles in both Martha and Karen, two unmarried women who opened a school and ran a business together, professionally and financially independent. When Karen learns, too late, that proof of her innocence has been discovered and the most influential woman in town is planning a public apology, she refuses forgiveness, saying, "I won't be your confessor. Take your conscience some place else, get somebody else to help you be a 'good' woman again. . . . Get out of here and be noble on the street."[6] Hellman's creation of Karen is not that of a gentle, feminine woman living by the Christian doctrine of forgiveness. She created a woman who had lost everything and was filled with rage.

With a decidedly unhappy ending that includes admissions of forbidden love, denials of forgiveness, and suicide, Hellman's play was consid-

Florence McGee (seated), Anne Revere, and Katherine Emery in the 1934 Broadway production of *The Children's Hour*. *Photofest*

ered so scandalous, productions were banned in Boston, Chicago, and London.[7] But It was warmly received in New York. Declared a "stinging tragedy" by Brooks Atkinson of the *New York Times*, the play was praised for its "hard, clean economy of word and action."[8] Atkinson continued, "Although [Hellman] writes her narrative with vibrant reticence she has also a gift for characterization. . . . It is as though Miss Hellman did not realize what a fine and sentient tragedy she has written."[9]

At the time, a lesbian relationship was considered significantly more scandalous than a same-sex relationship between men, and the idea that young schoolgirls were knowledgeable of same-sex relationships established the play as shocking—so shocking, in fact, that Hellman's script was labeled too unseemly for Pulitzer Prize consideration. In retaliation, New York writers formed the Drama Critics' Circle to bestow an award on the play. Running for almost two years, *The Children's Hour* earned Hellman $125,000 from its initial run and an additional $50,000 for a film adaptation. *These Three*, which was released in 1936, was written by Hellman but with all homosexual aspects of the plot erased. Reflecting the country's conservative culture, the film was critically praised, with some reviewers saying it even improved on the play.

The Children's Hour marked the first of many collaborations between Shumlin and Hellman. *The Little Foxes, Watch on the Rhine*, and *The Searching Wind* followed. Hellman recalled Shumlin as being supportive, writing in her memoir *Pentimento*, that when theater owner Lee Shubert was impolite to her at a rehearsal of *The Children's Hour*, Shumlin said, "That girl, as you call her, is the author of the play."[10]

Hellman's *The Little Foxes* portrayed a viscous power struggle among siblings to control a family business. Regina Giddens clearly resents the gender restrictions placed upon her by early twentieth-century society, a time during which only sons were considered legitimate heirs to their parents' estates. Instead of using her steely intellect for her financial well-being, the restless and scheming Regina is forced to employ her meek husband as a proxy and resort to blackmail and negligence to gain wealth and independence.

An unapologetically ambitious, conniving, and mercenary character, Regina was first played on Broadway by Tallulah Bankhead, whose performance in the "adult horror-play" was praised by *New York Times* critic Brooks Atkinson: "As the malevolent lady of *The Little Foxes* she plays with superb command of the entire character—sparring of the showy side, constantly aware of the poisonous spirit within."[11]

The play depicts Regina scheming against her family and employing her feminine wiles to obtain her material wishes—which she readily admits to her husband, informing him she only married him because she was lonely:

Not the way people usually mean. Lonely for all the things I wasn't going to get. Everybody in this house was so busy, and there was so little place for what I wanted. I wanted the world. Then, and then— Papa died and left the money to Ben and Oscar. . . . I told you I married you *for* something. It turned out it was only for this. This wasn't what I wanted, but it was something. [12]

Regina was hardly a "likable" female protagonist. Cold, calculating, and decidedly unsympathetic, she deliberately sits still and ignores her husband's pleas for help when he suffers a heart attack. But she was also representative of the societal confines of 1900. Unable to work, confined to domestic life, she couldn't do what her brothers could and was patronized by them even when discussing business deals, being told, "You'd get farther with a smile, Regina. I'm a soft man for a woman's smile."[13] Regina pays for her actions, losing her daughter's respect, her brother's devotion, and her husband's life. Although her actions are not understandable, her frustration is. "It's men who have the things that Regina has always longed for: money, freedom, prestige," wrote Hilton Als in the *New Yorker*. "Reading Hellman's script, one feels a pang, every once in a while, for Regina's dark hopes. How far could she—or any woman— really go in a small Southern town in 1900?"[14]

Following its Broadway bow, *The Little Foxes* ran for 410 performances and toured the United States before Hellman penned the screenplay for its 1941 Academy Award–nominated fim adaptation.

After the success of *The Children's Hour* and *The Little Foxes*, Hellman was admitted into the club of American "dramatic literature"—the first woman to be so honored.[15] She went on to integrate politics into her stories and shine the spotlight on the struggles and triumphs of individuals with such plays as *Watch on the Rhine*, *The Autumn Garden*, *Toys in the Attic*, and *Another Part of the Forest*.

The theme of misrepresentation in *The Children's Hour* was frequently explored by Hellman in *Watch on the Rhine*, *The Autumn Garden*, *Toys in the Attic*, and *Another Part of the Forest*, and offstage in her publicized and politically active life. *The Children's Hour* received a revival in 1952, directed by Hellman herself, when the Red Scare was sweeping the country. When called to testify in front of the House Un-American Activities Committee, she adamantly refused to name names, writing in a letter published by the *New York Times*, "To hurt innocent people whom I knew many years ago in order to save myself is, to me, inhuman and indecent and dishonorable." She added, "I cannot and will not cut my conscience to fit this year's fashions, even though I long ago came to the conclusion that I was not a political person and could have no comfortable place in any political group."[16]

Speaking of the timely revival of *The Children's Hour*, Hellman said, it was "not really a play about lesbianism, but about a lie. The bigger the lie, the better, as always." The play's themes—paraonia, dishonesty, and prejudice—were not lost on the country.[17]

But her refusal to testify for the House Un-American Acitivites Committee resulted in Hellman being blacklisted and unable to work for years. Her income dropped to almost nothing. Never one to hide her opinions, she shared her contempt for the events decades later when presenting the award for Best Documentary Film at the 1977 Academy Awards:

> I was once upon a time a respectable member of this community. Respectable didn't necessarily mean more than I took a daily bath when I was sober, didn't spit except when I meant to, and mispronounced a few words of fancy French. Then, suddenly, even before Senator Joe McCarthy reached for that rusty and poisoned ax, I and many others were no longer acceptable to the owners of this industry. Possibly they were men who had been too busy to define personal honor or national honor. Possibly. But, certainly, they confronted the wild charges of Joe McCarthy with a force and courage of a bowl of mashed potatoes. I have no regrets for that period. Maybe you never do when you survive, but I have a mischievous pleasure in being restored to respectability, understanding full well that a younger generation who asked me here tonight meant more by that invitation than my name or my history. I thank them for that because I never thought it would happen, and to make them and myself feel better I hope that the rest of my life will not be too respectable.[18]

Despite Hellman's accomplishments, her work was consistently viewed through the lens of sex, and her gender and appearance dominated any news about her, notably reviews of her work. Her nose and skin were topics of commentary, and she was described as "butch" and a "tough broad . . . the kind of girl who can take the tops off bottles with her teeth."[19] And when the *National Review*, founded by conservative author William F. Buckley, ran a feature story on the writer, its cover featured Hellman gazing into a mirror and asking, "Who is the ugliest of them all?"[20] He also stated that referring to Hellman as the "greatest woman playwright" was the "same as talking about the downhill champion on the one-legged ski team."[21]

Hellman scoffed at the title "woman playwright"—she thought it was demeaning—and she was aware of the prejudice against her due to her gender.[22] When an article that named Edward Albee, Tennessee Williams, and Arthur Miller as America's three greatest living playwrights, Hellman was outraged.[23] But she remained inexhuastibly active, penning three memoirs, along with movie scripts, and remaining politically involved, as well as socially contentious. One of her later feuds involved author Mary McCarthy, who, on Dick Cavett's television show in 1979, described Hellman as "tremendously overrated, a bad writer, and a dishonest writer, but she really belongs to the past." McCarthy also challenged the truth of Hellman's memoirs, stating, "I said once in some interviews that every word she writes is a lie, including 'and' and 'the.'"[24]

A lawsuit—filed by Hellman against McCarthy, PBS, and Cavett for $2.25 million—quickly followed. It was dissolved following Hellman's death in 1984, until which she remained active, and her work remains popular and frequently produced and revived.

Long after her death, Hellman herself remains the source and subject of drama. A one-woman show about her life, titled *Lillian*, played in New York in 1986, starring Zoe Caldwell. Written by William Luce, the play draws from Hellman's three memoirs, *An Unfinished Woman*, *Pentimento*, and *Scoundrel Time*. The play was criticized by *New York Times* critic Frank Rich for glossing over the deeper conflicts and darker moments of Hellman's life, with focus on her treatment of people who shared her political beliefs.[25] He commented,

> Were her most vociferous literary opponents to see *Lillian* en masse, Broadway might have its first riot in years. . . . It's hard to reconcile the rather sugary, only slightly curmudgeonly figure presented here with the vinegary rebel who stirred up tempests for almost five decades on the public stage.[26]

It was after Hellman's death, apparently, that her personality would be honored.

Peter Feibleman, a former colleague and lover of Hellman's, also attempted to bring the playwright to life in *Cakewalk*, an autobiographical play about the pair's relationship. Adapted from Feibleman's book *Lilly:*

Reminisces of Lillian Hellman, the play received similar criticisms of glossing over Hellman's famously challenging personality and addressing why she maintained her status as a subject of fascination, as well as presenting her as an endearingly cantankerous elderly woman.

Ben Brantley of the *New York Times* described Feibleman's script as a "featherweight excursion down memory boulevard" and wrote, "*Cakewalk* is frankly presented as a memory play, with all the telescoping and distortions the term implies. (The relation between fact and fiction is tenuous, of course, when you're talking about Hellman the memoirist, but that's not the issue here.)"[27]

The same criticism could be applied to the subject of the play, whose honesty was frequently called into question, especially regarding the content of her memoirs. But these criticisms did little to stifle the playwright, who declared, "When I'm dead they'll kill me."[28] In that case, at least, Hellman was wrong: She and her work continue to endure, despite her declaration made in a 1966 lecture: "I do not like the theater at all. I get restless."[29]

"INTELLECTUAL REVOLUTIONARY"

A fellow but extremely different boundary breaker from the early 1900s was Lorraine Hansberry, who, in 1959, became the first African American woman to have a play produced on Broadway. Both Hansberry and Hellman channeled their political ideals into drama, broke new ground for women, and were the subject of biographical plays written about them. Born into a family of activists, Hansberry witnessed and was part of political engagement at a young age. Her father fought racial restrictive covenants in their Chicago town through the lawsuit *Hansberry v. Lee*. The case, which Carl Hansberry won, served as inspiration for Lorraine's trailblazing drama *A Raisin in the Sun*.

Long before Hansberry began writing *A Raisin in the Sun*, she was politically engaged, developing an awareness of financial classism even as a child and uncomfortable with her family's material comfort when living amongst struggling families. After attending kindergarten wearing a white fur coat in the middle of the Depression, she recalled, "The kids beat me up; and I think it was from that moment I became a rebel."[30] Dinner guests at the Hansberry household included Walter White, director of the NAACP; W. E. B. DuBois; Langston Hughes; Paul Robeson; Duke Ellington; and Jesse Owens.[31] After her writing was discovered by her family, Hansberry was encourged to channel her activism into words and send letters to the government.[32]

It was after Hansberry saw her first play, a folk musical by Howard Richardson and William Berney titled *Dark of the Moon*, that she became determined to write her own play.[33] And a production of *Juno and the Paycock* convinced her that the theater was her future.[34] She enrolled in a class in set design, but her teacher gave her a failing grade because, he said, he didn't want to encourage her to pursue a field led by white people.[35]

Hansberry moved to New York after college, where she wrote for the Young Progressives of America and worked at the left-wing, socialist paper *Freedom*. Launched by singer, actor, and activist Paul Robeson, the paper's editorial policy was to "keep the African American community informed about issues ignored by the mainstream press, especially the exploitation of African countries by colonial powers, McCarthy's intimidation of American citizens, and racism."[36] Hainsberry's writing, which spoke of "literature's social accountability and ethical obligations," earned her the title "intellectual revolutionary."[37] Her activism extended far beyond the paper: The night before Hansberry's wedding to songwriter and producer Robert B. Nemiroff, the bride and groom-to-be had taken part in a nationwide demonstration against executing Julius and Ethel Rosenberg.

"THERE WASN'T A THEATER IN NEW YORK THAT WOULD TOUCH IT"

Hansberry began writing *A Raisin in the Sun*, originally titled *The Crystal Stair*, with the intention of writing a "social drama about Negroes that will be good art."[38] She had become "disgusted with a whole body of material about Negroes. Cardboard characters. Cute dialect bits. Or hip-swinging musicals from exotic sources."[39] Determined to depict working-class black people who triumph over racial discrimination, Hansberry was inspired by the people and personalities of her childhood. Frustrated with her lack of progress, she threw the script into her apartment's fireplace, but her husband retrieved the pages and stored them for a few days before she resumed work on the play.[40]

An unexpected and rapid-fire journey brought *A Raisin in the Sun* to Broadway. It began at a dinner party in 1957, with a spontaneous reading of the script. Hansberry had no intention of completing the entire play, but her friends encouraged her to continue, and the story of the Younger family captivated guests throughout the night. The following morning, Hansberry received an impassioned phone call from Philip Rose, a guest who had only gotten home at 4:30 in the morning. He had already decided he wanted to produce the play.[41]

Raising the money took work. Director Lloyd Richards told the *New York Times*, "The smart money did not invest in the show. There was no audience for this sort of play. We went on the road without having a Broadway theater to come back to."[42] And Hansberry herself told the *New York Times* just before the play opened on Broadway, "Potential backers read my play and cried: 'It's beautiful! Too bad it isn't a musical. White audiences aren't interested in a Negro play.' I told them this wasn't a 'Negro play.'"[43]

So, Rose took *A Raisin in the Sun* out of town, with tryout performances in New Haven, Philadelphia, and Chicago. The play, with ten parts for black actors and actresses, offered such rare opportunities that almost 1,000 people auditioned.[44] The plan was to open on Broadway if reviews were good, but a theater was not booked in advance. The house was half-empty for the first performance on the road, but word quickly spread. This show was different, people said, and they were buying tickets because, as one black woman told director Lloyd Richards, "The word's going around my neighborhood that there's something here that has to do with me."[45]

"Mama, it is a play that tells the truth about people—Negroes and life," Hansberry wrote to her mother from New Haven,

> and I think it will help a lot of people understand how we are just as complicated as they are—and just as mixed up—but above all, that we have among our miserable and downtrodden ranks—people who are the very essence of human dignity. That is what, after all the laughter and tears, the play is supposed to say. I hope it will make you very proud.[46]

"SOMETHING OF A MIRACLE"

On March 11, 1959, *A Raisin in the Sun* opened on Broadway at the Ethel Barrymore Theatre—the first work by a black woman to be produced on Broadway. As Nan Robertson remarked in the *New York Times*, "That the play ever got to Broadway at all is something of a miracle." Only three other black playwrights—Langston Hughes, Richard Wright, and Louis Peterson—had "straight plays" open on Broadway, and none of them were women.[47] Hansberry had chosen Richards, a black director with no Broadway experience, to direct.[48] She had made history at just 28 years old.

Producers, who had been uncertain of the play's reception, watched opening night as it opened to a standing ovation that went on for 15 minutes until Sidney Poitier went into the audience and escorted Hansberry to the stage.[49] Michael Anderson recalled, "They had never seen anything like it," adding,

A Raisin in the Sun with Sidney Poitier, Claudia McNeil, Ruby Dee, Glynn Turman, and Diana Sands. *Photofest*

Until that evening, Broadway had never seen a play written by a black woman, nor a play with a black director, nor a commercially produced drama about black life, rather than musicals or comedy. The Broadway premiere of *A Raisin in the Sun* was as much a milestone in the nation's history as it was in American theater. "Never before," commented James Baldwin, "had so much of the truth of black people's lives been seen onstage."[50]

Remarking on the play's honesty, Brooks Atkinson, who described the show as a "Negro *The Cherry Orchard*," wrote,

> *A Raisin in the Sun* has vigor, as well as veracity, and is likely to destroy the complacency of anyone who sees it. . . . What the situations are does not matter at the moment. For *A Raisin in the Sun* is a play about human beings who want, on the one hand, to preserve their family pride and, on the other hand, to break out of the poverty that seems to be their fate. Not having any axe to grind, Miss Hansberry has a wide range of topics to write about—some of them hilarious, some of them painful in the extreme.[51]

Three weeks after opening, Hansberry was awarded the Drama Critics' Circle Award for Best Play of the Year. The first African American and youngest playwright to win the award, she beat Tennessee Williams's *Sweet Bird of Youth*, Eugene O'Neill's *A Touch of the Poet*, and Archibald MacLeish's *JB*.[52]

But the praise for *A Raisin in the Sun* wasn't universal. Some considered the play too conservative, while others found it too radical. Playwright and poet Amiri Baraka thought the play was "middle class—buying a house and moving into white folks' neighborhoods," and author Nelson Algren described it as a "good drama about real estate."[53] As white critics embraced the play without fully comprehending its themes and message, some black critics thought Hansberry had "sought integration through the whitening of her characters" and accused her of attempting to "convince whites that blacks were exactly like them, and that therefore full integration could take place without seriously disturbing the status quo or forcing hard sacrifices."[54]

Some of the praise *A Raisin in the Sun* received was for its universality—coming from white journalists reviewing the show who implied the story would be as effective if the black characters had been white. But Hansberry, who asserted that the Younger family was from Chicago's

South Side and specifically Negro, said, "I don't think there is anything more universal in the world than man's oppression to man. One of the most sound ideas in dramatic writing is that, in order to create the universal, you must pay very great attention to the specific."[55]

The play and Hansberry herself received criticism for writing about a struggling black family when she herself had been raised in an upper-middle-class background, but the playwright responded as follows:

> I come from an extremely comfortable background, materially speaking. And yet, we live in a ghetto . . . which automatically means intimacy with all classes and all kinds of experiences. It's not any more difficult for me to know the people I wrote about than it is for me to know members of my family. This is one of the things that the American experience has meant to Negroes. We are *one* people.[56]

A Raisin in the Sun ran for 530 performances on Broadway,[57] and its success propelled it to Hollywood, where Hansberry, determined to present an accurate representation of black people, insisted on writing the screenplay herself. Movies about African Americans released before the 1960s had been few and far between, and their few black characters— usually maids, servants, and entertainers playing themselves—experienced incomplete characterization and pejorative presentation. So, Hansberry negotiated herself as the screenwriter.[58] It took her three tries to produce a script the studio accepted.[59] The entire Broadway cast performed in the film, which was directed by Daniel Petrie and premiered in 1961, to mixed reviews, but it drew a record number of audiences.

Hansberry's fame was on the rise, but neither her race nor her gender went unnoticed in the press, which was largely male: A *New York Times* profile of her began its second paragraph by referring to her as "Mrs. Robert Nemiroff, wife of a music publisher and songwriter," before describing her as "voluble, energetic, pretty, and small."[60] And the second sentence of a *New Yorker* article about her described her as "a relaxed, soft-voiced young lady with an intelligent and pretty face, a particularly vertical hairdo, and large brown eyes, so dark and so deep that you get lost in them."[61]

Hansberry continued to write, questioning social restrictions and boundaries, her unwavering devotion to political activism and social justice apparent on the page. The playwright, who had declared that black people "must concern themselves with every single means of the strug-

gle: legal, illegal, passive, active, violent, and nonviolent" tackled slavery, anti-Semitism, homosexuality, prostitution, and suicide—all in just
two scripts.[62] *The Drinking Gourd*, written for television, addressed slavery from multiple points of view. It had been commissioned by producer-
director Dore Schary for NBC as part of a series of dramas memorializing
the Civil War's centennial, but Hansberry's script was never produced,
having been deemed too controversial.[63]

Following *A Raisin in the Sun*, Hansberry's next play, *The Sign in
Sidney Brustein's Window*, featured a protagonist struggling to find his
place in Bohemian culture. Prior to its opening in 1964, the play was
discussed among journalists for its departure from the "Negro problem,"
instead featuring numerous white characters—a "somewhat startling departure for a Negro playwright."[64]

The Sign in Sidney Brustein's Window, which opened on Broadway on
October 15, 1964, received mixed reviews and has been criticized for its
ambitious, complicated story. Howard Taubman of the *New York Times*
praised one particular scene for being "more searing than anything on
Broadway," but he also faulted Hansberry for attempting "to cover too
much ground and to touch on too many issues." Declaring that the play
"lacks concision and cohesion," he stated, "One remembers isolated pas-
sages rather than the work as a whole."[65]

The lack of enthusiasm for Hansberry's second Broadway play was
noted: A letter to the editor of the *New York Times* lamented the cool
reception, contrasting it with the adoration *A Raisin in the Sun* had received, asking,

> How can it be that, of the hundreds of thousands who roared with
> pleasure and wept tears at her *Raisin in the Sun*, so few have the
> intellectual appetency to hear what her mind has been at work on
> since? . . . Is it a compliment to our culture that one season a writer can
> be voted the best playwright of the year and another season be ignored
> like a novice?[66]

But the play has endured. More than fifty years later, *The Sign in
Sidney Brustein's Window* was warmly received, as a Chicago revival
earned critical acclaim. Writing for the *Chicago Tribune*, Chris Jones
questioned why the play was not better known and credited its absence
from the canon to racism and sexism among theater critics:

Gabriel Dell and Rita Moreno in *The Sign in Sidney Brustein's Window* (1964). Photofest

With *Sign*, white, male critics in New York in 1964 simply could not get their heads around a black woman from Chicago showing such extraordinary range. . . . Hot on the heels of *Raisin*, Hansberry was writing not about a domineering mother and a shiftless son, moving to a different neighborhood in a distant, racist city, but of the fevered souls of white Manhattan liberals. She was peering at the insecurities of the struggling people of the theater, the art world, and the nascent alternative media—living in Greenwich Village and fighting for progressive societal change and personal happiness, only to find the one as elusive as the other.[67]

Hansberry's devotion to politics went beyond race; it also included women. Influenced by Harriet Tubman, Sojourner Truth, Mary Church Terrell, Ida B. Wells-Barnett, and Mary McLeod Bethune, she believed that mothers helped to prolong sexism by teaching their daughters to devote their lives to marriage and parenthood instead of success and careers.[68] She declared in an interview with Studs Terkel, "Obviously, the most oppressed group of any oppressed people will be its women, who are twice oppressed. . . . So, as oppression makes people more militant, women become twice militant, because they are twice oppressed."[69]

Beneatha, Lena's adult daughter in *A Raisin in the Sun*, personified these beliefs. Rebellious, independent, unapologetic, and independent, the aspiring doctor declines the advances and even a marriage proposal from two different men and rejects the notion that her brother should be the head of the household. And, to her mother's shock, she declares herself to be athiest, despite living in a devoted Christian home, saying,

Mama, you don't understand. It's all a matter of ideas, and God is just one idea I don't accept. It's not important. I am not going out and be immoral or commit crimes because I don't believe in God. I don't even think about it. It's just that I get tired of Him getting credit for all the things the human race achieves through its own stubborn effort. There is simply no blasted God—there is only one man, and it is he who makes miracles![70]

Hansberry and Nemiroff divorced in 1964, but they remained friends and colleagues. The two had collaborated on her plays, he providing feedback and encouraging her to write, but the partnership was intellectual and professional. Hansberry was romantically involved with women, moving within a small lesbian set of which she was one of few, if any, black women. Nemiroff said her sexuality "was not a peripheral or casual part of her life but contributed significantly on many levels to the sensitivity and complexity of her life on human beings and of the world."[71] It was after she was diagnosised with cancer that the two separated.

Even after being diagnosed with pancreatic cancer, Hansberry continued her activist work. Her voice continued long after her death on January 12, 1965, at thirty-four years old. But Hansberry's voice was far from silenced following her death. It was spoken from the stage, in her own words, when the play *To Be Young, Gifted, and Black: The World of Lorraine Hansberry* opened in 1969. Adapted by Nemiroff, the script drew from the playwright's letters, plays, and novels. It told her story, beginning with her childhood in Chicago, and chronicled her years in college, her moving to New York, and the obstacles she had to overcome for *A Raisin in the Sun* to be produced on Broadway, before concluding with her battle with cancer. An ensemble production, the show featured several actors playing Hansberry. Reviewed by Richard Shepard in the *New York Times*, the play was lauded for its lack of sentimentality, as well as its portrayal of grief, humor, and anger. *To Be Young, Gifted, and Black* ran from 1968 to 1969 Off-Broadway and was subsequently adapted into an autobiography with the same title.

Another posthumous work by Hansberry, *Les Blancs*, was produced by her husband, and *A Raisin in the Sun*, one of the most revived plays in the world, and has been translated into thirty-five languages.[72] Her writing inspired many works, notably the Tony Award– and Pulitzer Prize–winning *Clybourne Park*, by Bruce Norris, which portrays events both before and after *A Raisin in the Sun* in the home the Youngers moved into, and *Beneatha's Place*, by Kwame Kwei-Armah. Kwei-Armah's script focuses on Beneatha Younger and Joseph Asagai, her Nigerian boyfriend, examining racism in a white neighborhood in Lagos, Nigeria, in 1959. Further enhancing the timelessness of prejudice, both plays are set in two different time periods, decades apart.

Hansberry, who believed that "living is a protest,"[73] was praised by Howard Taubman posthumously as a writer who "brought a burning passion and mature, sensitive viewpoint to a theater where they are in short supply."[74]

Both Hellman and Hansberry were women of whom the likes had not been seen before offstage and who brought people who had never before been seen onstage. Hellman found the title "woman playwright" demeaning, and Hansberry advocated activism and equality offstage, speaking at town hall meetings just months before her death. The women broke new ground, but it would take much more effort to keep their work going.

4

REVOLTING WOMEN

As the 1970s approached, women's voices grew louder and began challenging societal norms everywhere. Betty Friedan's *The Feminine Mystique*, questioning the truth of the "happy housewife," was published in 1963, inspiring women to think to themselves, "Is this all?"

Women began organizing. When the 1964 Civil Rights Act made its way through Congress, feminists campaigned for an amendment outlawing sex discrimination in employment. The act, and the amendment, Title VII, were passed, despite Title VII being introduced as a strategy to derail the bill. But women were far from protected in their places of work. In 1965 came the formation of the Equal Employment Opportunity Commission, but it refused to enforce Title VII, as the *New Republic* asked, "Why should a mischievous joke perpetrated on the floor of the House of Representatives be treated by a responsible administration body with this kind of seriousness?"[1]

Women were mad, and they were mobilizing. The National Organization of Women was formed in 1966, in the United States, and, in 1967, women's lib crossed the pond to England, where the Abortion Act was passed in 1967, the Equal Pay Act in 1970, and the Sex Discrimination Act in 1975.[2]

It was inevitable that these voices and issues would find their way to the stage. A notable step forward took place in 1968, in England, when the Theaters Act eradicated theater censorship by the state. The passage ended a centuries-long act, passed in 1737, and modified in 1843, that gave Lord Chamberlain, the most senior office of the Royal Household of the United Kingdom, the power to license plays and regulate restrictions on dramatic works. Productions approved by Lord Chamberlain, who had become established as the arbiter of morality in the performing arts, forbid the use of profane language, references to homosexuality, and explicit heterosexual behavior.

It seemed fitting that the tribal love-rock musical *Hair*, whose book and score included explicit depictions of drug use, references to homosexual relationships, a strong antiwar message, and an infamous nude scene, opened the following day. Theaters could now stage political works, responding to current events through their productions, but women's voices and issues continued to be underrepresented.

"WE'RE NOT BEAUTIFUL, WE'RE NOT UGLY. WE'RE ANGRY."

So, women began forming their own groups. Their names included Monstrous Regiment, Spare Tyre, Mrs. Worthington's Daughters, Cunning Stunts, and Beryl and the Perils, among others. They seized upon opportunities to bring women's voices and stories to the stage, and a variety of collectives began taking shape, devoted to promoting parity and equality, and challenging the traditionally established roles women held in society.

But despite their efforts, much of the new, female-focused work was met with patronizing attitudes and obligatory indulgence by arts reporters and theater critics—men who, according to their archives, were reluctant to take women's theater seriously or even view it as theater at all.

One of the first collectives began by taking to the streets. After assembling in 1970, the Women's Street Theatre Group did not limit themselves to the stage. They made public statements, celebrating International Women's Day in March 1971, by dancing to the song "Keep Young and Beautiful" from the Depression-era musical *42nd Street*, along with marchers, and performing their first play in Trafalgar Square. Titled *Sugar and Spice*, the script satirized the sexualization of women and their entrapment in traditional family units.[3] In 1971, the group picketed the Miss World Contest at Royal Albert Hall.[4] This followed the notorious protests of 1970, during which people hurled tomatoes and stink, smoke, and flour bombs at comedian Bob Hope and distributed leaflets brandishing the slogan, "We're not beautiful, we're not ugly. We're angry."

The following year, the Women's Street Theatre Group parodied the pageant by performing *The Flashing Nipple Show*, wearing dark pants and shirts with flashing lights affixed on their breasts and vaginas.[5] The group took to the streets again, by invitation, at a demonstration coordinated by the Christian Festival of Light. Accompanied by a group of gay men dressed as nuns, protestors brandished a placard that read "Holy Family" on one side and "Fuck the Family" on the other, while large "hands" demonstrated familial violence. The men and women were arrested, forcing the police to determine in which cell the men, dressed as women, should be held. They were placed in a separate cell.[6]

Street theater found its way underground when the group held an "auction" of women in the London Underground, and onto Oxford Street when they protested in the women's lavatory in the Miss Selfridge store by pretending to shave their faces, presenting a comparison to the women applying makeup in the powder room.[7] The group then changed its name to Punching Judies and began work on a show that reflected both the accomplishment of the Equal Pay Act being passed in 1970 and the concerns that remained regarding its loopholes. *The Amazing Equal Pay Show* was based on the 1968 strike at Ford for equal pay—from which women received 92 percent of what they were requesting—and encouraged women to recognize the connection between work and home, and the challenges women faced at each.[8]

Playwright and critic Michelene Wandor wrote of the show in *Carry on Understudies: Theatre and Sexual Politics*,

> The exhortatory message behind the play is directed mainly at women in the audience, urging them to see the connections between the struggle at home and the struggle at work. At the same time the play ridicules the men, the trade union bureaucracy, and the Labour Party in a way that was theatrically effective but politically naïve, since it appeared to attack political organisations as such. However, it was uncompromising in pushing the interests of ordinary women to the fore, showing how deep the division between working-class men and women can be, and pointing out the conflicts between working people's needs at the grassroots and the demands of the Realpolitik at the top.[9]

The question of representation was brought to audiences in the West End in 1978, when the Feminist Theatre Study Group picketed five shows, distributing questions that asked whether the characters in this play impied that,

Blondes are dumb?
Wives nag?
Feminists are frustrated?
Whores have hearts of gold?
Mothers-in-law interfere?
Lesbians are aggressive?
Intellectual women are frigid?
Women who enjoy sex are nyphomaniacs?
Older women are sexless?

They said, "We are a group of theater workers who are tired of portraying these cardboard cutouts. We want theater managers, directors, and writers to stop producing plays which insult women."[10]

The groups kept coming together, staging both comedies and dramas, but they were far from respected by the people determining their funding.[11] Cunning Stunts, which was formed in 1977, performed cabarets using circus techniques on the streets, at children's shows, and for community projects. The Arts Council of Great Britain, which, from 1977 to 1978, consisted of sixteen men and four women, condensed into this group of "talented, zany women doing crazily funny things because they liked doing them." But, as Jonathan Lamede wrote, "No doubt, you can aim at all these things and you can do some of them some of the time, but it would take a lifetime's genius to fulfill them in one body of work."[12]

The council was not impressed with Cunning Stunt's productions: They sought professional-quality performances and frequently complained about the quality of productions by these enterprising new groups. Drama officer Clive Tempest reported on their 1981 show *Winter Warmer*, saying,

> If they wish to entertain simply as an all-woman clown company, I suspect they will have to work very hard on their skills. . . . If they are interested in narrative, they will have to find ways of creating stronger material. And some directorial authority, no matter how it is arrived at, seems necessary.[13]

The collective's application for funding a series of public workshops was denied by the council, and the group presented one last show before disbanding in 1982.

Cunning Stunts was far from alone in their provocative performances. Another controversial theater group was Clean Break, a collective that specialized in working with female prisoners. The group, which formed in 1979, was also reprimanded for its lack of professionalism, noted by Lamede, who wrote that one of the actors was giving the "sort of self-indulgent performance that would pass for bravura acting at secondary school but had little place in professional theater."[14] The collective did not receive regular ongoing funding from the Arts Council until it began engaging professional theatermakers.[15]

One of the most enduring women's theater groups formed during this time was the Women's Theatre Group. First assembled in 1973, its declared mission was "directed towards exploration of the female situation from the feminist standpoint." The all-female company, which strove to build audiences, proved to be among the longest-lasting collaboratives of the decade.[16] The Women's Theatre Group's shows addressed the topics of women's careers, equal pay, contraception, artificial insemination, and female incarceration, with postshow discussions regularly held to encourage debate among the audiences.

Those discussions were necessary, a fact clearly seen when an established playwright named Pam Gems—whose *Dead Fish* had played the Edinburgh Festival, the Hampstead Theatre, and the West End—was rejected from the Royal Court Theatre after she penned *Queen Christina*, written for the Royal Court. Ann Jellicoe comissioned the work but left the theater before it was submitted, and the new, male management decided that *Queen Christina* was "too sprawly, too expensive to do . . . and it would appeal more to women."[17] The biographical play was then accepted at the Royal Shakespeare Company and went on to achieve success as the first play written by a woman to be performed at the Royal Shakespeare Company's the Other Place in 1977.[18]

The Royal Court did accept Mary O'Malley's comedy *Once a Catholic* in 1977, which proved to be the most commercially successful play by a woman in the 1970s.[19] The chronicles of 1950s schoolgirls struggling to reconcoile sexuality with religion was honored with several awards and established O'Malley as the Royal Court's resident dramatist for 1977, before being transferred to West End's Wyndham's Theatre for a two-year run.

"WE WORE DUNGAREES"

The influence of the Women's Theatre Group was widespread, but it was far from the only activist performance group putting on a show. In 1975, another Women's Theatre Festival, this time at Haymarket Theatre in Leicester, took place. Following the festival, two new theater collectives formed, one of which included several members who later helped assemble Monstrous Regiment. The group's name was a twist on the title of John Knox's 1558 pamphlet The First Blast of the Trumpet against the Monstrous Regiment of Women, an argument that female political authority existed in direct opposition to the Bible. But the women of the 1970s turned the insult on itself and made it into a mark of pride. Along with presenting new dramatic work featuring female writers and actors, Monstrous Regiment required women to direct, design, and perform technical work.[20]

Adele Salem told the oral history project "Unfinished Histories" about the excitement of working with an all-female group:

> We wore dungarees. I remember having a khaki flying suit when I was in the Women's Theatre Group. We could do what men could do. We [could] carry really heavy equipment, drive the big Mercedes van. It was a point of honour to us—to be seen by the young girls when we went into the schools carrying the equipment, setting up electric guitars, and all that kind of stuff. Saying yeah, we could do this. You can do this too. Look, we're doing it. That was very radical, very exciting, and very tiring—carrying all that stuff around.[21]

The groups had to work hard. With Margaret Thatcher elected leader of the Conservative Party in 1975, and appointed prime minister in 1979, grants funded by the Arts Council of Great Britain faced cuts—4.8 percent at the beginning of her time in office and 2.9 percent at the end—and the Arts Council evolved into a government instrument, having previously been an independent agency.[22]

When Monstrous Regiment first formed, funding was provided to artists through subsidies, distributed by the Arts Council, a body consisting of artists independent from the government that were provided money by the government. The group described itself as a "group of professional actors who wanted to make exciting political theater based on women's experience: Tired of seeing that experience marginalised or trivialised, we wanted to take it out of the wings and place it at the center of the stage."[23] But, as Peter Hall wrote in the *New York Times,*

> Then came Margaret Thatcher, and everything changed. Subsidy was anathema to a monetarist, so the arts had to change, too. For eleven years the performing arts were downgraded and diminished by a Government that could not and would not fit them into its economic philosophy. If the arts could not exist without subsidy and could not immediately make money, they were thought either inefficient or un-necessary—probably both. That the arts were subsidized so that they could serve the community, proliferate, be more productive, and, per-haps, finally, return something to the Exchequer was not admitted or discussed. [24]

The council granted money to Monstrous Regiment, which permitted the group to employ eleven people, both men and women, on a full-time basis.[25] The Regiment's works responded to societal sexism and patriar-chy, especially in theater, which often resorted to stereotypical depictions of gender.[26] They unapologetically examined sociopolitical issues affect-ing women, one pointed example being *Scum: Death, Destruction, and Dirty Washing,* by Claire Luckham and Chris Bond, subtitled a "musical celebration of the events of the Paris Commune of 1871."[27] The group continued to produce work that challenged and distorted cultural norms: *Vinegar Tom,* by Caryl Churchill, also came from Monstrous Regiment. Inspired by the Women's Rights Act in 1970, Churchill's play explored gender through England's seventeenth-century witch trials, illustrating patriarchal control in a society that rejects outcasts or anyone who devi-ates from societal norms. Violence against women was the subject of Ann Mitchell and Susan Todd's *Kiss and Kill,* and working conditions for women, both inside and outside of the home, were addressed in *Floor-show,* written by David Bradford, Bryony Lavery, and Michelene Wan-dor.[28] Wandor recalled of the production, writing, "The women in . . . [Monstrous Regiment] wanted to explore the notion of glamour in the performance process, to show that women can be as funny as men, and, as individuals, to experiment with adlib exchanges with the audience."[29]

The collective continued producing controversial work that was both embraced and opposed by feminists. The show was stopped—literally in 1978—during *Time Gentlemen Please*, Bryony Lavery's cabaret on sexuality, when feminists voiced their objections to the play's inclusion of heterosexual relationships,[30] while *Teendreams*, by David Edgar and Susan Todd, chronicled women's differing relationships with modern-day liberation as they attempt to carve out life paths that differ from the formerly prescribed straight and narrow journey of marriage and motherhood.

But the Regiment's bold, adventurous work was not welcomed by everyone: Loren Kruger stated that "stable" artistic institutions, rather than courageous, cutting-edge ones, are usually the recipient of subsidies, furthering women's marginalization and thus authorizing such marginalization.[31] The promise of subsidies was threatened as the Thatcher Era continued and funding decreased, and paid positions at Monstrous Regiment began to lessen. Payment shifted from annual salaries to a per-production basis, and the Regiment moved from a government-funded group to collective management.

Monstrous Regiment was far from alone in its patronizing reception from the male-dominated press. A similar perspective from critics was seen when Richard Edmond reviewed Byrony Lavery's *On the Origin of Species*, a critique of patriarchal history that featured women, rather than men, as the story's focus.[32] Writing for the *Birmingham Post* in 1984, Edmond wrote, "Bryony Lavery's latest farce is a complete confusion. Miss Lavery belongs to that modern breed of bellyaching feminists who protest the role of women in what is believed to be a male-dominated world, which is nonsense. The plays are naturally propagandist material."[33]

Along with staging "propaganda" about women's rights, the groups of the time were also addressing ageism in the industry. The Regiment began presenting stories about women who were past middle age—specifically, older than forty—holding workshops in which older and disabled women were encouraged to submit work. Topics also included stories of women in detention and elderly people's homes, seen in Jorge Diaz's *My Song Is Free* and Jenny McLeod's *Island Life*.[34]

The commercial value of the group's work remained in question and tension developed between the Regiment's mission and the government-sponsored funding. Janelle Reinelt, a professor of theater and performance, wrote of the growing strain, saying, "Although they have achieved a good deal of critical acclaim, even among traditional critics, they are definitely perceived as being politically suspect, linked (correctly enough) to the identity politics of feminism, and therefore 'marginal.'"[35] The Arts Council's influence was further evident when the Regiment was required to appoint an executive or artistic director to facilitate negotiations with the government. Their work continued for two more years before the group ceased producing in 1993.[36]

While Monstrous Regiment was dedicated to developing new works by and about women, the group Mrs. Worthington's Daughters focused on recovering plays by women that were "lost" or "neglected." The Daughters produced their first season in 1979. Assembled by women who had previously run the consciousness-raising collective the Feminist Study Group, the Daughters presented West End theatregoers with pamphlets asking, "Do you want to see women represented other than as men's wives, mothers, lovers, and daughters?" It was the study of women's suffrage drama, by Julie Holledge, that inspired the group to produce works by female artists from the past.[37] They brought their fight to Equity, which resulted in the creation of the women's subcommittee.

After discovering more than 500 female playwrights from 1900 to 1920, the collective began producing plays examining motherhood, marriage, and gender roles. In the 1980s, they revived Githa Sowerby's critically acclaimed *Rutherford and Son*, first produced in 1912. But when their arts officer died and was replaced with someone unfamiliar with their work, the Daughters' application for project funding was denied by the Arts Council. The Daughters dissolved in 1982.[38]

"BEING GAY WAS NOW A CAUSE"

Progressive theater's mission went beyond just gender, as sexual identification featured prominently in activist works onstage. The 1970s included an outpouring of plays featuring gay and lesbian characters, centered on political and social issues. Gay Sweatshop was formed in 1975, by a group of men that included Roger Baker, Lawrence Collinson, Alan Wakeman, Drew Griffiths, Gordon MacDonald, Gerald Chapman, and John Roman Baker.[39]

Gay Sweatshop's formation took place eight years after the repeal of the Labouchere Amendment, which, in 1885, had established homosexuality a "gross indecency" punishable by life imprisonment in the United Kingdom. The repeal's effect was immediately visible, as Simon Callow recalled in the *Guardian*:

> A whole new life had sprung up overnight it seemed in the wake of that sudden enfranchisement, with bars, clubs, and discos nakedly—in many cases, literally—celebrating and fomenting sex between men. Being gay—gay, not queer, not homo, not poof nor pansy, faggot nor fairy—was now a cause, a crusade; we were a separate and self-sufficient subdivision of human kind, our lives centrally predicated on desire. Let groin speak unto groin was all the law. [40]

The Sweatshop set out to present a realistic portrayal of gay life. Its 1975 Manifesto stated the group's intention as follows:

> To counteract the prevailing perception in mainstream theater of what homosexuals were like, therefore providing a more realistic image for the public, and to increase the general awareness of the oppression of sexuality, both gay and straight, the impact it has on people's lives, and the society that reinforces it. [41]

Two shows presented by the sweatshop in 1975 and 1976 had a far-reaching impact on awareness and recognition of gay and lesbian life: Roger Baker and Drew Griffith's *Mister X* and Jill Posener's *Any Woman Can*. A story of coming out and self-oppression, *Mister X* was performed at the 1975 Sheffield Campaign for Homosexuality Equality conference before it opened the season of plays at the ICA in 1976. The show, which examined the need to identify as gay and the consequences of denying one's core identity, and concluded with a climactic speech of self-affirmation, toured throughout Britain, often alongside *Any Woman Can*.[42] Posener's play, inspired by her own experience of coming out, was the first play produced by Gay Sweatshop that was written by a woman. [43]

Gay Sweatshop, which began involving women after its Almost Free season, presented Posener's play, a series of monologues that also addresses coming out. The production marked an exception to what had become the norm: A significantly larger number of plays about homosexual males were produced during that time than about females. [44] One of the better-known works was *Care and Control*, by Michelene Wandor.

The realist drama about lesbians entangled in custody cases was inspired in part by *Any Woman Can* and presented by Gay Sweatshop, opening in 1977, at Action Space Drill Hall. Its program read, in part, as follows:

> Single mothers, lesbian and heterosexual, face the same kind of prejudice when they come before the judicial system.
>
> A woman is suspect in the eyes of the State when she asserts her right to live independently of men. She is seen as a direct challenge to family life and the traditional sexual roles which the court upholds.
>
> It is against these attitudes and assumptions, which deny all of us the right to decide the most basic and intimate matters of our lives, that women are organising to fight the custody battle. It is a dramatic development—one which the women of Gay Sweatshop wished to explore, not only for the sake of representing the struggle, but to advance it!
>
> Gay Sweatshop wishes to increase general awareness of the oppression of sexuality; to raise questions (leading to discussion) about the nature of oppression, the society which reinforces it, and the resultant effects on people's lives. [45]

The cause and the work continued to gain momentum. Women from Gay Sweatshop, including Julie Parker, Nancy Duiguid, and Kate Crutchley, helped to organize the Women's Festival at London's Drill Hall. Running for three weeks, the festival exemplified the relationship between the women's movement and Gay Sweatshop. [46] And, in 1978, Gay Sweatshop was featured at the Gay Times Festvial at Action Space's Drill Hall. [47] Following the three-week festival, the Drill Hall would become the Gay Sweatshop's producing theater for the next twenty years.

Queer theater was performed far beyond the Drill Hall. The lesbian company Hormone Imbalance was formed in 1979, by some members of the Sweatshop and Pirate Jenny. The two groups collaborated in 1979, on the production *Iceberg*, and then worked independently.

Wandor explained the separation:

> The first was simliar to the split that had occurred within the Gay Liberation front itself, in that lesbians felt that many features of their oppression were shared more with other women than gay men. One of the consequences of this was to be seen in a conflict between theatrical styles, in that the men drew on an already familiar camp and drag tradition, which they had both celebrated and tried to stand on its head,

whereas the women leaned more towards the newer agitprop, documentary-based styles, as a means of showing hitherto suppressed lesbian experience. The problem of male dominance in the organization of the group and the clash of styles was acknowledged on both sides, and the plays done in 1977 reflected this divergence of emphasis.[48]

Gay Sweatshop toured throughout the 1970s, during which time they were met with protests, picketing, and threats.[49] But the group faced new challenges when the Arts Council of Great Britain scaled down their status to project subsidy, which resulted in the Sweatshop losing its administrator. It temporarily ceased production in 1981, before reconvening two years later.[50]

"I FOUND GOD IN MYSELF/AND I LOVED HER"

The ripples of the second-wave movement were not confined to just one side of the Atlantic; theater artists were bringing their anger and activism to the stage in the United States as well. A landmark piece of black feminism arrived in New York, moving from downtown to midtown and eventually landing on Broadway, where it offered an experience truly unique to Broadway audiences.

In a departure from the expected norms of Broadway, *for colored girls who have considered suicide/when the rainbow is enuf* was neither a traditionally structured play nor a conventional musical. A series of twenty different poems set to music, Ntozake Shange referred to the show as a choreopoem, interweaving stories about women living—and struggling—with relationships, oppression, and empowerment, celebrating sisterhood as the women find unity in a society that is both racist and sexist. Shange deliberately wrote in a colloquial tone, imitating how women spoke in everyday life, using vernacular language and unconventional punctuation.

Inspired by events in Shange's own life, the poems in *for colored girls* encompassed sex, losing one's virginity, abortion, rape, and domestic and sexual violence. She had attempted suicide several times[51] and credited the play's title to an experience she had when witnessing two parallel rainbows when driving down Highway 101. Passing under them, it became clear to Shange she wanted to live and use her voice to speak for herself and other women of color. "I was overcome. . . . I had a feeling of near-death or near-catastrophe. Then I drove through the rainbow, and I went away. Then I put that together to form the title."[52]

The women in *for colored girls* were named after the colors of the rainbow. These stories of African American women coming of age and the obstacles they faced in a patriarchal world were first staged in the California women's bar Bacchanal. It bowed in New York in 1975, at the Studio Rivbea and the New Federal Theatre, before it was brought to Joe Papp's attention and opened at the Public Theater in June 1976, with Shange playing the Lady in Orange. Clive Barnes, in the *New York Times*, praised the "totally extraordinary and wonderful" production, reflecting on his own experience as a white man while watching it:

> Black sisterhood. That is what Ntozake Shange's totally extraordinary and wonderful evening . . . is all about. It has those insights into life and living that make the theater such an incredible marketplace for the soul. And simply because it is about black women—not just blacks and not just women—it is a very humbling but inspiring thing for a white man to experience.[53]

Jack Kroll from *Newsweek* was equally rhapsodic in its review, declaring,

> These pieces are tremendously effective mini-dramas that explode on-stage, showering shrapnel of significance. Shange's poems aren't war cries—they're outcries filled with a controlled passion against the brutality that blasts the lives of *colored girls*—a phrase that in her hands vibrates with social irony and poetic beauty. These poems are political in the deepest sense, but there's no dogma, no sentimentality, no grinding of false mythic axes. . . . Your scalp prickles at the stunning truth of her characters: The high-school girl ponders whether or not to surrender her virginity in 'the deep black Buick smelling of Thunderbird and ladies in heat,' the dancer who has all the earth-force of the Mississippi, the sexpot who turns men on with a Babylonian arsenal of seductive machinery but then emerges from her postcoital bathtub with the soul sadness of a "regular colored girl."[54]

For colored girls quickly transferred to Broadway, opening at the Booth Theatre in September 1976—the second play by a black woman to be produced on Broadway—and surprising those who thought it too radical for a commercial Broadway run. But in its yearlong run, *for colored girls* reached new audiences, showing many theatergoers something they had rarely seen before on Broadway—representation. The play "definitely spoke to a generation of young women who didn't feel invited into a theater space," playwright Lynn Nottage told the *New York Times*, "who suddenly saw representation of themselves in a very honest way, and understood that they could occupy space for the first time."[55] The praise and attention that was showered onto *for colored girls* was so intense, Shange's lawyer considered hiring her a bodyguard. She departed the cast after three weeks of performances.[56]

"We hadn't seen a black girl's body promoting anything literary since Kali published her book of poems, in 1970, at the enviable age of nine," *New Yorker* theater critic Hilton Als recalled.[57] But the play did more than simply cast people of color on a Broadway stage. It defied established social norms and introduced new kinds of characters. Recalling when one character shouted, "i will raise my voice/& scream & holler/& break things & race the engine/& tell all yr secrets bout yrself to yr face," Als wrote, "That call undid something in me. It shattered the Negro propriety I knew and lived by. The force of Shange's writing seemed to say, 'Fuck the old rule of not airing your female business in front of colored men, white people, let alone the rest of the world.' You own the copyright on your life."[58]

The play opened to an ecstatic review from Mel Gussow in the *New York Times*, who declared, "The final question is not whether *colored girls* find an audience on Broadway, but will it should find an audience on Broadway. The answer is a very enthusiastic affirmative. Uptown or downtown, in a bar or at the Booth, *colored girls* is a play that should be seen, savored and treasured."[59]

With a female author and choreographer, and an all-female cast, as well as women in charge of costumes, and lighting and composing music, *for colored girls* presented a specific demographic onstage, and its candid and personal dialogue regarding abuse and trauma spoken by black women was perceived by some as an insult.[60] Shange came under fire for her portrayal of black men, with Erskine Peters of the *Journal of Ethnic Studies* declaring that she "portrays Black men basically as pasteboards or beasts."[61] The play was described by sociologist Robert Staples as having a "collective appetite for black male blood,"[62] with Curtis E. Rodgers of the *Amsterdam News* writing,

For colored girls who have considered suicide/when the rainbow is enuf. **From left: Leona Johnson, Roxanne Reese, Sharita Hunt, Robbie McCauley, Laurie Carlos (standing), and Rise Collins (kneeling).** *Photofest*

> In her unrelenting stereotyping of Black men as always "shucking" and "jiving" . . . [Shange], without realizing it, just as insistently caricatures Black women as being easily duped and emotionally frivolous. This is so because Ms. Shange's *colored girls* invariably takes up with those Black men whom she damns as mean and trifling. [63]

The reaction surprised Shange, who years later wrote, "There was quite a ruckus about the seven ladies in their simple colored dresses. I was truly dumbfounded that I was right then and there deemed the biggest threat to black men since cotton pickin', and not all women were in my corner either." [64]

For colored girls won the Obie Award for Distinguished Production and was nominated for two Tony Awards, for Best Play and Best Featured Actress, which Trazana Beverley, who played the Lady in Red, won. It ran for 742 performances, until July 16, 1978, and its impact was long and far-lasting. Shange adapted the play into a book and received a Grammy nomination for Best Spoken Word Recording. Moreover, the play was made into a made-for-television movie that premiered on *American Playhouse* in 1982, and it inspired a theatrical film written and directed by Tyler Perry in 2010. The play is frequently performed at schools and in local theaterical productions, and has become a touchstone for black women, inspiring many playwrights, including Dominique Morisseau, Lynn Nottage, Anna Deveare Smith, Aleshea Harris, Jackie Sibblies Drury, Ngozi Anyanwu, and Suzan Lori-Parks.[65]

Shange continued to write throughout her life, including novels, children's books, plays, poetry, and essay collections, but *for colored girls*, her first play, remains her most well-known work. It received a New York revival in 1995, which Shange herself directed. Revisiting the show was necessary, she said, because, "The silence has been broken and our voices are not so unknown in the universe as they were. But the condition of women is materially worse in the world today than it was twenty years ago."[66] It continues to be frequently performed at local and regional theaters. Following Shange's death in 2018, Jane Carr wrote,

> To say that her words were revolutionary is insufficient. To say that *for colored girls*, with its searing portrayals of life, death, rape, abortion, and struggle, changed people's lives is undeniably true. Whether they encountered Shange's words onstage, onscreen, in the classroom, or by other means, generations of women of color—and others who felt marginalized, traumatized, or held locked in place by an unforgiving world—found themselves in Shange's choreopoem.[67]

"PUT IN A PACKAGE AND SOLD"

One of the most unabashedly feminist musicals in the United States to date was Nancy Cryer and Gretchen Ford's *I'm Getting My Act Together and Taking It on the Road*. Originally produced by Joe Papp and New York Shakespeare Festival at the Public Theater, the pop-rock chamber, with music by Ford and book and lyrics by Cryer, follows Heather, a 39-year-old singer, as she attempts to break from her history of crooning torch songs and love ballads, and burst into songs about women's liberation.

Heather's story was a collaboration of Cryer and Ford, one of the first prominent female songwriting teams, who had written 1967's *Now Is the Time for All Good Men* and 1970's *The Last Sweet Days of Isaac*. In

1973, their futuristic computer-centered musical *Shelter* opened on Broadway, albeit for a brief, thirty-one-performance run.

I'm Getting My Act Together, which opened on June 14, 1978, and ran until May 15, 1981, offered an intimate look at Heather's growing self-empowerment and Joe, her manager and former lover's lukewarm response. With such songs as "Strong Woman Number," "Lonely Lady," and "Put in a Package and Sold," *I'm Getting My Act Together* unapologetically compelled audience members to face what, or who, might be holding them back as women's roles changed inside and outside the home. The lyrics both pleaded and commanded, "Look inside for the part of me that can't be put in a package and sold."

I'm Getting My Act Together was originally scheduled to run for six weeks at the Public Theater, and its lackluster reviews forebode an early closing. It was after Papp noticed the conversations taking place after the performances and introduced postshow talk-backs that word began spreading about this new show. Even if the critics had dismissed their work, Cryer and Ford had tapped into the cultural and political zeitgeist.[68]

Despite *I'm Getting My Act Together*'s triumphant conclusion, with Heather parting ways with Joe and performing her show, Cryer and Ford initially stated that the show was not meant as an assertion of feminist ideals. "We were writing about relationships between men and women, not about women's roles in society as a whole," Ford told *Breaking Character* magazine. But she said the show was "pigeonholed . . . as a feminist show, and [people] assumed we were militants."[69]

The musical sold out at the Public Theater and ran for three years Off-Broadway before touring the country. But its commercial success was not paralleled with critical acclaim. Reviewers did not warm to the show, especially Richard Eder of the *New York Times*, who wrote,

> There is a touch of wit here and there. Gretchen Cryer, who wrote the book and lyrics, and plays the leading character, is trying to say something honest about age and feminine identity. Her perception fails her; she falls into platitude after platitude and comes up with a show that is both insubstantial and very heavy.

In fact, the confidence with which Cryer and Ford crafted their show and gave to name was the subject of Eder's scorn: "Self-celebration is the affliction of *I'm Getting My Act Together*. . . . But *I'm Getting My Act*

Together and Taking It on the Road is not so much a title as a pious hope."[70]

A brief concert production at New York's City Center in 2013 didn't fare much better, with Charles Isherwood at the *Times* dismissing the show as irrelevant. Women's rights had come so far, he thought, that the show no longer had an impact. Isherwood opined,

> The production, directed by Kathleen Marshall, places the show firmly in period, which is unavoidable since its themes—of women's self-empowerment and men's ornery responses to it—are now mostly obsolete, at least in the specific terms they are addressed here. . . . *I'm Getting My Act Together . . .* struck a reverberant chord at the time, when questions of the changing roles of women in American culture were matters of heated concern. They remain so today, but the conversation often focuses on how women with established careers can maximize their potential at work while raising a family and pursuing sever-

I'm Getting My Act Together and Taking It on the Road. **From left: Margot Rose, Gretchen Cryer, and Betty Aberlin.** *Photofest*

al fulfilling hobbies. Instead of being asked to fetch ginger ale, today's women are more likely to be wondering how they can find a couple of free hours in a frantic week to bottle their own. [71]

Critic David Finkle echoed Isherwood's sentiments, lamenting in the *Huffington Post* the lack of development dedicated to Joe's character and devoting four paragraphs to his defense and defending his objections to Heather's material. Joe, according to Finkle, was "right on the money, just about every time." Finkle also considered the show outdated, writing,

> Appreciated then as a strong feminist statement, it now seems practically antiquated in its outlook and outrage. Much of the complaints Heather makes about her infuriating plight—they're incorporated as skits worked into the new act she's about to debut—may have seemed necessarily blunt then but now come across as simplistic, as crude, as insultingly humorless. . . . Whereas in 1978, Heather represented a large segment of the women fighting fervently for raised consciousness, she now impresses as a woman who wants social improvements but is going about it the wrong way. [72]

The progress these male critics were espousing was not quite as drastic as they seemed to think. In 1978, the year of *I'm Getting My Act Together*'s Off-Broadway premiere, one hundred thousand people marched in Washington, D.C., in support of the Equal Rights Amendment. By 2013, when Cryer and Ford's musical was revived in New York, the amendment still had not been ratified. Birth control was a part of pop culture; in 1975, Loretta Lynn's country song "The Pill" was released, and, by 1978, the Supreme Court had ruled that couples have a right to contraception and that a law prohibiting unmarried women from buying contraceptives was unconstituional. By 2013, the 40th anniversary of *Roe v. Wade*, seventy provisions aimed at restricting access to abortion had been enacted by as many as twenty-two states. [73] The Pregnancy Discrimination Act was passed in 1978, prohibiting sex discrimination on the basis of pregnancy, and by the fiscal year 2013, 5,342 pregnancy discrimination charges had been filed with state and local Fair Employment Practices agencies and the Equal Employment Opportunity Commission. [74]

The revival of Cryer and Ford's musical had held a mirror to the audience and the critics, but the reflection was smudged.

"THE GREAT UNCHARTED WATERS"

Women weren't satisfied with the roles being written for them, so they were taking matters into their own hands. In 1978, Women's Project Theater opened. Producer Julia Miles founded the nonprofit theater in response to the lack of opportunities for female artists. While producing at the American Place Theater, Miles became aware of the lack of female playwrights being produced in comparison to male.

"Can you name many women playwrights?" Miles asked the *New York Times* in 2001. "Maybe there are five that are well known. If I knew why this is, then I would have done something about it sooner. The more women who are produced, the more women will write for the theater. The body of work by women writers has to be increased."[75]

Opening at a time when only 6 percent of professional directors in New York were female, Women's Project premiered with the play *Choices*, which explored questions of female identity. Conceived by Patricia Bosworth and adapted from female authors, including Dorothy Parker, Joan Didion, Virginia Woolf, and Colette and Gertrude Stein, among others, the play was performed by Lily Lodge. The *New York Times* wrote of the show, "*Choices* serves as a brief introduction to the artistic energy of literary women. Given the variety of versatile people who are engaged in the 'Women's Project,' we look forward to the plays, playwrights, and directors that should emerge from the American Place."[76]

The desire for better roles also motivated Bryony Lavery to start writing. The author of *Frozen* and *A Wedding Story*, *More Light*, *Goliath*, and *The Magic Toyshop* cofounded the theater company Les Oeufs Malades—which produced only her work—in 1976, with Gerard Bell. She also set up the feminist cabaret troupe Female Trouble and served as artistic director of Gay Sweatshop.

Lavery contributed plays to Monstrous Regiment, Women's Theatre Group/Sphinx, and Theatre Centre, among others, and much of her earlier writing called for entirely female casts. She authored *Her Aching Heart*, a lesbian romance that parodies the tropes of romantic fiction, for Women's Theatre Group to provide more and better roles for women, and told the *Guardian* that when she wrote the play, "way back in the day . . . I did see my job as providing lots of great female roles, which I sometimes still do. There's a lot to redress."[77]

A prolific writer and outspoken feminist, Lavery had said that anger fueled her writing. One of the few women whose work was produced on West End's main stage when *Frozen* opened at the Royal National Theatre's Cottesloe Theatre in 2002,[78] Lavery has also written many adaptations of popular works, including *A Christmas Carol*, *Treasure Island*, and *The Lovely Bones*, often adding a feminist undertone to the well-known stories.[79]

Another popular playwright of the time, Pam Gems, made space for women with her work. Her many scripts chronicling the lives of important and controversial women helped to restore their overlooked places in male-dominated society. Men were not allowed in these spaces created for women, and oftentimes the plays focused on a group of women, rather than a single woman, in direct contrast to the heroic lead that is so often seen in male-authored work.

"It's not that I don't feel that I can write about men, but when you see the great uncharted waters, the notion of dealing with two thousand years of men's history just isn't very tempting," Gems told the *Guardian*. "When I came to the theater in the early 70s, I realized that there was no authentic work about women: They were occasionally celebrated but never convincingly explored."[80]

Gems, who hoped to present her plays as artistic, rather than political, statements, objected to the purported "antimen" stance of feminism and distanced herself from such labels such "feminist icon" and "woman playwright." While in 1977, she declared the phrase "feminist writer" to be inconsequential due to its argumentative connotations[81] she later acknowledged her work's feminist perspective and her own feminist ideals but would "steer would-be dramatic writers away from the preaching-to-the-converted," which "had been so prevalent in committed theater."[82]

The female experience was explored in such pieces as the monologues *My Warren*, *After Birthday*, *Betty's Wonderful Christmas*, and *The Amiable Courtship of Miz Venus and Wild Bill*. *Go West, Young Woman*, about female pioneers, produced by the Women's Company at the Roundhouse in London, was met with protests from two different feminist groups on its opening night in 1974, when women objected to there being men in the cast.[83]

Premiering at the Edinburgh festival in 1976, *Dusa, Fish, Stas, and Vi* follows four women sharing a flat in London. One of the first plays to delve into the inner lives of women questioning their roles in society

Pam Gems. *Photo © Suzie Maeder/Bridgeman Images*

during and after the women's movement, it transferred to the West End in 1976, with a female director and female creative team. Ted Whitehead wrote in his review in the *Spectator*, "It's reasonable to expect that such a production will tell us something about what women are thinking today, and I have an awful fear that it does." He went on to ponder the playwright's view of men, writing,

> Pam Gems's writing is quick, nervy, and spontaneous, with a humor that can bubble, as well as bite. What is she actually saying? Given this dramatic situation, it's hard to assess her view of men, as they are relegated to offstage monsters or idiots pumping drivel through the pop programs on the radio. . . . Any man who had written it would have been flayed alive by the feminists—who should approach it with care. But I think it's worth seeing, not least for the arguments you can have afterwards.[84]

Why assessing Gems's view of men was necessary when reviewing a play about four women was not explained. Despite its ambiguous perspective on the male sex perceived by Whitehead, Gems's play earned a spot in the National Theatre's list of 100 plays of the twentieth century.[85]

Gems shifted her focus from writing about everyday women to famous ones, but she didn't simply want to write about women; she wanted to examine what had been projected onto them by men and the disparaging effects of the male gaze: "If you're writing as a woman . . . you want to explode some of the grosser myths that have been erected by men; the sentimentalization of women and therefore the reduction of them."[86]

Gems's *Queen Christina*, accepted at the Royal Shakespeare Company, achieved success as the first play written by a woman to be performed at the Royal Shakespeare Company's the Other Place in 1977.[87] With its exploration of gender roles and femininity and power, the Swedish queen, whose parents strove to "make a man" of her, was a rich subject for Gems to explore. Christina is expected to embody the "manly qualities of a king and fecundity of a woman."[88] She was raised as a prince; trained in traditionally masculine skills like hunting, fighting, and studying politics and military tactics; and faced the challenges of surviving and ruling in a patriarchal society. Gems symbolizes Christina's internal war, presenting her success with handling the "bloody [Thirty Years'] war" alongside her struggles in handling her monthly menstrual cycle. *Queen Christina* explored gender and sexual identity, as well as motherhood, illustrating restrictions established by gender and later mourning her missed chance at motherhood after firmly resisting it throughout her life.[89] Despite the centuries between the character and her audience, Christina represented present-day women struggling to balance a career and motherhood, and the typically masculine and feminine identification that accompanied such choices.

The next woman Gems brought to the stage was French singer, actress, and cabaret performer Edith Piaf. The biographical play named after the singer opened at the Royal Shakespeare Company's the Other Place in Stratford-on-Avon in 1978, before moving to Broadway in 1981. Gems offered an unapologetic portrayal of the singer in her play, illustrating her drug and alcohol use and sexual promiscuity rather than idealizing her due to her gender or creative accomplishments. The reception of the play, both in topic and creator, illustrated the gender-based biases of arts critics and the deep-rooted connection between women's appearances and their work.

In an article for the *New York Times* about the show, Cliff Jahr described the real-life Piaf as a "sad little dumpling of a woman who sang songs about the underside of life and amour in Paris," and added, "Neither beautiful nor shapely, she still managed to attract a parade of lovers, among them Yves Montand, the prizefighter Marcel Cerdan, and John Garfield." He also notes that Gems, the playwright, is a "heavyset blonde woman of 55."[90] *New York Magazine*'s John Simon espoused on the leading lady's talents, writing, "She can do a perpetual scrunched-up grin, and she can do Cockney. She cannot begin to sing like Piaf, and she apes her gestures wretchedly. Though she is quite ugly as Piaf, she is ugly in the wrong way—with a shallow, jokey ugliness rather than the sad sobbing plainness that Piaf could, through her art, transform into beauty."[91]

Gems's *Camille* was produced by Royal Shakespeare Company in 1984. Her adaptation of the tragic love story, drawn from Alexandre Dumas' novel and play *La Dame aux Camellias*, illustrated the price a woman pays for love, but its message was lost upon the critics. While *Camille* was praised for its sincere and sympathetic portrayal, the same attributes were also the focus of criticism. Benedict Nightingale of the *New York Times* wrote that Gems was trying just a little too hard with the play:

Miss Gems's feminism is the moderate sort that believes in the possibility of genuine understanding and reconciliation between the sexes. . . . It's clearly a very well-intentioned play, and that, as it happens,
is what's wrong, as well as right, with it. We're just a bit too aware of
Miss Gems's overriding aim, which is to show a no-sexist, classless
relationship struggling into transitory existence in a sexist, class-ridden
world and then being destroyed by it. We're a bit too aware of the
contemporary moralist, the earnest constructor of meaningful case
studies, lurking inside the narrator of what is, after all, still one of the
more fabulous nineteenth-century love stories. If Miss Gems had been
content to make romance as realistic as possible, all might have been
well, or at least only intermittently preposterous.[92]

In his review of *Camille*, Gussow wrote that Gems had failed in her
attempt to craft a unique new drama: "The play is a potboiler, as it was in
its premiere two years ago at Stratford-on-Avon. This was not, of course,
the playwright's intention when she decided to revamp the classic tear-
jerker as a relevant feminist statement, allied with her other dramas of
independent women (including *Piaf*)."[93] But, according to Gussow, Gems
did not succeed, instead writing dialogue "purple with portent" that
downplayed the severity of prostitution, saying it "seems like an extended
glossy night on the town."[94]

This dismissive attitude toward female-centric plays was seen in the
United States with the Broadway opening—and immediate closing—of
Trafford Tanzi, Claire Luckham's play that ran for just one day on Broad-
way in 1982. Originally titled *Tuebrook Tanzi, the Venus Flytrap*, it was
performed at the Everyman Theatre in Liverpool before it transferred to
Manchester as *Trafford Tanzi*, achieving commercial success in England.

The *Times* reported on the production in Great Britain, stating, "The
outrageous comedy with music keeps the audience cheering its favorite
(Tanzi) and hissing the villains (everyone else, including the referee/
master of ceremonies). A cross between a vaudeville, a sideshow, and a
contact sport, 'Tanzi' is a feminist play to end all feminist plays." *Tanzi*,
which was described by its playwright as being "about the basic struggle
any woman faces in growing up," tells the story of the title character, a
tomboyish girl who marries a professional wrestler and supports his career. She then pursues wrestling herself and challenges her husband to a
match, the loser of which has to take responsibility for the housework.[95]

The play opened on Broadway in 1983, under the title *Teaneck Tanzi: The Venus Flytrap*, to universal critical pans. The critics claimed it was badly written, the characters were not believable, and the plot was too predictable. Its failure could also be blamed on its feminist message, according to some; Frank Rich of the *New York Times* implied in his review that its portrayal of women's oppression was simply not believable.

> The author's metaphor cloaks a feminist message-play, set in some anachronistic land (surely not New Jersey) where women are so oppressed they are denied higher education and any career other than housewife. Tanzi's despotic husband, a professional wrestler, is dressed as a 1950s greaser and, in a typical sample of the evening's wit, is named Dean Rebel. (Another sample: Tanzi's lascivious school psychiatrist is named Dr. Grope.) After much tedious biographical exposition, which charts the heroine's progress "from potties to panty hose," we reach the "main event": Tanzi becomes a lady wrestler so she can finally challenge hubby to a do-or-die battle for her liberation from the kitchen. Anyone who can't guess the winner in advance deserves a lifetime pass to *Rocky III*.[96]

Teaneck Tanzi: The Venus Flytrap fared no better with United Press International, where Glenne Currie wrote,

> Once the basic symbolism has been established, the individual scenes become simplistically feminist, and the play has nowhere to go but to a final, sensational, realistic best-of-three-falls match between husband and wife. This does not even have the advantage of suspense, as it is obvious that Tanzi—fighting for the right to live her own life and not just as a housewife—will win out. Incidental songs are undistinguished. "Teaneck Tanzi" doesn't strain the brain, but it's a different sort of entertainment for Broadway.[97]

Luckham was criticized for underdeveloped writing, but playwright Louise Page received the opposite response, for writing with too much thought. The playwright explored gender dynamics in sports (*Golden Girl*), warfare (*Falklands Sound*), and breast cancer (*Tissue*), and was met with patronizing critical responses. Rich described her play *Salonika* as an "emotionally dead drama about mothers, daughters, and lost love," adding, "Exactly the same is true of *Real Estate*. The fault, I think it's safe to assume, is not in the stars. . . . Jenny and Gwen are not people but pawns in a conceit—the brittle, neatly manicured creations of a controlling writer who seems to be thinking much too hard."[98] And *Tissue*, reviewed by Stephen Holden in the *Times*, was critiqued as feeling "like a skillful exercise in form" and a "bit too long and repetitive to be entirely gripping."[99]

"WHY ARE WE ALL SO MISERABLE?"

One of the most prolific writers of the time was Caryl Churchill, who examined worldwide patriarchal systems in plays that frequently explored political and financial quandaries, as well as personal and moral ones. Landlords and greed were the subjects of *Owners*, a satire on property rights that was poorly received during its New York premiere in 1973. "It is an absurdist play about property that owes much to many other writers," wrote Clive Barnes, who further stated, "Absurdity needs to have roots in reality to be dramatically viable."[100]

The Putney Debates were dramatized in *Light Shining on Buckinghamshire*, and Churchill continued her daring, explorative writing with *Cloud 9*, which earned her the title "daft" writer from Frank Rich of the *New York Times*. Rich said her joke "wear[s] thin too quickly," while he praised Tommy Tune's direction for keeping the "performances at a realistic level" and called him her "most powerfully ally."[101] Other critics described the work on Victorian sexuality, society, and colonialism as the "most confusing show in Manhattan," as well as "brilliant," "transcendant," and "madness."[102] *Cloud Nine* ran Off-Broadway for more than two years, followed by *Serious Money*, in which Churchill took on the British stock market, set immediately following Thatcher's deregulation.

Women's professional ambition and the price they pay to succeed in business, and the definition of success for women of that era, were the topics of *Top Girls*, which premiered in the United States in 1982. *Top Girls* uncompromisingly examined the price of feminism and the difference between British and American feminism.

Top Girls opens with its protagonist, Marlene, hosting a dinner party to celebrate her recent promotion to managing director of the Top Girls employment agency. Her guests, fittingly, are powerful women from history: Pope Joan, who reigned disguised as a man; Dull Gret, figured in

Pieter Bruegel's painting, which depicts her leading a female charge dressed in armor and an apron; Victorian explorer Isabella Bird; Lady Nijo, a Japanese emperor's courtesan and later a Buddhist nun; and Patient Griselda, the obedient wife of "The Clerk's Tale" in Chaucer's *The Canterbury Tales*.

The women's conversation, naturally, features their experiences as women in a patriarchal world. Marlene, a caricature of Margaret Thatcher, is later seen in her office and her home, where the sacrifices and price of her ambition are made abundantly clear. It turns out she has a daughter, born out of wedlock, who she left to be raised with her sister and feels little affection toward. Focused on advancing professionally, Marlene begins to adopt the characteristics of a patriarch herself and is scorned by the wife of the man who she beat for her promotion. Arriving uninvited at Marlene's office, Mrs. Kidd claims if her husband had been passed over for a man, he'd consider it normal, but seeing a woman promoted for a job he sought has left him distraught and sleepless. Marlene responds professionally to her unexpected visitor and suggests sleeping pills, only to be told, "You're one of those ballbreakers. . . . You'll end up miserable and lonely. You're not natural."

While the harsh portrayal of women's circumstances may have been intended to communicate their burdens to an otherwise uninformed audience, Frank Rich thought otherwise. The *New York Times* critic described *Top Girls* as "trying" and said the play took it too far, writing,

> The absence of the middle range—of women who achieve without imitating power-crazed men and denying their own humanity—is an artificial polemical contrivance that cuts the play off at the heart. We're never quite convinced that women's choices are as limited and, in the play's final word, "frightening" as the stacked case of *Top Girls* suggests. Even in England, one assumes, not every woman must be either an iron maiden or a downtrodden serf.[103]

Top Girls was revived twenty-six years later, on Broadway, with a cast that included Martha Plimpton, Elizabeth Marvel, and Marisa Tomei. The *New York Times* reviewer—also a man—praised the show's performances but offered little commentary on its relevance, and some critics went as far as to say gender politics had evolved so greatly that the play's relevance was questionable. But Marlene's abandonment of her daughter continued to beg the question of whether a successful career and family life are possible—not the first play to ask this and far from the last—and given the ongoing lack of paid maternity leave in the United States, the denial of *Top Girls'* pertinence by a cluster of male critics could be summed up in the play's final word: "frightening."

5

VOICES, NEW AND NOW

If bell-bottoms, long hair, and the peace sign encapsulated the heady activism of the 1970s, a makeover was in store. The modern woman of the next decade wore suits sporting shoulder pads and walked to work in sneakers, with her heels stashed in her purse. "We have it all!" the women of the 1980s gloated—or lamented. Following the inspired advocacy of the 1970s, the consumer-driven frenzy of the Me Decade both gifted and burdened women with new expectations, new demands, and new anxieties regarding work–life balance, motherhood, and biological clocks. The Equal Rights Amendment was defeated in 1982, and "family values" became a conservative political buzzword as more women found employment outside of the house. Professional jobs held by women went up by 5 percent, from 44 to 49 percent, and 36 percent of women held "managerial" jobs held—an increase from the previous 20 percent.[1] In 1984, Geraldine Ferraro became the first female vice presidential nominee for a major political party, and although losing to the Reagan–Bush ticket, she made history. Headlines proclaimed that the women's movement had suceeded, and many seemed to agree.

It took years for the mainstream media to begin acknowledging that the gender wars were not, in fact, over.[2] Anita Hill's testimony to Congress about alleged sexual harassment by Supreme Court nominee Clarence Thomas rocked the nation the same year that Susan Faludi's *Backlash* hit the bookshelves, outlining her examination of why so many people were renouncing feminism and blaming the women's movement for their problems and struggles. Rather than "having it all," some felt they had lost.

CHANGING ROLES, CHANGING WRITING

Despite women assuming more responsibilities—and thus failing at times to meet more expectations—they remained underrepresented in the theater. If women had it all, "it all" did not include the stage. Between 1969 and 1975, according to Action for Women in Theatre, only 7 percent of playwrights and directors working at Off-Broadway and regional theaters were women.[3]

Entertainment began challenging traditional gender roles, some attempts succeeding more than others. In 1980, Jane Fonda, Lily Tomlin, and Dolly Parton triumphed over their chauvinistic boss in *9 to 5*, while Glenn Close's career-driven Alex Forrest in *Fatal Attraction*, seemingly driven to insanity due to her ticking biological clock, was defeated by a stay-at-home mom. Onstage, women were questioning work–life balance, aging, and romance, which defied a tidy two-act play with a happy ending.

In England, the stage seemed set for female playwrights and composers as the number of plays written by men began to decline. But men's voices continued to dominate the press, and theater criticism remained a male-dominated profession.[4] The writing that could ensure a show's success or failure was typically authored by one demographic: white and male. Theater was being viewed through a narrow, and patriarchal, lens, clearly demonstrated when Michael Billington, film critic for the *Guardian*, claimed that, despite the many new works by women, the British theater of the 1980s was characterized by "a crisis in new writing."[5]

Perhaps his statement could be understood, as women were severely lacking in representation on the main stages, Timberlake Wertenbaker recalled when discussing her resignation from the Royal Court Theatre with Billington:

> There was a particular moment when there were all these plays by men about men with really no women present. You go to the theater partly to be mirrored in some way, and you begin to feel you don't exist. I don't think women have ever been a welcome voice. You sense a relief that we can shut those women up and get back to what really matters,

which is what men are saying. It's not complete paraonia. I think we're trained from birth to listen to men. The disappearance of women from the stage may also have discouraged aspiring writers. Word got around that there was little point in sending your play to the Court or the National. So women just stopped. Or went into TV and films.[6]

Women were writing and producing, touring on the small-scale circuit, as well as in local companies, including Black Mime Theatre Women, Mrs. Red Ladder, Siren, Talawa, Theatre of Black Women, and Women's Playhouse Trust. Billington's declaration ignored the alternative, off-the-main stage works by women that were flourishing in smaller spaces. Apparently, in Billington's eyes, works by women were not works of theater.[7] Instead, works by women were viewed as the other, the outlier, rather than the norm. "Contemporary women's plays are more likely to be excluded," noted professor and author Sue-Ellen Case, "because there is no precedent or tradition of development towards them," and the spectator's "'horizon of expectation' is established by 'the traditional male form.'"[8]

And when women were represented, attempts to ensure equality were considered catering or pandering—to 51 percent of the population.[9] When Annie Castledine, director at the Derby Playhouse, announced her 1988 season lineup, she was asked why she exhibited a noticable bias toward female playwrights. Castledine's reply was that there was a "precisely balanced 50 percent of plays in the season by women—quite proportionate to the British population."[10]

The contradictions in society and politics were onerous, as women were encouraged to work but were punished for it, and female playwrights were exposing these double standards on the stage. The number of British playwrights increased,[11] as did productions of experimental theater in the form of visual, "nonliterary" experiences that used new forms of technology and a growing interest in mime, according to the 1986 Court Report.

These conflicts were apparent in American society as well, none more clearly than when Anita Hill accused Clarence Thomas of sexual harassment. After she was called to testify before an all-male Senate committee, the televised hearing inspired a new series of conversations examining sexual harassment and treatment of women in the workplace. Following the hearings, which confirmed Thomas, Hill was credited with making "sexual harassment the great connector among women," according to

Irene Natividad, chairwoman of the National Commission of Working Women. Her testimony inspired a "new and potent wave of feminism," said the president of New York Women's Foundation, Marion Kaplan,[12] and the conversations about sexual harassment changed in both content and volume.

"VENOM-SPITTING VIRAGO OF RADICAL FEMINIST THEATER"

Sarah Daniels was writing those conversations for more people to see and hear onstage. The playwright's work depicted and chronicled abuse and violence against women, earning her recognition as a man-hater—or, more specifically, the "venom-spitting virago of radical feminist theater."[13] But Daniels, according to professor and author Elaine Aston, was the only feminist lesbian playwright who achieved status among mainstream audiences following years in the alternative performance groups.

Daniels took on such subjects as pornography (*Masterpieces*), child abuse and women's mental health (*Head-Rot Holiday*), nuclear war (*The Devil's Gateway*), and reproduction (*Byrthrite*). In *Ripen Our Darkness*, she made middle-aged women the center of attention onstage and in the public eye—a marked contrast to the role they played in society offstage.

Central to Daniels's work is the abuse and exploitation of women, a decision that inspired continuous backlash. This attitude was demonstrated in the commentary on her work by critics—most of them male—who complained of being alienated by her work and accused the playwright of making a "clean sweep of the male sex with no pretense of fairness."[14] The importance of being fair seemingly hadn't occurred to male playwrights who excluded women from their scripts.

The reaction to Daniels's work and her depiction of women mirrored the backlash to feminism that had infused society, chronicled in Susan Faludi's book of the same name. Feminism, which had been declared the "great experiment that failed" in many publications, was inspiring caustic reactions from the public—especially women. Their rejection, Faludi wrote in *Backlash*, was motivated by a strategic, insidious smear campaign aimed to inspire women to question if they actually wanted an existence that was equitable to men.

What had been exciting and idealistic was now impractical and exhausting. Throughout the 1980s, as Reaganism and "family values" swept through the United States, feminism had come to symbolize disparaging motherhood and selfishly pursuing one's own professional goals and accomplishments. Feminism had become the scapegoat for many of the problems women were facing, and government support for programs supporting equality decreased or ceased to exist altogether. Ronald Reagan failed to fulfill his campaign promises to "enthusiastically appoint women to all levels of government," and his proposals to eliminate Social Security and cuts to the social services block grant, the Comprehensive Employment and Training Act, and Aid to Families with Dependent Children, among others, directly and negatively affected women. [15]

The conflict-ridden setting of feminism was reflected in the personal, as well as the political. In the days before Anita Hill's testimony, only 21 percent of Americans thought she was telling the truth, and 47 percent of Americans thought she was lying. Following the broadcast of the testimony, 54 percent of Americans did not believe her—twice the amount of the 27 percent who did. [16]

It was a tension-laden society watching Daniels's unflinching portrayal of the oppression and exploitation of women. Mary, the central character in *Ripen Our Darkness*, strongly resembled the women written in and reading Betty Friedan's *The Feminine Mystique*—about a housewife who does not work with four children approaching adulthood, three of whom live with her. The first of Daniels's plays to be published and garner praise from the public, *Ripen Our Darkness* unflinchingly examines the oppression an average woman suffers from the blind compliance of patriarchal institutions, including marriage, mental health, and religion. It is only through death—at her own hands—that Mary achieves real freedom.

Mary is an archetype of the women seen in many of Daniels's plays. *Byrthrite* focuses on the persecution of women in the seventeenth century, and *Blow Your House Down* follows the Yorkshire Ripper, the brutal murderer of women in England in the 1970s. *Head-Rot Holiday*, written after conducting lengthy interviews with former detainees, psychologists, and nurses, is located in a psychiatric prison from which the women have no chance of escaping. They resort to attempted suicide. One character declares of the self-inflicted violence, "It's keeping me alive. Every other fucker's done things to me. I'm going to things to myself for a change." [17]

This autonomy—social, political, religious, or even economic, was noted by the public—with both joy and scorn.

> *Beside Herself, Head-Rot Holiday*, and *The Madness of Esme and Shaz* all focus on the difference between women doing things *to* themselves and doing things *for* themselves, with the latter being constructed as empowering and the former as disempowering. . . . One might argue that most of the plays end with the defeat of the female characters. More commonly, they exit from the male-dominated context in which they exist, aided by other women. [18]

Works by Daniels, described as a "leading female playwright whose work has been persistently under attack from male critics,"[19] were received with condescension by many; the playwright said of *Ripen Our Darkness*, her first professionally performed play, "nobody, except women, thought the men were drawn with any accuracy."[20] *The Madness of Esme and Shaz*, a story of a woman released from prison and paired by probation services with her aunt, whom she has never met and with whom she forms an unlikely friendship, was dismissed by critic Paul Taylor as an "unpersuasive version of *Travels with My Aunt*," with the main character described as a "lonely, recently retired suburban spinster,"[21] a pejorative term used to describe unmarried women of a certain age, synonymous with the derivative title "old maid."

Another critic noted in his review that *The Madness of Esme and Shaz* consisted of an "all-female cast" of "largely steretypes," and he suggested that the play "may lack a male response."[22] Men's voices were prominent in *Masterpieces*, Daniels's brutal examination of pornography featuring men telling jokes about rape while in the company of women, but hardly in the form of a typical leading man. A blistering attack on a patriarchal culture, *Masterpieces* invited the audience to consider the harm done to women by pornography and consider the consequences of women fighting back and instigating, rather than receiving, violence.

Inspired by Andrea Dworkin's groundbreaking book *Men Possessing Women*, in which the activist argues that pornography contributes to violence against women, *Masterpieces* was written for and produced by the Royal Court Theatre Upstairs. Its 1983 premiere coincided with the height of the feminist antipornography movement, when activists were striving to increase awareness of pornography's dangers without inspring accusations of censorship, and Daniels's play openly connects jokes and actions—especially misognyistic ones—with pornography and violence, portrayed through the actions of a variety of characters.

Luc Gilleman wrote in "Drama and Pornography: Sarah Daniels's Masterpieces and Anthony Neilson's *The Censor*,

> Of the three couples, the men represent three different degrees of offensiveness (hypocrisy in Trevor, condescension in Ron, and blatant misogyny in Clive); the women, three different reactions to victimization (eccentricity in Jennifer, withdrawal in Yvonne, and aggression in Rowena). The exposition takes the form of several direct addresses of an informative nature delivered in Brechtian style. . . . The universe of *Masterpieces* is dismal and hopeless, recalling Dworkin's dark vision of an all-encompassing, inescapable masculine evil: "In the system of male sexual domination explicated in pornography, there is no way out, no redemption." . . . Neither is there in *Masterpieces*. The play does not raise the possibility for these women to find fulfillment in an alternative, lesbian, sexual relationship. They are trapped in an impossible and repugnant heterosexuality, in a world where not having sex becomes a source of satisfaction.[23]

Jules Wright, who directed the original production of *Masterpieces*, recalled, "[Daniels] was one of the hardest-hitting playwrights of her generation. *Masterpieces* shocked, disturbed, and angered every audience. It remains one of the most serious and provocative attacks on pornography written for the British theater."[24] Gender representation in the script was also noted: As Aston stated in an introduction to the play, "Unlike the moves towards intrasexual understanding, this verbal sparring is indicative of a gender divide that cannot be broached or healed given the men's entrenched sexism."[25]

As the pornography wars were waged, debates about the depiction of sexual violence and oppression became so heated the National Organization for Women (NOW) weighed in, taking the side of antipornography feminists. NOW declared that sadomasochism and pornography did not constitute sex; they comprised violence and were dangerous, because of the clear link between pornography and sexual violence.[26] The movement swept college campuses, and the tug of war between pornography and the First Amendment continued. It entered local politics when Dworkin and feminist legal scholar Catharine MacKinnon contributed to antiporn legislation introduced in the Indianapolis city council. Defining pornography as a civil rights violation, the legislation inspired more debates about censorship and the First Amendment, along with new divides among the feminist movement.

"When pornography is debated, in or out of court, the issue has been whether government should be in the business of making sure only nice things are said and seen about sex, not whether government should remedy the exploitation of the powerless for the profit and enjoyment of the powerful," Dworkin and MacKinnon wrote. "Whether pornography is detrimental to the 'social fabric' has therefore been consiered; whether particular indivduals or definable groups are hurt by it has not been, not really."[27] The campaign was controversial, and it inspired a deep divide within the feminist movement.

Disparaged by many male critics following its opening, *Masterpieces* was dismissed by Irving Wardle as "consciousness-raising seances," referring the popular group sessions in which women applied experiences from their personal lives to the larger issues and goals of the movement, and he also publicly revoked the "patronizingly masculine compliments" he had paid the playwright in previous reviews. Robert Hewison also dismissed the play as "subjective, not objective truth."[28] The male-centric criticism, which decried her depiction of men as "male bigots," "bestial exploiter," and "domestic Hitlers," communicated much more about society's reaction to feminism than it did about Daniels's writing.

Masterpieces wasn't subtle, nor was it supposed to be, Daniels said, describing her controversial work as an "issue-based play," adding, "And in that sense it is didactic." She told *Rage and Reason*,

> I don't necessarily think I would write like that anymore, but I don't feel apologetic for it. People said it was like a sledgehammer, but it was more like a scream really. If it had been more subtle, I don't think it would have had the impact that it did. . . . I tried to ensure that nobody could misinterpret *Masterpieces*. I felt so strongly about the ideas in the play that, in an attempt to guard against being misunderstood, I censored myself from writing the detail and contradictions which give a character depth.[29]

Daniels was accused of "overkill" by some, those reactions further communicating the accusers' resistance to the subject and acknowledging that violence against women was more common than one assumed, Aston wrote, adding, "One feels tempted to reply with a statistical analysis of child abusers, rapists, men who commit acts of domestic violence, etc."[30]

Daniels's unapologetic depiction of men in her plays, especially *Masterpieces*, was noticable and noticed. The culture of backlash fostered the reaction to her work, with one male critic repeatedly complaining he felt "ill at ease in [Daniels's] universe."[31]

It was Daniels's determined examination of these conditions and the complicity within them that repulsed the male critics, Aston wrote. And they were repulsed: Both Daniels's characters and Daniels herself were despised by the men of the press, who described the playwright as "'manhating,' 'fanatical,' 'raging,' 'wrathful,' 'vitriolic,' 'embittered,' 'furious,' 'savage,' 'bilious,' 'rancorous,' 'blasphemous,' 'outrageous,' 'incensed,' 'aggressive,' 'obsessive,' 'strident,' and 'shrill.'"[32]

But these accusations did not phase the playwright, who wrote,

> I was tempted to answer each distorted point that the fraternity of theater critics made up about *Masterpieces*, but their narrow, shallow view of the world has taken up too much space already. . . . I make no apology for what my plays say. I make no apology for the anger which is intrinsic to *Masterpieces* for I know it to be justified.[33]

TELLING THE UNTOLD STORIES

Another unapologetic reenvisioning of women's societal roles was seen in the plays of April De Angelis. The actress-turned-playwright began her career performing with the group Monstrous Regiment during the height of exploring identity politics through alternative theater. As a writer-in-residence for Paines Plough in 1990, she adapted John Cleland's eighteenth-century erotic novel *Fanny Hill*. In *Ironmistress*, she depicted the power struggles between a Victorian widow and her daughter after the widow inherits her husband's iron foundry. *Hush*, commissioned by the Royal Court Theatre, chronicled the effects of a woman's disappearance on the community she left behind.

De Angelis was a woman who wrote about women, but she resisted being defined by that single characteristic: "When I first started writing, it was for a women's theater group called ReSisters, and the question of what to write about never really entered your head," she told the *Independent*. "You wanted to put women on the stage and to talk about women's issues, and you wanted to do it as well as you could. For years that's how we wrote."[34]

Sarah Hemming wrote,

> *Ironmistress* was written like that, you know—there was no question. One could write plays supported by a movement and a consensus, there were rules and regulations and sound and unsound things to do. Now those sorts of plays aren't very satisfying; they tend to be the kind that come to a good, strong conclusion. Everything is now more confusing. Also I don't want—as a person or a writer—to keep repeating that formula. It's quite old-fashioned, and the audience is rather bored of it—"Oh, another play about women being oppressed." The world is much more complex than that anyway. So you are thinking, "What do I write about?" You have to take on your society in a broader way.[35]

Examining the feminine identity through her work, De Angelis reenvisioned the role of the helpless Victorian heroine and the Creature from Frankenstein in *Breathless*. In *Playhouse Creatures*, she narrated the experiences of four female actors in 1669 London, just after women were permitted to perform onstage, exploring modern-day issues of gender and equity in a historical context. She took on the topic of motherhood, determined to portray it in a realistic, nonidealized way—a marked departure from much popular entertainment. "You are often disempowered as a mother and denied [the opportunity to be] self-defining," she told the *Guardian*.

> The stories of mothers are stories that largely remain unwritten. A lot of women's lives and experiences are overlooked, not thought of as interesting. The heroic struggle of bringing up children and all the emotional caretaking that entails; these things are seldom recognized and written about in theater and culture.[36]

Mother–daughter dynamics were also explored in 2011's *Jumpy*, in which a middle-aged mother and former activist struggles with her daughter's political apathy. In *After Electra*, which opened in 2015, she set a middle-aged woman center stage, while examining conflicting attitudes toward motherhood by commandeering the myth of Electra through the story of a mother, Virgie, and her daughter Haydn. De Angelis told the *Guardian*, "I wanted to try and rewrite it and reconfigure the relationship between mother and daughter so they are not always set against each other, which is how Freud sees it."[37] In *The Positive Hour*, the pressures of modern feminity are explored through sessions with a social worker whose cases include a single mother earning extra income through sex work, a student with a troubled family, and a failed artist.

LOVE, MARRIAGE, AND MOTHERHOOD

Onstage, women were defying conventions, challenging societal norms, and breaking conventional gender roles, while offstage, attempts to re-move women from the office and return them to the kitchen, often by inspiring fear, were abundant in the media and politics. A now-infamous study in 1986, reported that a single, college-educated woman older than thirty only had a 20 percent chance of ever being married. Fast forward ten years, and her chances of wedded bliss were down to 1.3 percent. In June 1986, the cover of *Newsweek* blared the headline, "The Marriage Crunch/If You're a Single Woman, Here Are Your Chances of Getting Married," while the interior asked, "Too Late for Prince Charming?" The article, which reported that women older than 40 were more likely to be killed by a terrorist than marry, was based on an unpublished study (and was retracted 20 years later), but it inspired panic among women. Pursu-ing their careers came at a cost, women were told, because their time to find a husband and have children was running short.[38]

"I want it all!" the leading ladies of *Baby* sang joyously when it opened on Broadway in 1983. With a book by Sybille Pearson and music and lyrics by David Shire and Richard Maltby, the musical chronicled three very different pregnancies in a small college town. Based on a story developed with Susan Yankowitz, at first glance *Baby* could have easily been described as a feminist show. One of the expectant mothers (Lizzie) is a college student living with her boyfriend but has no desire to get married, even though she does want to have the baby. Another (Pam) defies the typically feminine ideal—an athletic coach who prefers track pants to dresses. And the third (Arlene) is in her forties, having just celebrated her twentieth anniversary with her husband.

Between 1983 and 1984, *Baby* played for 283 performances on Broad-way and was nominated for seven Tony Awards. While it did challenge some traditional gender roles of the time, it embraced others, perhaps unconsciously. Lizzie didn't want to marry Danny, but his repeated declarations that they *would* get married did not upset her, nor did his shock and apparent disgust when she referred to their child as "she"—to which he loudly corrected her with "he!" Out of her range of hearing, he declares he is "not going to let her get away with this" and will make her marry him. And, in the show's final act, despite her repeated declarations, Liz decides she will marry Danny after all, thus adopting the patriarchal "family values" the free-spirited college student had defied.

Baby contained some positive depictions of women—academic, professional, athletic—but that's all they were: depictions, not characters. Liz's joyful embracing of her unexpected pregnancy at age twenty, while a junior in college, is never contextualized or explained. Her reasons for keeping the baby could be religious, familial, or otherwise, but they are never explained. She is written as a lighthearted, loving, optimistic New Woman who happily accepts her role as a mother without hesitation.

The confusing contradictions of a woman's identity—personal, professional, and maternal—in the 1980s are personified in Pam, who, after thinking she is pregnant, shames herself for her appearance, asking, "What kind of mother wears gym clothes all day?" While recalling her childhood as a tomboy, Pam says she "set out to be a girl and almost achieved it." She equates motherhood with femininity, changing from her track uniform into in a flowing skirt and heels when she and her husband visit a reproductive specialist. When waiting to learn why she and Nick are having trouble conceiving, Pam assumes it is her fault, lamenting, "I know what I'm going to hear. I have an irregular cycle, I'm an irregular woman," equating infertility with failure and shame. In *Baby*, childless women are still the other, even following the efforts of the Second Wave movement. When the specialist informs them that Nick's low sperm count is the reason they're not pregnant, Pam insists that it couldn't be, it must be her—adopting the blame to protect her husband's ego and protect his masculinity.

Pam and Nick's marriage is loving, and her husband is the most progressive in the musical, happily telling one of the students he coaches that he doesn't mind that his wife is in better shape than him or that he cooks. But when he sings lovingly of Pam, "At home late at night there's a woman I make her see," some of his traditional mindset is revealed. While Nick appears to be the ideal modern man, and in many ways his actions are admirable, he assumes responsibility and ownership of his wife's identity. In *Baby*, it's only through the male gaze that the strong and muscular Pam is seen as feminine.

Empty nesters Alan and Arlene also defy the gender norms of the time—he wants to keep the baby, and she wants to end the pregnancy, sell their family home, buy a small apartment, and travel the world. Alan idealizes parenthood, while Arlene is more pragmatic, remembering the challenges and stress, as well as the joy. They agree to not keep the baby, but she abruptly changes her mind. Alan and Arlene's relationship offers the most realistic look at marriage. When they realize they had existed more as parents than as partners, they decide to try to rebuild their relationship with more love.

Despite its seemingly progressive approach to family structures—three principal female characters, one older than 40, and a story line that defied the typical love, marriage, and baby plot—*Baby* offered an unrealistic, idealized look at pregnancy. Money is almost never discussed except in the vaguest of terms. Health insurance is not mentioned. And aside from a brief mention—and denial—of morning sickness in the doctor's waiting room, the frightening and dangerous aspects of pregnancy don't seem to exist. Even though "not having" the baby is discussed between both Danny and Liz and Alan and Arlene, the word "abortion" is never spoken onstage—a trend that continued into and past 2016.[39]

One of the chief complaints about feminism in the 1980s was that it caused women to behave like men—and the worst parts of men. This sentiment was shared by Robert Brustein, who taught playwright Wendy Wasserstein at the Yale School of Drama, and who wrote, "[Wasserstein] seems to suggest that the feminist movement, instead of reforming society, has succeeded largely in introducing women to the ravening competitiveness of the given circumstances, which is to say it has encouraged women to imitate the worst qualities of men."[40]

Examples of this backlash permeate *Baby*, for instance, when Pam shares that she had been "expecting" for many years but "made sure not to expect too much." Women couldn't have everything they wanted. When Liz asks Arlene, "Did you agonize over working or staying at home?" Arlene's response is, "I wanted to stay at home. Now why is that so embarrassing to admit? . . . What's worse is I loved making totem poles out of fruit cans." It's a subtle jab at some of the stereotypes of feminism, which many perceived as expecting women to work and shaming them if they did stay home.

While waiting at their doctor's office, Liz, Pam, and Arlene meet and discuss their respective pregnancies and relationships. Subdued at first, they soon burst into song, declaring proudly that they "want it all"—even Arlene, who, at first, informs the women they will have to make choices and sacrifices. Liz, only twenty and a junior in college, tells her new friends she made a list to help decide her future, but all she could come up with was, "I want it all! Adventure, love, career, kids large and small." Liz, in her youth and excitement, longed for domestic, as well as professional, fulfillment—a "simple quiet life and some glory, and Stephen Spielberg filming my story." It's never acknowledged in *Baby* that Liz will not be able to achieve all of her desires. Nor does the audience see her share these desires with her partner, Danny. It's only in the safety of an all-female setting that these women can share what they truly hope for. The book *Baby*, written by a woman, was largely derided by critics, but the music and lyrics—by men—were praised.

THE TRAPPED WOMAN

Breaking free from the entrapment of a patriarchal society took new form in 1983, when *'night, Mother*, Marsha Norman's play chronicling a woman's decision to die by suicide, opened on Broadway. The play, which was nominated for three Tony Awards, won the Pulitzer Prize for Drama and inspired debates about its intention and message, as well as its dramatic impact.

Norman's two-person play examined the relationship between Jessie and her mother Thelma, as Jessie prepares for her death and Thelma struggles to prevent and then understand her daughter's decision. First developed at the Circle Repertory Company and opening on Broadway in 1983, following performances at the American Repertory Theater, Norman's intimate look at the women's lives was viewed by some as a depiction of women entrapped in postmodern society and patriarchal culture, and by others as a defeatist work encouraging death as an escape from what a woman considered a problematic world.

Taking place entirely in Thelma and Jessie's home, *'night, Mother* is unapologetically realist, described by Dorothy Chansky as a "kind of experimental, underground feminist tool."[41] It portrayed two women alone: a widowed mother and divorced daughter whose survival depends on one another, the daughter caring for her mother and the mother providing a home for her daughter. And one was being abandoned by the other.

Jessie's decision is hardly spontaneous. Instead, it is a carefully prepared and executed decision. She calmly informs her mother, "The gun is for me. . . . I'm going to kill myself, Mama," before methodically going through the necessary steps to prepare her mother for living alone. [42] Suffering from epilepsy and depression, divorced and disappointed in her son, Jessie does not see a reason to continue living. Frustrated by the futility of her life and seeing no way out, she views her choice through a pragmatic and practical lens, telling her mother, "We're not going to just sit around tonight. I made a list of things." She teaches Thelma how to use the washer, goes over the specifics of ordering groceries, and gives her mother a manicure. She even plans to lock her bedroom door so the police won't suspect Thelma in her death.

Jessie's decision is even presented as empowering, an opportunity for her to take control of an existence in which she has felt disempowered. Thelma begs Jessie to postpone her decision for two more weeks, pleading, "But something might happen. Something that might change everything. Who knows what it might be, but it might be worth waiting for!" Jessie replies, "No, Mama. *This* is how I have my say. This is how I say what I thought about it *all*, and I say No." [43]

Described by critic Frank Rich as a "shattering evening," the play divided many critics concerning whether it was a feminist work with a political message or a drama that either succeeded or failed to move audiences. "Does *'night, Mother* say no to hope?" Rich asked in his review. "It's easy to feel that way after reeling from this play's crushing blow. But there can be hope if there is understanding, and it is Marsha Norman's profound achievement that she brings both understanding and dignity to forgotten and tragic American lives." [44]

Opening during Ronald Reagan's first term as president, as "family values" swept the country, the play surprised and shocked many. "It is a very scary play," Norman said. "It is trapped girl, writ large." [45]

Norman had previously introduced the trapped girl in her 1979 drama *Getting Out*. Inspired by a young woman Norman had known who was imprisoned for murder, *Getting Out* chronicled one day in the woman's life after she was released from prison. Led to a dreary apartment arranged by her mother, Arlene attempts to begin building a normal life, but her past continues to haunt her. The play became an Off-Broadway hit, praised by film critic Richard Eder for its "central fragility of conversions and the need to accept the evil inside one." Eder continued that the idea "is not, of course, a new one; and sometimes it is set down a trifle schematically. The play's achievement is not intellectual; it is dramatic and emotional, and as such, it is a triumph of the season."[46]

The praise for Norman's plays quickly evolved into expectations: A "Marsha Norman play" had to have a certain kind of woman going through a certain kind of story. It was those expectations, Norman said, that contributed to her decision to stop writing plays. Following *'night, Mother* she authored more scripts but was frequently told, "We want a Marsha Norman play." She wanted to reply, "This is a Marsha Norman play. I wrote this."

"That takes you all the way to, 'I realize now I can't write anymore plays,'" Norman said, adding,

> *'night, Mother* really is the end. I can't write plays about anything without the expectation being here of, "If it's not *'night, Mother*, we don't want it." . . . Plays that win the Pulitzer tend to be the end of a particular line of thought. It's an exploration. That's about as far as you can go with the trapped girl.[47]

She recalled when *New York Times* critic Mel Gussow told her, "Marsha, people like the plays of yours when women have guns." That moment explained so much to Norman, who said,

> If you've got a gun, you can be in a show. If you've got agency and power, you can create danger and havoc. But if you're just going to write a play about a woman poet who's decided to stop writing poetry and go live in France, which is what my last play was, we don't want that. "There's no gun? You're Marsha Norman. You're supposed to write the plays where the girls have guns." . . . In other words, if you write like a man you can get in. If you write like a girl, no.[48]

THE UNCOMMON WOMEN OF WENDY WASSERSTEIN

It wasn't until 1988 that feminism proudly arrived on Broadway in the form of Heidi Holland, the title character of *The Heidi Chronicles*. Written by Wendy Wasserstein, who had narrated the lives and conflicts of modern women in several other plays, *The Heidi Chronicles* was considered groundbreaking for its time, giving voice to the frustrations and disappointments women were experiencing in their careers, friendships, and families. The leading lady of *The Heidi Chronicles* was Heidi Holland, an art historian and activist for women, who the audience follows from a high school dance through an accomplished career and the feminist movement of the 1970s.

Heidi arrived on Broadway in the heat of the antifeminist backlash; the same week the play opened at the Plymouth Theatre, the "New Traditionalists" ad campaign was launched in *Good Housekeeping*, featuring women who left the workplace in favor of marriage and children.[49]

Ms. Holland was far from the first unique woman seeking fulfillment in an uncertain future Wasserstein had brought to life; the playwright had already penned several scripts that found critical acclaim Off-Broadway. "It's where my imagination goes and sticks," she told the *Washington Post* in 1994. "Women's issues are still interesting enough to me to make me want to sit alone in a room and write."[50] In *Uncommon Women and Others* (1977), a group of students at a woman's college attempt to decide how to shape their futures following academia. As the young women discuss love, marriage, and careers, they personify the tension women of that generation faced. These women were encouraged to continue their studies or seek employment after graduating—"Today, all fields are open to women, and more than 50 percent continue in professional or graduate school," the play's narrator announces—after having been raised by parents who extolled the virtues of marriage and family.

These women are not ignorant of the world they are entering into. As the character Rita states,

> This entire society is based on cocks—the *New York Times*, Walter Cronkite, all the buildings and roads, the cities, philosophy, government, history, religion, shopping malls, everything I can name is male. When I see things this way, it becomes obvious that it's very easy to feel alienated and alone for the simple reason that I've never been included because I came into the world without a penis.[51]

Years after graduating, the women gather for lunch and share their various accomplishments. One of the longtime friends hesitates to share with her friends that she is pregnant, admitting it was difficult to share the news and that she was even embarrassed. She fears her friends' disap-

The Heidi Chronicles. **From left: Robert Curtis-Brown, Amy Irving, and Michael Sandels.** *Photofest*

proval of her becoming a mother—another demonstration of the confusion women were facing regarding their roles inside and outside of their houses.

Personal and professional fulfillment was again debated in 1981, in Wasserstein's *Isn't It Romantic*, in which a young unmarried woman living alone in New York is forced to shape her own life, much to the chagrin of others and herself. After years of relying on humor and indecision, Janie Blumberg is forced to confront both her parents' and her best friend's expectations of her and acknowledge her own hopes and desires. Her parents want her to find a nice man and marry, as they remind her in daily phone calls and messages, and unannounced visits, in which they simultaneously celebrate and criticize her choices.

Janie's romantic relationships, or lack thereof, are mentioned frequently by her mother. In the middle of a visit, presumably to celebrate her daughter's new apartment, Tasha reminisces, "I remember my first apartment in New York. Of course, I was much younger than you, and I was already married to your father. Toasts: To Janie. Congratulations, welcome home, and I hope next year you live in another apartment and your father and I have to bring up four coffees." Janie responds, "You want me to have a roommate?"[52]

Janie, an unfashionable aspiring freelance writer, and her best friend Harriet, a chic, ambitious career woman, are both, in different ways, trying to "have it all." The two attempt to balance love, fulfillment, and independence, as well as the weight of family expectations, and feel panicked by the expectations placed on them. Harriet, who regularly lunches at the Four Seasons with her single, successful mother, tells Janie she can't look up to women unable to fend for themselves:

> Maybe it's because I'm Lillian's daughter, but I never respected women who didn't learn to live alone and pay their own rent. Imagine spending your life pretending you weren't a person. To compromise at this point would be antifeminist, well, antihumanist, well, just not impressive. I'm not being too harsh.[53]

That kind of woman is exactly who Janie's boyfriend wants. Marty, a Jewish doctor from a wealthy family, dotes on Janie, affectionately nicknames her "Monkey," and frequently reminds her that she is a "sweet." Janie drifts along in the relationship, uncertain of whether or not to commit; her parents encourage her, while her best friend disapproves.

Through Janie and Harriet's lives, Wasserstein comments on women of the time and what they could and should expect from the world. Harriet, entangled in an office affair that is clearly going nowhere, asks her mother, "Do you think it's possible to be married, or living with a man, have a good relationship and children that you share equal responsibility for, and a career, and still read novels, play the piano, have women friends, and swim twice a week?" Her mother, from another generation

Isn't It Romantic with Joan Copeland and Christine Estabrook. *Photofest*

and seemingly unable to comprehend what it is her daughter wants out of life, who has found professional success but spends her evenings alone watching *The Rockford Files*, responds, "You mean what the women's magazines call 'Having it all?' Harriet, that's just your generation's fantasy."[54]

Wasserstein gives voice—although not necessarily a sympathetic one—to the men in her plays, articulating their confusion regarding what they've been raised to expect and what they are experiencing. Harriet's lover patronizingly attempts to comfort her when she invites him to spend the night with her, saying, "I see what's going on here. It's the old, 'I'm afraid of turning thirty alone and I'm beginning to think about having a family.'" He later speaks of his own confusion regarding women:

> When I graduated from Yale, I thought I'd find a nice wife who would cook me dinner, we'd have a few kids and I'd support the family, and a few years up we'd get a house in Madison, CT, for the weekends. The girl I married never cooked, and she wasn't lucky like you. Girls didn't assume they'd have careers then. My wife was just very bright and

very unhappy. And the girls I date now, the ones like you, the MBAs from Harvard, they want me to be the wife. They want me to be the support system. Well, I can't do that, Harriet, I just wasn't told that's the way it was supposed to be.[55]

Deciding what is "supposed to be" for their own lives leads both Janie and Harriet down unexpected paths, with Janie deciding to not move in with Marty and Harriet getting engaged to a man she has only been dating a few weeks. Rather than a romantic happily ever after, Wasserstein bluntly illustrated the fact that these characters were not happy and couldn't "have it all." In a foreshadowing of Heidi's speech in *The Heidi Chronicles*, Wasserstein described Harriet as someone who "has all the externals." She continued,

Harriet could be a cover on *Savvy* magazine. The girl who "has it all." You know, the person who gets up at eight o'clock in the morning, spends twenty minutes with her daughter and ten minutes with her husband, then they jog together, she drives to work, comes home to a wonderful life, studies French in the bathtub, and still has time to cry three minutes a day in front of the mirror.[56]

Wasserstein's examination of women's confusion and sadness due to societal expectations, as well as personal ones, was overlooked by the largely male press, who seemingly viewed the playwright's intention with patronizing appreciation. Many, when reviewing the play, commented on the leading actress' physical appearance before her actual performance. Richard Christiansen, of the *Chicago Tribune*, wrote, "Alma Cuervo, a veteran of the play's Off-Broadway productions, is a perfect embodiment of the plump, sweet-faced Janie, and she's a fine actress as well, despite a tendency to prolong her elfin grins and exaggerate her pixieish frustrations."[57] And Mel Gussow, of the *New York Times*, remarked,

Miss Cuervo's identification with the character is complete, as it was in *Uncommon Women*, giving a clownish twist to every glint of self-mockery. For the sake of the actress's versatility, perhaps we can look forward to some future incarnation of the character in a play by Miss Wasserstein about a formerly fat princess passing thirty and becoming svelte and secure.[58]

The modern woman's isolation was further explored in *The Heidi Chronicles*, culminating in Heidi's speech to her alumni in which she admits to feeling "stranded." Her confession comes close to the end of Wasserstein's play, the first production on Broadway to examine the shortcomings of the feminist movement.[59] Wasserstein credited the play's birth to her imagination of a woman actually daring to articulate her unhappiness: "I wrote this play because I had this image of a woman standing up at a women's meeting saying, 'I've never been so unhappy in my life.' . . . The more angry it made me that these feelings weren't being expressed, the more anger I put into that play."[60]

Wasserstein was inspired by her personal experiences, she said, notably feeling out of place at social events with women her age. "When I wrote *Heidi*, I was 35, I had just written a movie for Spielberg that didn't work out, I wasn't married, and I was beginning to feel like the odd man out at baby showers," Wasserstein told *People* magazine. "I didn't know whether the sacrifices I had made were worth the road I was taking. So I decided to write a play about all that."[61] Heidi personifies the feeling of being the "odd man out," hovering at the edge of the play's larger scenes, observing but rarely interacting until invited to do so.[62]

Heidi's isolation, if self-imposed, continues to build, culminating in her confession, "I'm just not happy. I'm afraid I haven't been happy for some time." Having been invited to discuss her accomplishments, as well as those of the women's movement, Heidi declares, "I don't blame any of us. We're all concerned, intelligent, good women. It's just that I feel stranded. And I thought the whole point was that we wouldn't feel stranded. I thought the point was that we were all in this together."[63]

Heidi introduces this speech—or lack thereof, because she doesn't have one prepared, inspiring the stream-of-consciousness confession—by sardonically listing the things people expected her to have done just the night before: attending a low-impact aerobics class, cooking a free-range mesquite chicken, having sex with her husband in the kitchen "so he wouldn't feel old," and reading forty pages of *Dante's Inferno* in Italian. Her hyperbolic list of a day in the life of a successful woman who appears to "have it all" concludes with, "She's exemplary and exhausted."[64] Again, Wasserstein exposes the incredible pressure women were feeling during the years following the intensity of the Second Wave movement as they attempted to do everything they said they could. There was too much for women to do and too little time.

Heidi first arrived in New York in 1988, Off-Broadway at Play-wright's Horizons, earning positive reviews. It opened on Broadway in 1989, and ran for 622 performances, winning a Tony Award for Best Play—establishing Wasserstein as the first woman to win a Tony Award for Best Play—and the Pulitzer Prize for Drama. Wasserstein, long praised for her comedic approach to writing, was praised for her deeper, more serious approach. As Heidi seeks fulfillment, her anxiety was illustrated more clearly than any of Wasserstein's previously written women. Mel Gussow of the *New York Times* praised the play, writing, "Heidi's search for self is both mirthful and touching. Ms. Wasserstein has always been a clever writer of comedy. This time she has been exceedingly watchful about not settling for easy laughter, and the result is a more penetrating play."[65]

Feminism's shortcomings were commented on by men as well but with a decidedly different point of view. *Heidi* wasn't a hit with everyone she met. Wasserstein was criticized for writing her title character as too passive, someone who watched history pass her by rather than participating in it. And the show's conclusion, which has Heidi adopting a baby as a single mother, was considered too traditional and privileged of a reaction to her isolation and disappointment.

"The play assures us that modern, intelligent women are funny for the same traditional reason that women have always been funny: They hate their bodies, can't find a man, and won't believe in themselves," wrote Alisa Solomon in the *Village Voice*. "Its vision of feminism, like its dramaturgy, is entirely bourgeois."[66] Solomon was not alone: Betty Friedan, author of the famed *The Feminine Mystique*, the best-selling nonfiction text challenging the widely held belief that "fulfillment as a woman had only one definition for American women after 1949—the housewife-mother," which is largely credited with sparking the Second Wave feminist movement, wrote,

> I'm proud of Wendy Wasserstein. She's a very good playwright, and I'm happy she won the Pulitzer Prize, but I was disturbed by the play. In depicting Heidi as troubled over career and family, Wendy Wasserstein inadvertently fed a media hype, a new feminine mystique about the either/or choices in a woman's life. Either/or is a false and a no-win choice that comes of a new antifeminist traditionalism. These articles about women putting down their briefcases and putting on aprons are detours. They take us away from the real agenda, which

should be for us to stop being the only nation in the advanced world, besides South Africa, without a national policy of child care and parental leave. [67]

Feminist activist Gloria Steinem also commented on the play but was gentler in her criticism, saying *The Heidi Chronicles* was "clearly a step forward." Steinem also credited the rumored divide among feminists regarding the play an attempt to instead divide women, saying,

> There is no essential controversy among feminists. . . . Individual women have discussed with each other their responses [to the controversial ending], but of course there's public support for the play. To have a play on Broadway about the change that a woman goes through in her life; to be in a situation where hundreds of thousands of people have sat completely absorbed in the life choices of a particular woman . . . this is a revolution in itself. [68]

In breaking new ground for women on Broadway, Wasserstein, and Heidi herself, was now shouldering the burden of representation. The pressure for Wasserstein—a woman who wrote a play about a woman to represent all women—was evident and, in part, due to the fact there were so few plays representing women at all. Professor and author Jill Dolan wrote, "Before she died, Wasserstein urged people to not saddle her with such responsibility and argued forcefully and rightfully that there should be more plays about women and feminism, so that she could tell her story without the impossible necessity that it represent *all* women's stories." [69]

The lack of diversity in *The Heidi Chronicles* became a symbol and a scapegoat for the lack of diversity on Broadway because *The Heidi Chronicles* was the only play by a woman to open on Broadway that season. This inequality was noticeable. Mary Remnant, who was the second editor of the series, noted that, in Metheun's 1981–1982 catalog, seventy-five playwrights were listed, and only two were women. The "Plays by Women" series was launched in 1982, first edited by playwright and critic Michelene Wandor. [70] Despite many women proving this assumption wrong, one reason contributing to why women playwrights were less frequently published was the divide between work and family: Cheryl Robson wrote the introduction to the play collection *Female Voices Fighting Lives* and wrote that,

Theater publishers are not only looking for good plays, but also bankable writers who'll be writing plays in ten years' time, so they can recoup their initial publishing investments. Women playwrights are so often considered to be unsuitable for long-term investment because they may take time out from their writing career to have children. [71]

The activism went beyond writing, expanding to backstage and offstage altogether. The advocacy organization the League of Professional Theatre Women was established in 1986, to increase the visibility of and advocate for opportunities for female theater professionals. In 1989, the Women in Arts and Media Coalition was founded to help establish and further interdisciplinary connections.

Women were ready to work for change, and they knew it would take a long time. As Steinem said of Wasserstein's play, "Wendy Wasserstein is not saying that women are led astray by the movement. It takes a long while to overthrow 5,000 years. The question is not, 'Is it perfect now, but is it better than it used to be?'" [72]

6

WINNING AWARDS FOR DOING A "MAN'S JOB"

The stage was set for change, but it was coming slowly. Women were working. They were writing, producing, directing, and organizing—but they were rarely seen in leadership positions backstage on Broadway. It wasn't until 1996, when women were admitted to one of the most illustrious clubs in the theater community, that they began to make their mark.

It's ironic that, in decades that had passed since the first Tony Awards, so few women had won a trophy honoring the best of Broadway—a trophy that was named after a woman. Many have been surprised to learn that "Tony" refers to actress, director, producer, and philanthropist—and woman—Antoinette Perry.

"DOING A MAN'S JOB"

Introduced to the theater at a young age, Perry first desired to be an actress. "When I was six," she later wrote, "I didn't say I'd become an actress. I felt I was one. No one could have convinced me I wasn't."[1] She made her stage debut in her uncle George Wessells's company at age fifteen. Versatile and industrious, Perry made herself useful in almost every department, recalling, "I watched and learned. I did everything from helping in wardrobe to selling tickets. I was petite and blonde, and soon was playing the ingenue in melodramas and farces. Eventually, Uncle George trained me, mainly in the Shakespearean male roles."[2]

Marriage took Perry from the stage in 1909, when she wed Frank Wheatcroft Frueauff. Two children soon followed, and, at her husband's urging, Perry focused on motherhood and left the theater. But marriage did not completely remove her from the industry. Flouting the established societal conventions for women, Perry handled business and money independently. She proudly refused to limit her life to the conventions of marriage and motherhood, remarking to a reporter, "Should I go on playing bridge and dining, going in the same old monotonous circle? It's easy that way. But it's a sort of suicide, too."[3]

Following her husband's death in 1922, which left her with a $13 million estate, Perry returned to the stage in 1924, in *Mr. Pitt*, a play by Zona Gale. That performance was followed by George S. Kaufman and Edna Ferber's *Minick* in 1924, Kate McLaurin's *Caught* in 1925, George Dunning Grible's *The Masque of Venice* in 1926, and *Electra* in 1927.[4]

Inspired by Rachel Crothers, an actress and playwright who often wrote about women's issues and directed her own works, Perry turned to directing and began years of daringly unconventional work.[5] She made her directorial debut in 1928, codirecting Ransom Rideout's *Goin' Home*, with Brock Pemberton as the staging producer, followed by the comedy *Hotbed*. The duo also collaborated on Preston Sturges's *Strictly Dishonorable* in 1929. The romantic comedy ran for 557 performances, marking Perry's first hit production,[6] for which she was praised by a critic for "doing a man's job."[7] The show opened in London and film rights were sold, establishing Perry and Pemberton on solid ground just before the stock market crashed in 1929.

But even that didn't stop the pair. Perry and Pemberton teamed up for Valentine Davies's *Three Times the Hour* in 1931; *Christopher Comes Across*, by Hawthorne Hurst, in 1932; and *Personal Appearance*, by Lawrence Riley, in 1934. But Perry also led productions on her own. She directed *Divorce Me, Dear*, by Katherine Roberts, in 1931, and 1935 saw her directing *Ceiling Zero*, by Frank Wead. The wartime adventure story earned mixed reviews, with the *New York Sun* noting, "One minor point in the acting of *Ceiling Zero* had been pilloried by several critics on the grounds that it had been done by a woman director, and Miss Perry was so gleeful when she found the same bit of action in another play which was done entirely by a man."[8]

Perry multitasked in 1937, directing three Pemberton-produced shows and alternating rehearsals to accommodate all three. Her daughter Margaret recalled rehearsals taking place in the living room, with her mother peeling peaches for preserves as she directed.[9] In 1938, Perry directed two plays: *Eye on the Sparrow*, by Maxwell Selser, and *Kiss the Boys Goodbye*, by Claire Booth Luce.

Perry went on to direct many more shows and found one of Perry's greatest successes in 1944, with *Harvey*. Praised by critics before winning the Pulitzer, Mary Chase's play enjoyed a Broadway run of 1,775 performances. *New York Times* critic Clive Barnes praised Chase's script and Perry's direction, writing,

> Miss Perry has staged the show for laughter, and she should have, but she has not failed to underline it with considerable profundity. Harvey is a Pooka, a large animal spirit, originating in Celtic folklore. "Harvey" is a full-bodied and irresistible comedy which no theaterlover can afford to miss.[10]

"I'M JUST A FOOL FOR THE THEATER"

Perry delighted in her work and made no attempt to mask her enjoyment. When a reporter asked her, "Why do you devote so much of your money and time to such thankless activities?" her response was, "Thankless? They're anything but that. I'm just a fool for the theater."[11] Her self-proclaimed foolishness took her involvement in the community offstage and behind the scenes, where she contributed to the American Theatre Council's Apprentice Theatre, the Stage Relief Fund, the Actor's Thrift Shop, and the Actors' Fund of America.[12] She was a cofounder of the American Theatre Wing of Allied Relief, now known as the American Theatre Wing, which opened the Stage Door Canteen. Stars including Lauren Bacall and the Andrews Sisters served food, washed dishes, and gave performances at the Canteen, where American servicemen could enjoy entertainment.[13] The Canteen was the title subject of a 1943 film that featured Tallulah Bankhead, Lynn Fontanne, and Helen Hayes,[14] and whose profits funded USO tours to entertain soldiers in battle.[15] Following the war's conclusion, Perry helped recloate the American Theatre Wing to a new position. Perry's philanthropy was notable, and praised by Pemberton, who said, "Probably a third of her life was given to our work, the other two-thirds to helping people individually or through the organizations she headed."[16]

Her support extended to artists as well. As president of the National Experimental Theatre, she collaborated with Actors Equity and the Dramatist's Guild to financially support new artists. More than 7,000 auditions were financed by Perry throughout and following the war.[17]

When Perry returned to performing, using her unmarried name, she frequently chose plays written by women or featuring daring women defying societal conventions.[18] Her "angel investment," *Miss Lulu Bett*, was authored by Zona Gale, who adapted it from her own book of the same name. According to the *New York Times*, Gale "rebelled against everything that she regarded as unjust or oppressive,"[19] and the play portrayed a woman's attempts to assert herself and build a new life. Gale, the first woman to win the Pulitzer Prize for Drama, was described in the script's foreword as having "violated many sacred dramatic rules." The foreword further explains,

> She has given us characters who talk as people really talk and who therefore are dull. . . . The result of such adherence to uninspiring reality might well have been expected to be a failure in its appeal to an uninspiring nation of theatergoers. But Miss Gale took the chance. She wrote the play, as she had written the book, without compromise, and was rewarded by an enthusiastic public.[20]

Perry's performances brought women's stories to the stage: Kate McLaurin's *Caught* chronicled the tragic consequences of a man's dishonesty with two women and Sophocles' *Electra* chronicled a woman seeking revenge for the unjust death of her father. Her interest in women's stories was also apparent in her directing, which she often undertook for a play by a woman. Women writers seen onstage under Perry's direction included Clare Boothe Luce (*Kiss the Boys Goodbye*); Katherine Roberts (*Divorce Me, Dear*); Mary Chase (*Now You've Done It* and *Harvey*); Florence Ryerson, with Colin Clements (*Glamour Preferred*); Josephine Bentham, with Herschel Williams *(Janie)*; and Rose Simon Kohn (*Pillar to Post*). She also chose progressive and challenging subjects, for example, interracial marriage and divorce. A collaborative director, she often worked with the writers on their scripts, sometimes receiving writing credit herself.[21]

Perry's collaboartion with Pemberton continued until Perry died in 1946, from a heart attack. She was memorialized by Pemberton as an "individualist who met life head-on, dramatized life, and gave of a generous nature."[22] It was Pemberton who, after Perry's death, proposed that an award in Perry's honor be established for accomplishments in stage acting and technical work. During the first ceremony, held in 1947, Pemberton referred to the award as a Tony. The name stuck.

Following her death, Perry was remembered by *Time* magazine as "one of Broadway's few successful women directors." The article continued, "Tony Perry, ever the angel of tyro actors, was the wartime guiding spirit of the American Theatre Wing, [and] left her heart at its seven Stage Door Canteens across the nation."[23]

SO FEW FEMALES

Even though the awards had been established in honor of a trailblazing, groundbreaking woman unafraid to challenge the expectations of society, the Tonys remained dominated by men for decades to come. As of 2017, seventy plays had won the Tony Award. Of those seventy, five have included women on their writing teams. It was only the third time the Best Play nominees included more than one play written by a woman. This scarcity also includes nominees: A total of 267 plays have been nominated for Best Play, and thirty-two have included women on their writing teams. Never before for more than three years in a row had the Best Play nominees included at least one woman, and the number of nominated plays written solely by women totaled twenty-seven as of 2017—slightly more than 10 percent.

Frances Goodrich, the first woman to win a Tony for Best Play, shared it with her male writing partner, Albert Hackett, for 1956's *The Diary of Anne Frank*. Five years later, in 1961, *Beckett*—translated by Lucienne Hill but originally written by Jean Anouilh—was awarded Best Play.

It wasn't until 1989 that a woman took home the Tony by herself, when Best Play went to Wendy Wasserstein's *The Heidi Chronicles*. Yasmina Reza was next in 1998, for *Art*, and she took home the honor again in 2009, for *God of Carnage*—the only woman to win twice.

Since the first awards in 1947, no more than two female nominees for Best Play have been honored with nominations simultaneously. The first year the Best Play category included more than one work by a female playwright was in 1960, with Lorraine Hansberry's *A Raisin in the Sun* and Lillian Hellman's *Toys in the Attic*—an occurrence that did not repeat itself until 2002, with *Topdog/Underdog*, by Suzan-Lori Parks, and *Meta-morphosis*, by Mary Zimmerman, and it happened again in 2017, with Paula Vogel's *Indecent* and Lynn Nottage's *Sweat*.

For more than a decade, between 1962 and 1973, no female play-wrights were nominated for Best Play, the trend concluding in 1974, when Marjorie Barkentin's *Ulysses in Nightown* was nominated and, in 1977, with *for colored girls who have considered suicide/when the rain-bow is enuf.* In 1983, Marsha Norman's *'night, Mother* was nominated but did not win the Tony, despite winning the Pulitzer Prize. Female playwrights were also completely absent from the nominations between 2005 and 2008.

Musicals have not fared much better, although the musical form does offer more categories within which women can be employed. Approxi-mately one-third of the 248 Best Musical nominees as of 2017, including original musicals, revues, and jukebox musicals, featured work contrib-uted by a woman—either as a composer, lyricist, or book writer.

Only once—1978—has a woman been on the writing team of every Best Musical nominee. But even then, only two featured original works were by women—Elizabeth Swados (*Runaways*) and Betty Comden (*On the Twentieth Century*). The other two—*Dancin'* and *Ain't Misbeha-vin'*—were revues consisting of numerous composers and included more work by men than women. Of the 29 composers and lyricists whose work was featured in *Ain't Misbehavin'* two were women: Ada Benson and Dorothy Fields. *Dancin'* had more—Melissa Manchester, Cynthia Weil, and Carole Bayer Sager were three of 26.

Out of the 195 nominees for Best Book, twenty have been written solely by women, and thirty-five have included a woman on the team. Twice—in 1985 and 1991—has there been more than one nominee for Best Book written completely by women. Of the fifty-one times the award for Best Book has been given, four women have won.

The first time was in 1949, when *Kiss Me Kate*, which featured a book by Samuel and Bella Spewack, won Best Book, and in 1978, with Best Book going to *On the Twentieth Century*, cowritten by Betty Comden and Adolph Green. Thirteen years later, Marsha Norman won Best Book for *The Secret Garden*, becoming the first woman to independently win the award in 1991. *The Secret Garden* was written entirely by women—Norman authored the book and lyrics, the music was composed by Lucy

Simon, and it was directed by Susan Schulman. Heidi Ettinger produced the musical and also designed its set.

The next time a woman won Best Book it was Rachel Sheinkin for *The 25th Annual Putnam County Spelling Bee* in 2005, followed by Lisa Kron for *Fun Home* in 2015.

It wasn't until 2013 that Best Score was awarded to a woman working without a male writing partner. The first woman to share the honor was Betty Comden, who cowrote *Hallelujah, Baby!* with Adolph Green and Jule Styne, and won Best Composer and Lyricist in 1968. Comden shared the award with Adolph and Cy Colman in 1978, for *On the Twentieth Century*, and in 1991, for *Will Rogers Follies*. The second woman to win Best Score was Lynn Ahrens, for *Ragtime*, which she wrote with Stephen Flaherty, in 1998, and Lisa Lambert won for *The Drowsy Chaperone* in 2006, with her writing partner, Greg Morrison. In 2013, Cyndi Lauper, who wrote both the music and lyrics to *Kinky Boots*, won Best Score, making history as the first woman to win working alone.

As of 2017, a total of 248 musicals have been nominated for Best Musical, and sixty-nine have won. Of those sixty-nine, only fifteen, including jukebox musicals and revues, have had at least one woman contributing writing. Only six nominated musicals have been written entirely by women: *Don't Bother Me, I Can't Cope* (by Micki Grant); *Runaways* (by Elizabeth Swados); *Quilters* (by Barbara Damashek and Molly Newman); *The Secret Garden* (by Marsha Norman and Lucy Simon); *Fun Home* (by Jeanine Tesori and Lisa Kron); and *Waitress* (by Sara Bareilles and Jessie Nelson). It wasn't until 2015, at the sixty-ninth annual Tony Awards, that a musical written solely by women won Best Musical—*Fun Home*, by Jeanine Tesori and Lisa Kron.

If women writing musicals were scarce, women leading them were even more so. The lack of female directors on Broadway has been credited to latent (or open) sexism that resists women in leadership positions or entrusting women with significant financial responsibility. In 2014, more women were serving in the Senate than had directed a Broadway play in the past decade.[24]

Director Tina Landau emphasized the financial aspects of the bias, saying women are often thought of as "not as good at handling money as men. There is a large economic component [to directing], and producers need to trust that the person leading this endeavor is responsible for handling many-million dollars. Perhaps much of the unconscious weari-

The Secret Garden with Daisey Eagan as Mary Lennox and Alison Fraser as Martha.
Photofest

ness about trusting women in that role has had to do with that, rather than creative issues."[25]

The first woman to receive a nomination for Best Director of a Play was Joan Littlewood. In 1961, fourteen years after the Tony Awards were established, Littlewood received her first nomination, for the play *The Hostage*, which was followed four years later with a nomination for the musical *Oh! What a Lovely War*. In 1963, June Havoc was nominated for directing *Marathon '33*, her autobiographical play adapted from her memoir *Early Havoc*, about her time in dance marathons. The Second Wave feminist movement swept through the United States in the 1970s, but women were absent from Tony nominations until 1982, when Geraldine Mary Fitzgerald was nominated for *Mass Appeal*. The next directing nomination came in 1987—Carole Rothman for *Coastal Disturbances*. Eight years later, Emily Mann was nominated for directing her own play, *Having Our Say*, and, in 1998, a woman finally won.

Female directors of musicals did not fare any better, with the second nomination after *Oh! What a Lovely War* occurring in 1973. Vinnette Carroll, the first African American woman to direct on Broadway, received nominations for the musical revue *Don't Bother Me, I Can't Cope* in 1973, and the Biblical musical *Your Arms Too Short to Box with God* in 1977. But even when Cope's work was praised, a man's contributions were recognized as a part of them. When reviewing *Don't Bother Me, I Can't Cope*, *New York Times* critic Clive Barnes singled out Carroll's direction but mentioned the assistance of the show's creative team and cast in his review. It appeared Carroll's accomplishments could not exist without the help of others—namely, men:

> The show, which moves as fast as a carousel, has been very deftly staged by Miss Carroll. She is helped here by Richard A. Miller's handsome open setting, with its wide ramps and interesting playing areas, the bright costumes by Edna Watson, and the always effective lighting of B. J. Sammler. And, of course, by the cast.[26]

Women were not being encouraged to direct, playwright and director Emily Mann recalled. It was not considered a possibility when she graduated from college in 1974, and her male colleagues were planning on pursuing careers on the West Coast or in New York, or applying to the Yale School of Drama. When talking with her adviser about her plans following graduation, Mann, a leader of the Harvard-Radcliffe Dramatic

Gloria Foster and Mary Alice as Bessie and Sadie Delaney in *Having Our Say*, which premiered in 1995. *Photo by T. Charles Erickson, courtesy of Emily Mann*

Society, was told, "Oh, I should have told you earlier. You may be very talented Emily, but, in fact, women can't write or direct in the professional theater. And you should start thinking about children's theater."[27]

That attitude was not limited to academics/college. After she was accepted to the Bush Artist fellowship—the first woman to do so—Mann was told, "Oh no dear, you can't possibly direct professionally. I heard you can act."

Said Mann, "I said, 'I came here as a directing fellow, and that's what I want to do.' He insisted I audition, and he said, 'You're rather good, you should do this.' I said, 'No. I'm going to be the directing fellow.' It was really, really, really tough. That was not considered to be my place."[28]

This sexism fueled her career. Despite the belief that women couldn't direct—and countless puns about her name in the media—Mann went on to be the first woman to direct on a major stage in the United States. She eventually took on the role of artistic director and resident playwright of the McCarter Theatre Center in Princeton, New Jersey.

Mann made her Broadway debut, both writing and directing, when she helmed a production of her play *Execution of Justice* in 1986. Nine years later, in 1995, she directed another one of her own works, *Having Our Say*, which earned her Tony nominations for writing and directing. One way that women could direct on Broadway, it seemed, was to lead productions of their own works. This success, driven by independence and self-sufficiency, existed in stark contrast to the feminist backlash that had begun to infiltrate social and political culture. *Runaways* secured Elizabeth Swados a directing nomination the following year, a musical for which she also wrote the book and music, and choreographed. When Barbara Damashek was nominated in 1985, it was for *Quilters*, for which she also wrote the music and lyrics, and contributed to the book.

"Women were kept off the Great White Way for a very long time," Mann recalled.

> If you look at the data, we were still in the single digits for women directing on Broadway and writing on Broadway. Even with Marsha [Norman], Wendy [Wasserstein], and me and Tina Howe—there were a few of us who broke through. If we weren't the ones up there, it was zero. And if we were, it was 1 or 2 percent. It was outrageous and pathetic until quite recently.[29]

Several years passed before the absence of female directors was noted in the *New York Times*, in 1989—following Wendy Wasserstein's history-making win at the Tony Awards for the overtly feminist play *The Heidi Chronicles* (which was directed by a man)—when Mel Gussow wrote,

> Though women have made a breakthrough as playwrights, they have still not achieved their proper recognition as directors—in contrast to England, where Deborah Warner is leading a new wave of directors in her nation's major national companies.
>
> This is not to suggest that there is a lack of directors among women in the United States. It is simply that they are not yet on Broadway and, in many cases, remain unfamiliar to the public. No woman has yet been named best director in the Tony voting, and in contrast to playwrights, very few have received nominations. Coincidentally, all of

those three Pulitzer Prize winners have had the major productions of their plays directed by men.[30]

THE YEAR OF THE WOMAN?

Wasserstein's playwrighting victory did not symbolize the feminist victory many hoped it would, as the feminist backlash of the 1980s gave way to the complicated social culture of the 1990s. The Second Wave had ended, the backlash had killed the Equal Rights Amendment, and women were visibly more prominent in notable ways. People were marrying and having children later in life, and women were assuming more leadership than ever before.

The "Girl Power" movement was prominent in both culture and politics, and 1992 was declared the "Year of the Woman," when the number of elected female representatives in the Senate tripled (from two to six).[31] Hollywood rode the wave, with the 1992 Academy Awards ceremony devoting itself to the empowerment of women, complete with a razzle-dazzle musical number performed by Liza Minnelli, but the message failed to land. The *New York Times* commented,

> Dedicating itself noisily to the "Year of the Woman," this year's show missed no opportunity to emphasize Hollywood's feminine side, no matter how misconceived that opportunity might be. . . . The show was determined to honor women as sanctimoniously as possible, provided it could retain the usual quota of dancing girls.[32]

TV screens saw women embracing their power but with mixed results. *Sabrina the Teenage Witch*, *Buffy the Vampire Slayer*, and the sisters in *Charmed* fought otherwordly evils, while the "Scully Effect" from *The X-Files* encouraged girls to pursue careers in science, medicine, and law enforcement. But much of this empowering entertainment also promoted unhealthy body image, as the gaunt, pale woman was established as the new norm for female beauty. Called "heroin chic," the look was personified by supermodel Kate Moss.

Theater saw "girl power" progressing offstage, where some women directors found themselves recognized—publicly—for their work. When Susan Schulman received a Tony nomination for her direction of Stephen Sondheim's dark thriller musical *Sweeney Todd*, her naturalistic production had been praised by the *New York Times* as "more upsetting than the first":

> One of the canards about Mr. Sondheim has always been that his musicals are longer on intellect than feeling. In keeping with the performance at its heart, Susan H. Schulman's production of *Sweeney Todd*, a remounting of her searing York Theater Company staging of last spring, reveals the nonsense of that assumption. . . . Ms. Schulman's new take on Mr. Sondheim's musical has less to do with her staging—some of which owes a debt to Mr. Prince's in any case—than with her distinctive reading of what the show is about. . . . By forcing us to face Mr. Sondheim's music and the feelings it contains so intensely, Ms. Schulman doesn't obliterate the Prince production; she creates an alternative.[33]

Schulman's nomination was followed by Graciela Danielle for her directing Lynn Ahrens and Stephen Flaherty's *Once on This Island* in 1991. The musical fable, set in the French Antilles, was described as a "joyous marriage of the slick and the folkloric, of the hard-nosed sophistication of Broadway musical theater and the indigenous culture of a tropical isle," and Danielle's direction was deemed the "most effervescent achievement of her career."[34] While the *Boston Globe* deemed the musical's plot a "feeble fable," it praised Danielle's direction for guiding performances that were "high, wide, and handsome," as well as her "knock-em-dead choreography."[35]

"A LONG LINE OF AWARDS FOR WOMEN AS DIRECTORS"

It wasn't until 1998, that not one, but two, women won the Tony Award for directing. Gary Hynes was awarded the Tony for her direction of Martin McDonagh's *The Beauty Queen of Leenane*, and just a few moments later, Julie Taymor won a Tony for directing the stage adaption of the animated Disney musical *The Lion King*—as well as for costume design.

"I'm so happy to be following in a long line of awards for women as directors," Taymor quipped as she accepted her award. Her wit was apt;

Julie Taymor. *Photofest*

Taymor had long been one of few women recognized for leadership positions in the theater.

Taymor, who began her career in theater at the age of ten with Boston Children's Theater, was considered a surprising choice to helm a big-budget Disney musical. She acknowledged this herself, saying,

> I wasn't afraid, but I was cautious. Everyone was asking me, "Why are you doing Disney? You do folklore and mythology." My aesthetic is not a Disney aesthetic at all, but when I met with the wonderful producers at Disney, they weren't looking for me to do their aesthetic. I'd already spent twenty years in the theater, so if they were going to hire me, they'd be hiring me for what I have to offer. . . . I had to take what had been a successful animated film, put it on the stage, and make it equally good. So I had to do what only theater can—to create a visceral experience that surrounds you.[36]

Taymor's distinctly unique style developed throughout her years spent traveling the world. As a teenager, she studied mime in France, and after majoring in mythology and folklore at Oberlin College she spent four years in Japan and Indonesia, where she founded the Teatr Loh, a group of dancers, actors, musicians, and puppeteers. Following her return to the United States, she led various Shakespeare productions, for the Public Theater and Theatre For a New Audience. Taymor made her Broadway debut with *Juan Darién: A Carnival Mass*. The musical adaptation of Horacio Quiroga's fable, which Taymor cowrote with Elliot Goldenthal, opened in 1996. The production showcased Taymor's fluid use of puppetry and masks, and she was Tony-nominated for her direction and scenic design with G. W. Mercier. The musical also received nominations for its score and lighting design, as well as Best Musical.

Taymor described her approach to directing to *Oprah Magazine*, saying,

> Here's what I feel: If you have a strong vision, then you're able to throw it away for a better one. The tyrant male directors who have everyone quaking in their boots—and by the way, women can't get away with being tyrants because they're seen as bitches—are so into their vision that they're terrified to let anyone see that there might be another way. That's a shame. I believe that if you really have a strong idea, you can say, "What do you think? Let's see how my idea plays off yours."[37]

One year after her first nomination, Taymor took home the Tony Award for *The Lion King*. Her innovative approach to adapting the film for the stage drew from a global repertoire of artforms, using masks and puppetry to bring the animated characters to life. The dazzling visual suggestions, rather than special effects, invited the audience to willingly suspend their disbelief while watching live actors perform the roles of animals. Taymor's direction, wrote the *New York Times*, was truly unique, something that had never before been seen on Broadway. Ben Brantley wrote in the *New York Times*,

> Ms. Taymor, a maverick artist known for her bold multicultural experiments with puppetry and ritualized theater, has her own distinctive vision, one that is miles away from standard Disney fare. Ms. Taymor has abandoned none of the singular, and often haunting, visual flourishes she brought to such surreal works as "Juan Darien," which was revived at Lincoln Center last season, and *The Green Bird*. . . . Ms. Taymor has introduced a whole new vocabulary of images to the Broadway blockbuster, and you're unlikely to forget such sights as the face of Simba's dead father forming itself into an astral mask among the stars.[38]

Taymor had accepted her award moments Garry Hynes won Best Director of a Play. Hynes, whose direction of *The Beauty Queen of Leenane* was praised as "finely modulated" by the *New York Times*, was the first woman to win. In Hynes' production of Martin McDonagh's story of a mother and daughter trapped in dysfunctional codependency, "nearly everything feels organic, an inevitable outgrowth of character and environment. . . . Ms. Hynes accordingly brings a haunting physical dimension to her production, an aura of mortal decay."[39]

Hyne's Tony win came after a career of theatermaking in her native Ireland. A graduate of the University College Galway, she cofounded the Druid Theatre Company with classmates Mick Lally and Marie Mullen in 1975. The first professional theater company based outside of Dublin, Druid was founded with a £1,500 grant from the Irish Arts Council and named after a character in the Asterix comic strip. The first production Hynes directed was described as "definitive"[40] and went on to produce classic playwrights Eugene O'Neill and Seán O'Casey, as well as emerging playwrights, and toured internationally.

Female directors were unusual in Ireland as Hynes set out on her career, but, she said, founding her own company helped her to avoid much of the sexism in the industry.

"It was unusual to be a woman theater director at the time, but I wasn't really aware of that until five or ten years later," she told *Post Magazine* in 2017. "By founding Druid, I more or less escaped all that. People think that in the 1970s and 80s, the feminist movement succeeded in changing things for women. But all the battles for women in Ireland have not yet been won, and not just in theater."[41]

Hynes served as the Druid's artistic director from its founding until 1991, and served as the artistic director for the Abbey Theatre from 1991 to 1994. She had initially rejected the offer, first made in 1986, but when it was extended again, she negotiated, gaining authority as a chief executive and securing artistic independence, obtaining professional authority in a largely patriarchal society where women in leadership were subject to scorn. The first woman to hold a cabinet position in Ireland was appointed in 1919, and sixty years passed before a senior ministerial office received another female appointee. When Mary Robinson was a candidate for president in 1990, she was desribed as a "Marxist, lesbian bitch" by a Catholic priest, and rumors circulated about her alleged "sham marriage." It wasn't until 1993, that two women held cabinet positions simultaneoulsy.[42]

It was a tumultuous time at the Abbey. Hynes was the sixth director to serve in seven years at the state-subsidized theater, and following the anticipation that preceded her appointment, her first show, *The Plough*, was strongly criticized. The *Irish Times* wrote of the "palpable sense of disappointment that the high expectations generated by her appointment have been so poorly realized so far."[43] Another production did not fare any better: *The Power of Darkness*, by John McGahern, was reviewed by the *Sunday Tribune* as follows: "To write a really dreadful play is easy. To have it put on in our national theater should be difficult. The finger should be pointed at Garry Hynes . . . responsible for staging a recycled farrago of risible melodramatic nonsense."[44]

Speculation spread, but Hynes responded. After mounting *One Last White Horse*, by Dermot Bolger, to negative reviews, a series of articles about "trouble at the Abbey" followed. In response, the theater ran a full-page advertisement in the *Irish Times* featuring positive critical reviews.[45]

Then Hynes came across a play called *The Beauty Queen of Leenane*, by the then-unknown Martin McDonagh. The playwright had submitted three plays to the Druid, which Hynes had returned to after three years at the Abbey, and while reading through previous submissions, she was struck by McDonagh's writing. Hynes directed the world-premiere production in Ireland before *The Beauty Queen of Leenane* opened on Broadway in 1998. Her history-making win surprised her, as she considered being a woman in Ireland to be a greater challenge than in the United States, where she thought women had progressed further. "There have been so many important women in the American theater," she told the *New York Times*. "I thought, 'How could this be?' It surprised me even more than that I had won."[46]

The second woman to win Best Director of a musical also made history, when *The Producers*, directed by Susan Stroman, broke the record for winning the most Tony Awards in history. Stroman had already won three Tonys for her choreography, but her direction of the musical adaptation of Mel Brooks's showbusiness satire, and her choreography, were two of twelve awards the musical took home that night.

The following year, Mary Zimmerman won for her direction of her own play, *Metamorphoses*. Zimmerman, a founding member of the Lookingglass Theatre Company, artistic associate of the Goodman Theatre, and a professor at Northwestern University, had already established a reputation for her ability to present unexpectedly theatrical productions of lengthy and academic texts, including *The Notebooks of Leonardo da Vinci*, *The Odyssey*, *Tales from the Arabian Nights*, and, from a sixteenth-century Chinese-Buddhist epic, *Journey to the West*.

Zimmerman, who had never written for or directed on Broadway before 2002, authored *Metamorphoses* as well, further establishing the pattern of women securing leadership positions on Broadway only when taking charge of their own work. After almost two years in Chicago, *Metamorphoses* originally played Off-Broadway at the Second Stage Theater, opening just days after the September 11 attacks on the World Trade Center in New York. It transferred to Broadway's Circle in the Square Theatre in February 2002.

Zimmerman's script was adapted from Ovid's lengthy poem, which spanned fifteen books and more than 250 myths, and narrated the stories of Orpheus and Eurydice, King Midas, Vertumnus and Pomona, and Alcyone and Ceyx. A large pool of water was central to each of the stories, highlighting the themes of change and rebirth. Containing hidden entrances for the actors, the pool permitted the characters to disappear into or emerge, transformed, from the water—as one of the narrators stated, "Bodies I have in mind and how they can change to assume new shapes."

The play's raw exploration of love, pain, and loss proved cathartic for audiences frightened and shaken following the shocking tragedy of September 11, and tears and other emotions were witnessed in the audience nightly.

Ben Brantley wrote in the *New York Times*,

> In another context, it might have registered as too precious, perhaps, too arts-and-crafts for Eastern urbanites. But for now it is speaking with a dreamlike hush directly to New Yorkers' souls. . . . Those who have known the loss of people they loved will surely feel echoes of their own pain. But it is what follows them—representations of those metamorphoses that find the solace in sorrow—that opens the emotional floodgates. [47]

It was cathartic, agreed Chris Jones, in *Rise Up! Broadway and American Society from "Angels in America" to "Hamilton"*:

> It was as if Zimmerman had found a way to express in the theater what an entire city—an entire nation—felt in their hearts. She had discovered how to let a broad popular audience into the healing story she wanted to tell. And she had done so in no small measure by explicitly acknowledging the sadness felt in that rehearsal room on Sept. 11. [48]

Zimmerman's production transferred to Broadway, winning the playwright and director the Tony Award for Best Direction—the second woman to do so, following Garry Hynes in 1997. Zimmerman was the only woman nominated in the category, alongside Howard Davies for *Private Lives*, Richard Eyre for *The Crucible*, and Daniel Sullivan for *Morning's at Seven*.

It wasn't until 2008, that the next woman to win Best Director of a Play was honored. The Tony went to Anna D. Shapiro for her leadership of the blistering, dark family comedy *August: Osage County*, that opened on Broadway in 2008, following its debut at Chicago's Steppenwolf Theatre in 2007. Like Hynes, Shapiro was awarded for her direction of a male playwright's work. In her speech, Shapiro acknowledged her cast and playwright, saying, "If you're really followed by a star, Tracy Letts hands you *August: Osage County* and says, 'Wanna?'"[49]

In his rave review of Letts's play, which ran more than one thousand words, *New York Times* critic Charles Isherwood made only one mention of Shapiro's work, describing the play as "superbly directed." Following her Tony win, Shapiro went on to direct several high-profile plays featuring Hollywood stars in their Broadway debuts: Chris Rock in *The Motherfucker with the Hat*, Michael Cera in *This Is Our Youth*, James Franco in *Of Mice and Men*, and Larry David in *Fish in the Dark*. All of the plays were authored by men.

When reflecting on her frequent collaborations with male artists, Shapiro remarked,

> They're very male. I think of myself as actually kind of prudish and girly, but I don't know if a lot of other people would see me that way. These writers are very muscular, but I don't think that has to do with them being male, because there are female playwrights who are very muscular in their expression. I just feel like for whatever reason, female playwrights don't really ask me to do their plays. Nothing would make me happier than finding the sisterhood, but I can't make them. So I'm waiting! Maybe it's the Steppenwolf thing. In a Steppenwolf play, usually somebody throws a chair.[50]

Shapiro was named artistic director of Chicago's Steppenwolf Theatre in 2014, following Martha Lavey. Praised for her leadership by many actors, Shapiro has been critical in interviews, describing herself as "deeply controlling but working on it." The (male) journalist profiling her described her by saying, "Shapiro is a type-A poster child."[51]

Shapiro, who was nominated for *The Motherfucker with the Hat*, hasn't won a Tony since 2008, and it wasn't until 2013 that another woman took home Best Director—two women, actually—in a repeat of the 1997 ceremony. Pam MacKinnon won for *Who's Afraid of Virginia Woolf?* and Diane Paulus won for *Pippin*. MacKinnon, nominated alongside three men—Nicholas Martin for *Vanya and Sonia and Masha and Spike*, Bartlett Sher for *Golden Boy*, and George C. Wolfe for *Lucky Guy*—had first directed Edward Albee's scathing depiction of an emotionally abusive marriage for Steppenwolf Theatre in Chicago in 2010. The play, which won the Tony Award for Best Play in 1963, was denied the Pulitzer due to "obscenity" and then revived in 1976 and 2005. In

2013, MacKinnon had developed a close relationship with Albee, having directed *The Play about the Baby* in 2002; *The Goat, or Who Is Sylvia?* in 2003; *Peter and Jerry* in 2007; *Occupant* in 2008; and *A Delicate Balance* in 2009. And she was the first woman to direct *Who's Afraid of Virginia Woolf?* on Broadway. While many of the reviews lavished praise on Tracy Letts for his performance as George, Scott Brown at *Vulture* declared,

> The star is Mackinnon herself, who has approached *Who's Afraid* as a symphonic piece. So much of its spell depends on its music, and under her baton, the insults and insinuations and bloviations flow into each other as if conducted by Bernstein. You could close your eyes and simply listen to this show and be satisfied—if, indeed, satisfaction is a word one would associate with *Woolf*. At the end of its three acts (in just over three hours), I felt full and, at the same time, emptied of everything. What a marvelous bloodletting.[52]

MacKinnon had moved to New York in 1997, just before Taymor and Hynes first won Tony Awards for directing. After accepting her award, and seeing Paulus and Lauper win during the same ceremony, the director said of women in the industry, "We're hitting our stride, absolutely."[53] Her fellow victor Paulus hoped for a future in which such victories would become the norm, rather than the exception:

> I'm hoping that after tonight we'll stop counting and women will be given the opportunity to be leaders, and I hope this encourages producers to trust women to think about the business of theater, which is what you have to do when you direct a musical. I'm thrilled, I hope that it gives courage to young, aspiring women directors all over the world to charge on.[54]

The 2015 and 2017 awards saw another woman at the podium. Marianne Elliott, who had won in 2011, with codirector Tom Morris, for *War Horse*, won Best Director for her inventive staging of the new play *The Curious Incident of the Dog in the Night-Time*. Elliott, Britain's National Theatre's associate director, had been recognized in a *New York Times* article that noted how her career defied expected [and archaic] gender norms by deliberately seeking what she wanted: "Best of all, whereas one might in some bygone era have expected a woman director to adopt a polite, reined-in approach to directing, leaving the big noises to the big boys, Elliott's style is as unabashed and up front as anyone around."[55]

Elliott went on to defy expectations of femininity when she secured the job directing *The Curious Incident of the Dog in the Night-Time* simply by asking for it. She told the *Globe and Mail*,

> Playwright Simon [Stephens] came out with this draft—and he didn't really know fully what to do with it and sent it to me. I read it as a friend, not as a prospective director. By the end of reading it, I was totally floored, devastated emotionally—and so I then took it to Nick Hytner, who was running the National Theatre at the time and said, "Please let me do it."[56]

Following her second Tony win, Elliott further established her professional independence, as she opened her own company with producer Chris Harper. Elliott and Harper productions debuted with a West End production of Stephens's *Heisenberg: The Uncertainty Principle*, and two years later they presenting a gender-switched production of Stephen Sondheim's *Company*—a groundbreaking and feminist first for the popular 1970s musical.

"It just seemed like an absolute no-brainer," Elliott said of launching Elliott and Harper—an ironic statement, given that the acclaimed artist hadn't considered a career in directing for a long time. Her father, theater and television director Michael Elliott, had died when she was a teenager, and Elliott "had never thought it was possible," adding, "which was probably a mixture of my own insecurities and because my father was a director; I'd seen directing as a male privilege, I suppose."[57] But her point of view changed, and Elliott and Harper was formed. "I'd have more control over what I did. I quite like to be in the driver's seat about how I do these shows or where I do them or when I do them," she commented.[58]

"WHAT TOOK THEM SO LONG?"

The year 2017 saw not only Rebecca Taichman win Best Director for the play *Indecent*, which she cocreated with Paula Vogel, but also the long-awaited Broadway debuts of two acclaimed, Pulitzer Prize–winning playwrights, Paula Vogel and Lynn Nottage. Vogel's Broadway debut came decades after her daringly controversial first production. The playwright and teacher has authored scripts about prostitution and sexual abuse, as well as familial conflict, beginning with *Swan Song of Sir Henry* in 1974. But it wasn't until 1997, that she rapidly rose to fame, when *How I Learned to Drive*, her chronicle of an incestuous relationship between an uncle and his niece, earned critical acclaim. The play premiered at New York's Off-Broadway Vineyard Theatre, earning an enthusiastic review from the *New York Times*, described by Ben Brantley as "both wryly objective and deeply empathetic; angry and compassionate; light-handed and devastating. Yet it seldom feels less than fully integrated."[59]

Vogel's play, narrated in a disjointed, nonlinear form as the niece, L'il Bit, recalls driving lessons with her Uncle Peck (which involved being sexually molested from the age of eleven to eighteen), was inspired in part by Vladimir Nabokov's novel *Lolita*. The playwright told Playbill.com, "I must have read that book a half-dozen times since high school. It was fascinating to me because it was so even-handed and so neutral. I couldn't stop thinking about what would happen if a woman wrote the story from Lolita's point of view."[60]

Vogel's script contained broad comedic moments from L'il Bit's uncouth family, each character defined by their sexual organs, depicting the objectification and misogyny that permeated L'il Bit's mentality as her relatives openly commented on her developing breasts and sexual appeal. Vogel created a contradictory world for L'il Bit: It is through driving that she can achieve physical independence from her family, but by learning how to drive from her uncle, her independence, both physical and mental, is violated and derailed.

How I Learned to Drive won the 1998 Pulitzer Prize and such Off-Broadway awards as the Lucille Lortel for Outstanding Play. It was the most-produced play in the 1998–1999 season and was seen throughout the country, at Center Stage, Arena Stage, and Mark Taper Forum. It received a New York revival in 2012, at Off-Broadway's Second Stage Theater.[61] But despite its success—both critical and commercial—the play never opened on Broadway.

While praised for its sensitivity, *How I Learned to Drive* was hardly Vogel's first staging of controversial subjects. *The Baltimore Waltz*, which premiered Off-Broadway in 1992, was crafted from a series of vignettes chronicling a brother and sister's European vacation, which doubled as a search for a cure for her fictitious terminal illness. Vogel had written the play in response to losing her brother Carl. The two had

Paula Vogel. *Photofest*

planned a vacation to Europe, but Carl died from complications due to AIDS before they could go.

Vogel's play was considered a crucial work about AIDS, as well as a moving family story. J. Wynn Rousuck, of the *Baltimore Sun*, praised it as a "rare and magnificent work," a "landmark" play, and declared, "Opening the same day that former tennis star Arthur Ashe announced he has AIDS, *The Baltimore Waltz* is perhaps the most glowing and creative theatrical effort yet to demystify this dreadful disease."[62] Malcolm Johnson of the *Hartford Courant* stated,

> Vogel's uproarious, searching, and finally devastating creation adds up to the very best of theater. . . . Vogel . . . obviously has mastered every discipline in her craft. Given the right director—and Bogart has never

seemed more lucid, witty, and varied—this writer can do as she wishes with an audience. [63]

But neither of the acclaimed plays received Broadway transfers. And, in 1993, *And Baby Makes Seven* earned Vogel the wrath of critics and audiences alike. Following a trio of friends, lovers Anna and Ruth, and their gay friend Peter, the play chronicles the lively fantasy life Anna and Ruth engage in as imaginary children Cecil Bartholomew, Henri Dumont, and Orphan McDermott—characters Peter is determined they should discard before their actual child is born. The women concede and obligingly kill off their imaginary selves, but they can't bear to abandon them and revive them before the play's conclusion.

Following Vogel's success with *The Baltimore Waltz*, Mel Gussow affirmed his disappointment in her next work, writing,

> In *The Baltimore Waltz*, Ms. Vogel overcame her penchant for whimsy and sent her central character . . . on an imaginative journey that dealt on a symbolic level with the anguish of AIDS. In contrast, *And Baby Makes Seven* operates on a single level and seems regressive, in several senses. [64]

It wasn't only the critics who disliked Vogel's play; the author was called "sick" because her show involved a lesbian couple and their gay male friend.

The play fared no better in Chicago, where Maura Troester criticized Vogel's script for presuming the audience understood the characters immediately upon the show's beginning and declared the play's message overstated in unnecessarily complicated terms. The *Chicago Reader* stated,

> *And Baby Makes Seven*, by New York playwright Paula Vogel, could be called warm, witty, bold, daring, even zany. They're the kind of words that make great banners for newspaper advertisements. They're also quite deceptive. For while *And Baby Makes Seven* has all these qualities, it's missing a more important one: a larger purpose. Its message is muddled. And when that message—"don't be afraid to play"— finally comes through, it seems incredibly wimpy. . . . All these shenanigans just to get that simple message across? Seems a waste of energy. [65]

In 1994, Vogel's one-act *Hot 'N' Throbbing (Because Obscenity Begins at Home)* premiered, examining the connection between pornography and domestic violence. First workshopped in New York in 1992, Vogel's play, which was funded by several grants,[66] premiered at the American Repertory Theater in 1994, followed by regional productions that continued through 1999. Vogel's script follows an uninvited reunion between a woman author of self-described feminist pornography that focuses on female desires and her ex-husband (against whom she has taken out a restraining order), who arrives at her door, lamenting that he couldn't afford a prostitute that night. Vogel's story, both chaotic and violent, was denounced as too ambitious for its topic and unresolved.

Variety's Markland Taylor declared,

> Given her new play's sexually explicit title, its subtitle ("Because Obscenity Begins at Home"), and its inflammatory subject matter, it is clear that Paula Vogel is venturing into deep, dark water. In her black farce *Hot 'N' Throbbing*, she sometimes swims, sometimes flounders, sometimes sinks, and the overall impression is that she isn't in complete control of her extremely difficult material.

Unfavorably comparing the play to *Oleanna*, by David Mamet, Taylor continued, "Vogel's play lacks the sly intellectual game-playing of Mamet's questionable work, and when all is said and done, it's really just another reworking of the dysfunctional family cliché."[67]

In its West Coast debut in 1996, *Hot 'N' Throbbing* was criticized for its uneven tone and pacing, with Laurie Winer writing, "Vogel never takes the easy argument by suggesting that Charlene's dabbling in porn brings about her tragic fate. She does suggest, however, that she is foolish to think that an advanced feminist rationale about how she is in control of her life and her body is enough to make it be true."[68] The play was "sophomoric drivel," according to the *Boston Globe*'s Bill Marx, and "often stilted and stubbornly enigmatic," according to the *Seattle Times*.[69] Others found it "profoundly disturbing" and compared it to a Greek tragedy.[70]

Few productions of *Hot 'N' Throbbing* followed, and, in 1997, Vogel spoke to *Playbill* about her exclusion from "mainstream theater," saying,

> There are theaters in this country that I call, "feet first" theaters. They don't produce you until you're dead. Yale Rep was like that, although

they did eventually do *Baltimore Waltz*. I've been pursuing Lincoln Center for twenty-five years. And there's no theater in the country willing to touch my 1994 play, *Hot 'N' Throbbing*, written a full year before the O. J. trial. There was a production in Boston that the *Globe* called "too disturbing." . . . I may be teaching, but in academia, they consider me the whore of Babylon, because I go against the basic academic thinking on plays and literature. We're *supposed* to approach these works through the brain, cognitively. But words attack meaning to get to emotion. An artist works viscerally, similarly to the way painting and music evoke an emotional language.[71]

Vogel's daring approaches to controversial subjects repeatedly earned less commercial recognition than work addressing similar subjects that were authored by men. She noted that *Blackbird*, David Harrower's play about a sexually abusive relationship, was produced on Off-Broadway in 2007, and on Broadway in 2016, but while *How I Learned to Drive* is produced worldwide, it is not considered "universal."[72]

In 2017, at the age of 65, Vogel saw her play *Indecent*, a dramatization of the production and subsequent controversy surrounding the play *God of Vengeance*, open on Broadway. The play received its New York premiere at Off-Broadway's Vineyard Theatre before transferring to the Cort Theatre. *Indecent* chronicles the birth of Sholem Asch's *God of Vengeance*, as well as the opening-night arrests of the entire cast on the grounds that the play included a lesbian relationship between a young woman and a prostitute, and prominently features a kiss between the women. Despite cutting the script, Asch's play was shut down by the police six weeks into its production and the cast charged with obscenity.

Exploring homophobia, as well as anti-Semitism, *Indecent* was described by Ben Brantley in the *New York Times* as "one of the season's most respectable—and respectful—plays." But this respect, Brantley said, diminished the play's impact:

The ardor that must have informed the writing and early performances of *Vengeance* only occasionally blazes forth in *Indecent*, which was created by Ms. Vogel and Ms. Taichman. Both women have described being deeply affected by their discovery of Asch's play in their youth. And you can sense how seriously they take their responsibilities as twenty-first-century curators of its reputation. . . . Such conscientiousness has its downside. For all its resourceful stagecraft—which in-

cludes the fluent use of period and original pastiche song . . . *Indecent*
can be deflatingly earnest in its dialogue and timeline exposition.[73]

Indecent was nominated for three Tony Awards in 2017, and it won
two. But it did not win Best Play, losing to *Oslo*, authored by J. T.
Rogers. Best Director went to Rebecca Taichman, for whom *Indecent*
marked her Broadway debut. Taichman, who had directed extensively
Off-Broadway, had collaborated with Vogel on the show's creation. Her
interest in the play went back to 1997, when, as a the first-year graduate
student at the Yale School of Drama, Taichman crafted her senior thesis
on *The God of Vengeance*, recreating the legal trial the show faced. She
then contacted Vogel, who was familiar with her work and knew of her
thesis project—and the two began the long road to Broadway.

When *Indecent* arrived at the Cort Theatre in 2017, female-authored
and female-led productions were still a rarity.

Taichman's Tony win marked the sixth time a woman had won for
directing since 1947. But despite the show's critical acclaim and two
Tonys, *Indecent*'s closing notice was posted shortly following the
awards. The public's support for the show was obvious immediately, as
ticket sales soared, and the play's run was then extended by producer
Daryl Roth, who postponed the June 25 closing until August 6. *Indecent*
was not Roth's first collaboration with Vogel; she was part of *How I
Learned to Drive*'s Off-Broadway producing team in 1997. Roth has long
supported works by and about women. These have included *Wit*; *Love,
Loss, and What I Wore*; *Mary Stuart*; and *The Testament of Mary*—
among others.

"I couldn't sleep," Roth told *Deadline* of posting the closing notice. "I
was totally tortured. But from the moment we posted, people were calling
and coming and lining up. I knew there was an audience for this play. I
felt it had more life."[74]

Lynn Nottage also made her Broadway debut in 2017, with *Sweat*, a
story of blue-collar workers in an industrial town. Like Vogel, Nottage
was a Pulitzer Prize winner who had earned critical and commercial
acclaim Off-Broadway and in regional theaters. Her first Broadway production came well into her career, at age fifty-three. She did not win the
Tony for Best Play, and despite critical acclaim, her play had a brief
Broadway run, closing June 25, after twenty-four previews and 105 regular performances.

Nottage, a playwriting professor at Columbia University, is the only person to have won the Pulitzer Prize for Drama twice. Her play *Intimate Apparel*, opening in 2004, Off-Broadway, was praised and extended, and won several awards, for its story of Esther, a skilled seamstress, whose financial self-sufficiency is stolen by a deceitful man. Nottage won her first Pulitzer Prize in 2009, for *Ruined*, a story of Congolese women at a bar and brothel, living with threats of physical and sexual violence, during the civil war. Despite its recognition, however, *Ruined* did not transfer to Broadway, a decision that frustrated Nottage.

"The two of us [Nottage and Vogel] write history plays, and we write political plays, and I think that that's why, perhaps, our journey has been a little different," Nottage told the *New York Times*. Known for the extensive research she undertakes before writing, she reflected on how a playwright's gender could affect the work's reception: "The plays are unabashedly political, and they're about very difficult subject matters and they tend to be unafraid of the darkness. And I think that women writers are supposed to embrace the light."[75]

Sweat, which was commissioned by the Oregon Shakespeare Festival for its American Revolutions cycle, was inspired by a phone call Nottage received from a friend who was struggling financially. The playwright proceeded to narrate the last breaths of an industrial town where both jobs and friendships were in danger.

When reviewing *Sweat*, Brantley described Nottage as a "justly acclaimed dramatist of ambitious scope and fierce focus" and praised the play for its foreshadowing of American politics: "Though it takes place in 2000 and 2008, and one of its characters swears he will never vote again, *Sweat* is the first work from a major American playwright to summon, with empathy and without judgment, the nationwide anxiety that helped put Donald J. Trump in the White House."[76] Jesse Green, at *New York Magazine*, declared,

> Lynn Nottage's *Sweat* . . . is a lot of great things: a deeply researched case history of the collapse of labor in America, a useful guide to understanding our own chaotic political moment, and a worthy attempt to put serious material before a wider public in a commercial environment. What it isn't, I'm sorry to say, is a great play; though improved in some ways, it remains pretty much as I found it downtown: gripping but disappointing. Why?[77]

Sweat, which was directed by a woman—Kate Whoriskey—had no famous stars and relied on word of mouth to bolster its ticket sales (two traits it shared with *Indecent*). The play received three Tony nominations, one of which was for Best Play, as well as the Pulitzer Prize for Drama, the latter ensuring Nottage a place in history as the first woman to win two Pulitzers for Drama. But these accolades did not inspire ticket buyers fill the seats at Studio 54. The show closed just after the Tonys, where it did not win any awards.

Vogel and Nottage's experiences further demonstrated the status women—even established, award-winning, history-making women—held in the mainstream theater industry. Both playwrights wrote stories about outcasts, conditions that they drew upon from their own lives; Vogel said her own sexuality had increased her awareness of marginalized people. "Being openly gay made me extremely aware of class, race, and gender," she told the *Washington Post*. "You see who's not getting the best table, and why."[78]

Nottage's writing often focuses on marginalized communities, painting vivid portraits of their lives. She declared to the *Guardian*,

> I write about people who are marginalized because, as an African American woman, particularly now I am a middle-aged woman, I walk down the street and people will bump into me. To much of the population I am invisible. I had one experience, when I had my two children with me, and we were standing in line to pay, and this young white man stepped in front of me. I said, *"Excuse me?"* And he said, "Oh my God, I didn't see you there." He was speaking on a much larger basis than that. He didn't recognize my presence, and I think that is why I write the stories that I write.[79]

For years, women had been making history at the Tony Awards as the first to be nominated for a category and the first to win the coveted prizes. But, in 2017, it was time for the firsts to be over. The Tonys still had a long way to go to truly represent their namesake.

7

A WICKED WAVE OF FEMINIST THEATER

"The fight is far from over," wrote author and activist Rebecca Walker in the article "Becoming the Third Wave." Published in *Ms.* magazine in 1992, following the Supreme Court confirmation hearings for Clarence Thomas and reflecting on gender roles in society and the impact of Thomas's confirmation, Walker's piece declared her commitment to "history, health, and healing of women" and called for others to do the same.

> So I write this as a plea to all women, especially women of my genera-
> tion: Let Thomas's confirmation serve to remind you, as it did me, that
> the fight is far from over. Let this dismissal of a woman's experience
> move you to anger. Turn that outrage into political power. Do not vote
> for them unless they work for us. Do not have sex with them, do not
> break bread with them, do not nurture them if they don't prioritize our
> freedom to control our bodies and our lives. I am not a postfeminism
> feminist. I am the Third Wave.[1]

Walker was far from alone. As Gen Xers, born in the 1960s and 1970s, progressed into the 1980s and 1990s, they saw some results of the Second Wave and civil rights movements carried out. People's lives now included increased power, both economic and professional, and they were using it to fight.

NEW GOALS FOR A NEW DECADE

In 1998, *Time* magazine's cover posed the question, "Is feminism dead?" The stark, black cover, bordered in bright red, featured photos of Susan B. Anthony, Betty Friedan, and Gloria Steinem next to a shot of popular TV lawyer Ally McBeal. Written by Ginia Bellafante, the article criticized the next wave of women for failing to honor the work of their predecessors and focusing on such frivolous concerns as their appearances instead. The subhead proclaimed, "Want to know what today's chic young feminist thinkers care about? Their bodies! Themselves!"[2]

In Bellafante's eyes, Ally McBeal embodied the shift in feminist thought in which a self-centered up-and-coming lawyer wore miniskirts to the office while navigating a chaotic love life and her career. Premiering in 1997, the show resonated with female viewers, so much so that Ken Tucker wrote in a review,

> A number of women I know are already devoted to this show; at *Entertainment Weekly* alone, I've been threatened by a vicious gang of female staffers who've vowed to hurt me if I knock *Ally*. . . . It's not hard to see what women respond to in Ally: She's complicated, ambitious, nervy, and vulnerably ambivalent—a walking, talking cross between a Cosmo girl, a *Ms.* feminist, and a *Sassy* editor. And if the show's female fans have no problem with the absurdly short skirts Ally wears to court, hey, who am I to suggest a certain lack of professionalism on her part?[3]

Ally McBeal predated *Sex and the City*, *Bridget Jones' Diary*, and countless stories of young women living in a city and seeking love, and Bellafante was not pleased with what these women represented.

It was clear that the next wave of feminists was targeting different issues than the previous, but it wasn't just lipstick and casual sex. Their efforts were focused on a worldwide scale to repossess the media surrounding women—beauty, sexuality, femininity and masculinity, and gender.[4] For these feminists, working to be inclusive of different races and cultural backgrounds, concerns regarding the environment, poverty, and marriage equality, were all part of the movement.[5]

The Third Wave's agenda had expanded, wrote Princeton University professor and author Stacy Wolf:

Third Wave feminism understands equality broadly. Explicitly non- or antidogmatic about gender and sexuality, Third Wave feminism is equally concerned with trans, queer, and shifting affiliations. From tastes in clothes to tastes in television, from choices about work to choices about domestic life, Third Wave feminists are irrefutably individualist. For some, Third Wave feminism encourages embracing irony, the playful reappropriation of typically misogynist representations, and aggressively against-the-grain spectatorship. For others, Third Wave feminism takes on a more earnest cast, a determined navigation of gender and race together. Contradiction and hybridity undergrid Third Wave feminist praxis. At the same time, Third Wave feminists place themsleves in a longer history of feminist movements.[6]

INTRODUCING INTERSECTIONALITY

Intersectionality entered the mainstream feminist discourse in the late 1980s. First introduced in 1989, by Kimberlé Williams Crenshaw, in a paper titled "Demarginalizing the Intersection of Race and Sex: A Black Feminist Critique of Antidiscrimination Doctrine, Feminist Theory, and Antiracist Politics," intersectionality addressed the erasure of black women in dialogues about discrimination due to the focus on privileged people that filled the feminist and civil rights movements. Crenshaw wrote that, without including intersectionality in an analysis, one is unable to adequately address the experience of the black woman:

> I argue that black women are sometimes excluded from feminist theory and antiracist policy discourse because both are predicated on a discrete set of experiences that often do not accurately reflect the interaction of race and gender. These problems of exclusion cannot be solved simply by including black women within an already established analytical structure. Because the intersectional experience is greater than the sum of racism and sexism, any analysis that does not take intersectionality into account cannot sufficiently address the particular manner in which black women are subordinated. Thus, for feminist theory and antiracist policy discourse to embrace the experiences and concerns of black women, the entire framework that has been used as a basis for translating "women's experience" or "the black experience" into concrete policy demands must be rethought and recast.[7]

The message of intersectionality—and all aspects of Third Wave feminism—was communicated more easily than the previous decades' messages. By the early-to-mid 2000s, more than half of the households in the United States owned computers, and 44 percent of households had at least one family member using a computer—an increase of 26 percent from two years before. More voices and more readers were sharing more ideas. Feminists began focusing on eradicating stereotypes rooted in traditional gender roles, as well as working to establish intersectionality, including a more diverse group of women, racially and culturally. The ideas were spreading, and they were reaching the theater.

"MY VAGINA IS ANGRY"

One of the most prominent voices, in both theater and feminism, beginning in the late 1990s, was Eve Ensler. The writer, peformance artist, and activist began one of the most well-known activist movements in the arts when she first performed *The Vagina Monologues* at HERE Arts Center in 1996.

Ensler wrote the series of speeches about women's sexuality to "celebrate the vagina" and foster empowerment in women. Inspired by a series of conversations with her friends, Ensler interviewed more than two hundred women—"older women, young women, married women, lesbians, single women, college professors, actors, corporate professionals, sex workers, African American women, Asian American women, Hispanic women, Native American women, Caucasian women, Jewish women"—about sex and relationships, violence against women, and empowerment, all of which she said was interconnected.[8]

Her monologues explore different aspects of the female experience: love, body image, menstruation, and masturbation, as well as sex work, rape, and genital mutilation. They encompass beauty standards and focus on removing body hair, traumas endured at rape camps, the meaning of the word "cunt," and a tirade against the injustices vaginas have to suffer, including tampons, speculums, and beautifying products.

"My vagina's angry," one monologue declares in furious defiance of beauty standards that prey on women's insecurities, as well as their finances.

It's pissed off. My vagina's furious, and it needs to talk. It needs to talk about all this shit. It needs to talk to you. I mean what's the deal—an army of people out there thinking up ways to torture my poor-ass, gentle, loving vagina. Spending their days constructing psycho products and nasty ideas to undermine my pussy.[9]

Word quickly spread about this daring show, and the limited run of *The Vagina Monologues* at HERE Arts Center was extended before it moved to the Westside Theatre Off-Broadway, where a rotating cast followed Ensler's solo performance.

Marketing for *The Vagina Monologues* honored its unapologetic aesthetic, but some found it alienating. Residents of Connecticut attempted to pass legislation that banned the employment of obscene words in outdoor advertising because of a billboard promoting the show. Subway advertisements read, "Eve Ensler, *The Vagina Monologues*: Spread the Word," adorned with a microphone going through a V shape, and producer David Stone recalled asking the *New Yorker*, "Do you have a problem with the word 'vagina'?" when the staff was "blanching." The reply: "No, we have a problem with the word 'vagina' in seventy-two-point type."[10] But the content wasn't objectionable or offensive to audiences in New York, who filled the theater.

The play's timing, was well as its pointed commentary on gender roles and norms, was noted by Charles Isherwood, who wrote of the price paid for "submitting to culutral taboos" and how surrendering to them can damage one's spirit, as well as sexuality, adding, "Much sorrow and confusion and loss have been occasioned by a 'Christian' propriety that includes silence on the subject of sex among its social diktats."[11]

Ensler's humor was praised by many, including the *New York Times'* Anita Gates (one of the few women to review the show for a major publication):

If Ms. Ensler is the messiah heralding the second wave of feminism, and a lot of people seem to think she is, it is partly because she's a brilliant comedian. *The Vagina Monologues* is alternately hilarious and deeply disturbing. But as important as the serious monologues are— the tribute to Bosnian rape victims, an eyewitness report about the wonder of childbirth—humor is the show's real strength.[12]

The show's impact went far beyond the stage. Two years after Ensler's first performance, the playwright and a group of women launched V-Day on February 14, 1998. In the movement working to end violence against girls and women, including transgender and nonbinary people, V stood for victory and Valentine, as well as vagina. Each year, the play is performed throughout the world, professionally in benetfit performances featuring casts of celebrities and on college campuses. Produced free of royalties, proceeds go to programs and projects working to ending violence against women and girls.

Ensler's play, which was adapted for an HBO TV movie, had become, for many, a staple of feminist theater. It was deemed "probably the most imporant piece of political theater of the last decade" by Charles Isherwood,[13] and Ben Brantley and Jesse Green stated, "No recent hour of theater has had a greater impact worldwide."[14] The script continues to be udpated as Ensler writes new monologues regarding global issues women are facing. "Under the Burqa" focuses on women in Afghanistan under the rule of the Taliban. "They Beat the Girl Out of My Boy . . . or So They Tried" was written after Ensler conducted interviews with people whose gender identities differ from what they were assigned at birth.

As feminism, as well as awareness of gender identities and sexual preferences and intersectionality, evolves, so has the reaction to Ensler's play. The show has faced criticism for its limited perspective on sexuality and lack of inclusivity regarding transgender people, its failure to mention the clitoris, and conflating women with a body part rather than their entire being. Ensler, a white woman, has also been criticized for writing monologues in the voice of people from different countries and backgrounds. Moreover, accusations of colonialism have been lobbed at the show, due to much of the violence described taking place in different countries.

Some productions of the play have been reenvisioned, using different demographics in its casting. A performance scheduled for Columbia University's V-Day fundraiser was cast entirely with women of color, and at Southwestern University a performance was cancelled following complaints from the students that it only offered the "white woman's experience" and didn't depict the "reality of womanhood." It was replaced by a series of works performed by women of color titled *We Are Women*.[15] And, in 2016, American University canceled its performance due to the show's binary represenation of gender and instead presented a new show consisting of original, student-authored monologues titled *Breaking Ground Monologues*.

Ensler has continued to write and work for women, authoring the plays *Emotional Creature*, *The Treatment*, *The Good Body*, *Necessary Targets*, *Lemonade*, and her memoir and subsequent play *In the Body of the World*.

"EVERYONE DESERVES A CHANCE TO FLY"

A feminist voice could be heard belting to the rafters when the new musical *Wicked* opened. Adapted from Gregory Maguire's novel *Wicked: The Life and Times of the Wicked Witch of the West*, Stephen Schwartz and Winnie Holzman's musical served as a prequel to *The Wizard of Oz*, telling the unheard story of Elphaba, the green-skinned girl who grew up to become known as the Wicked Witch of the West.

The musical, which starred Tony winners Idina Menzel as Elphaba and Kristin Chenoweth as Glinda, contained an unabashedly feminist message in a major Broadway blockbuster. In a departure from the standard norm of a romantic musical comedy in which a heterosexual romantic pairing drives the plot, *Wicked*'s central relationship was shared between two women. The complicated friendship of Elphaba and Glinda, who meet as roommates at the magical boarding school Shiz, was the musical's actual love story. Glinda, the pert and perky blonde who immediately establishes herself as the school's social leader and trendsetter, is unable to understand Elphaba, the awkward, impassioned, girl with bright green skin who recoils from socializing and popularity. A love triangle does take shape when Prince Fiyero arrives at Shiz, but he remains a supporting character, and the women do not engage in fights over him. Glinda is romanced by him initially, before he recognizes the passionate Elphaba as his match, and both lament their loss of Fiyero in renditions of "I'm Not That Girl." But rather than a song of jealousy or anger, the simple song is a wistful melody of grief.

When writing *Wicked*, Schwartz, who had composed the scores of the musicals *Godspell* and *Pippin*, as well as *Rags* and *Children of Eden*, knew he needed a female book writer, and Holzman, who created the popular female-focused TV series *Thirtysomething* and *My So-Called*

Life, had already expressed interest in adapting Maguire's novel before Schwartz asked.[16]

What followed was a decidedly, "surprisingly" feminist,[17] socially conscious story of friendship, political activism, and rebellion. The first duet between Glinda and Elphaba, "What Is This Feeling?" explores the newly felt emotion both girls are introduced to at school: loathing. As their voices soar and the two declare their feelings are "so pure, so strong," they thrill in the "strange exhilaration in such total detestation" and declare confidently they will be "loathing you my whole life long." Along with sending up the composition of a love duet, Schwartz's lyrics also satirize, with the word "loathing" echoing the sounds of "loving."

Rather than focusing on friends or boys, the teenage Elphaba directs her energy toward the rights of Animals in Oz, creatures who can speak and teach at the school but who are being silenced. The green-skinned girl's sensitivity to discrimination and impassioned sense of justice causes her to lose control of her powers, and when she meets the Wizard, she recognizes him for the fraud that he is and his role in suppressing the Animals.

Kristin Chenoweth and Idina Menzel in *Wicked. Photofest*

Elphaba's passion exiles her from Shiz and her new friendship with Glinda. In another defiance of the standards of musical theater, *Wicked*'s first act does not conclude with a rapturous love duet or a lengthy number establishing the conflict driving the second act. In the soaring climactic song "Defying Gravity," Elphaba breaks free from the societal conventions that imprisoned her and embarks on her own journey. Rather than remain with Glinda and apologize for her outburst, Elphaba goes her own way, literally soaring to the heights of the stage, singing, "If I'm flying solo, at least I'm flying free!"

The two women also share the final song of the show, "For Good." As they prepare to part ways, the friends reflect on their love for one another and how their friendship has shaped each of their lives. Rather than concluding the show with a happy reconciliation, Schwartz and Holzman have the women part ways in a bittersweet song of mutual respect and affection. Despite its heterosexual protagonists and romantic triangle, *Wicked*'s love story is that of Elphaba and Glinda.

Wicked, which was budgeted at $14 million when it opened in 2003,[18] received tepid reviews, especially from Ben Brantley in the *New York Times*, who decried the show, saying it so "overplays its hand that it seriously dilutes its power."[19] The *New Yorker* lamented, "Based on a clever novel by Gregory Maguire, the musical is an exercise in high camp—a universe turned topsy-turvy, where good is bad, normal is abnormal, and the purest well yields the sourest water."[20]

The musical's story of female friendship was praised by Linda Winer, who noted its ambitious, at times confusing, plot:

> Winnie Holzman, who wrote for TV's girl-sensitive *My So-Called Life*, has a keen sense of the complexities of friendship among teens, who happen to grow up to be witches we all know. This is lovely. But the story is also meant to be a political morality play about a place of bigotry against girls born green, oppression of Munchkins, and, most incoherently, a plot to cage all animals and stifle their ability to speak.[21]

Brantley stated in his review, "*Wicked* does not, alas, speak hopefully for the future of the Broadway musical."[22] The value of its impact is subject to personal perception, but, after fifteen years, tours, and productions, it's clear that *Wicked*'s impact is lasting.

"I'M HERE"

Female empowerment was given a soaring new voice in 2005, when *The Color Purple* opened on Broadway. With a score by Brenda Russell, Allee Willis, and Stephen Bray, and a book by Marsha Norman, the adaptation of Alice Walker's classic award-winning novel chronicled the emotional journey of Celie, a young woman who suffered years of physical and emotional abuse before beginning a journey into self-discovery and happiness.

After years of assault at the hands of her father, with whom she gave birth to two children who were taken from her, Celie is married to a local man, who also abuses her, and is separated from her sister and best friend Nettie after her husband attempts to attack her.

In *The Color Purple*, Celie's husband is only known as "Mister." Her denial of his name in her narrative removes him from the viewer, establishing him as less personal and less humane than those around him, shrouded in Celie's fear of his violence. Resisting, or retaliating, does not occur until Celie meets Sofia, her stepson's wife, who, when her husband attempts to beat her, fights back in the robust declaration, saying "Hell No."

"All my life I had to fight. I had to fight my daddy," Sofia sings. "I had to fight my brothers, my cousins, my uncles too. But I never, never, never, never, never thought I'd have to fight in my own house." By declaring ownership of her home, Sofia establishes her independence and autonomy. The house isn't just her husband's, despite property laws dictated by marriage; it is her house as well, and even though Sofia tells Celie that she loves Harpo, she says she will "kill him dead before I let him or anybody beat me." When Celie, who was shocked that Sofia would leave her husband, shares that her way of coping with Mister is to think of God and that she will die soon, Sofia responds to her weary resignation with, "What you ought to do is bash Mister's head open. And think on heaven later. You cain't stay here girl," before inviting her fellow women to join in the refrain of, "Hell no."

After meeting her husband's longtime mistress, Shug Avery, Celie begins a loving relationship for the first time in her adult life. She is then able to stand up to her husband, giving voice to how he has wronged her for years, cursing him and declaring, "Until you do right by me, everything and everyone you touch will crumble, everything you dream will fail." It is after Celie establishes her own identity, separate from a man, that she experiences true happiness for the first time and even establishes her own financial independence by sewing pants for women.

The power of sisterhood is prevalent in *The Color Purple*, seen in the individual relationships between Celie and Nettie, Celie and Sofia, and Celie and Shug. It's also apparent in the music, which features groups of women frequently singing inspiring refrains, whether it is "Hell, no!" in Sofia's song or an affirmation of Celie's independent life in "Miss Celie's Pants," as Celie declares, "But look . . . who's wearing the pants now!"

Celie is not alone in her transformation; the male characters in *The Color Purple* also undergo reflection and redemption. By moving beyond his own abusive childhood, Mister even seeks forgiveness from Celie and attempts to redeem himself. As the story draws to an end, Celie and Mister have even formed a kind of friendship.

The Color Purple earned eleven Tony Award nominations, including Best Actress for LaChanze, who played Celie, and recouped its $11 million investment within its first year on Broadway. But Celie's story of self-discovery seemed lost on critics, many of whom dismissed the production. Writing in the *New York Times*, Ben Brantley opined that book writer Marsha Norman brought a "refreshing if dogged writerly respect to Ms. Walker's work," but Brantley said the power of Walker's work had been lost in this adaptation:

> At the show's end, Celie has acquired, in addition to gray hairs and a personal fortune through the making and selling of pants for women, an air of matriarchal dignity that she wears like vintage couture. And it occurred to me that somewhere along the way in her odyssey of survival and triumph, Celie had morphed into a heroine of the kind of inspirational women's fiction found in airport bookstores, written by Barbara Taylor Bradford and Danielle Steel.
>
> These are authors I would never have thought to compare to Alice Walker. But such things happen in adaptations that emphasize sheer story over sensibility. Devotees of Ms. Walker's novel would be better off thinking of this show less as *The Color Purple* than as, say, *Celie: A Woman of Independent Means*.[23]

Michael Feingold of the *Village Voice* acknowledged the show's emotional impact but did not care for how the characters were portrayed, commenting on the disparity between the content the actors were bringing to life and the actual performances, writing, "The disheartening lack of quality in the material dilutes the quality of feeling with which it's being put over and makes the meanings behind it look questionable as well."[24]

David Rooney of *Variety* thought the character of Celie lacked autonomy, which contradicted the musical's story, writing,

> A chief weakness is the failure to give Celie (LaChanze) decisive ownership of the story. Inevitably, her personal journey from enslavement to empowerment, from battered insignificance to proud self-worth, allows the character to blossom only toward the final curtain; it's not until the penultimate song "I'm Here" that she gets to stake her claim on the center-stage position.[25]

Walker's story of self-discovery was marketed as a universal message of empowerment. The musical's triumphant message of individuality, along with its entirely black cast, exemplified the values of the Third Wave movement. "*The Color Purple's* liberal rhetoric is consistent with musical theater's political leanings," wrote Stacy Wolf in *Changed for Good.* "Around the millennium, the individualist message that *A [sic] Color Purple* espouses and the internet as a mode of communication also signal a Third Wave feminist movement."[26] This was a fitting setting, given that the term "Third Wave feminism" was coined by Rebecca Walker, daughter of Alice Walker, author of the novel *The Color Purple.*

In Celie, Walker created a woman who undergoes remarkable transformation throughout her life. Her daughter voiced her own need for a transformation to carry out her feminist mission:

> After battling with ideas of separatism and militancy, I connect with my own feelings of powerlessness. I realize that I must undergo a transformation if I am truly committed to women's empowerment. My involvement must reach beyond my own voice in discussion, beyond voting, beyond reading feminist theory. My anger and awareness must translate into tangible action.
>
> I am ready to decide, as my mother decided before me, to devote much of my energy to the history, health, and healing of women. Each of my choices will have to hold to my feminist standard of justice. To be a feminist is to integrate an ideology of equality and female empowerment into the very fiber of my life. It is to search for personal clarity in the midst of systemic destruction, to join in sisterhood with women

Playbill cover for *The Color Purple. Photofest*

when often we are divided, to understand power structures with the intention of challenging them. While this may sound simple, it is exactly the kind of stand that many of my peers are unwilling to take.[27]

PHYLLIS SCHLAFLY, OFF-BROADWAY

Women's stories were coming to the stage in fairy tales and historic stories, and, in 2012, a decidedly present-day drama regarding women's lives opened Off-Broadway. *Rapture, Blister, Burn*, by Gina Gionfriddo, provided a blunt examination of feminism that was described by many, including its playwright, as an homage (albeit, she claimed, unconscious) to *The Heidi Chronicles*. The show revolves around Catherine, a successful author and popular TV pundit, who returns to her hometown to care for her ailing mother. Back in familiar territory, she resumes a relationship with Don, her lover from graduate school, who married her best friend after the two broke up when Catherine chose to remain in London on a fellowship.

Fifteen years later, Catherine's success is unquestioned, but she is personally unfulfilled, questioning if her focus on her work came at the cost of marriage and family. Don and Gwen's marriage has slackened into a dull routine: He is unambitious, addicted to porn, and smoking pot, resigned to an administrative job instead of the academic fulfillment he once sought, and Gwen has abandoned her own academic pursuits to care for her family and focus on her sobriety. Gwen claims she is happy with the choices she has made and at one point references *The Feminine Mystique* author Betty Friedan, saying, "What was revolutionary about Friedan was her assertion that all women do not fit one mold."[28]

Don arranges for Catherine to teach a summer course at the local college, for which Gwen signs up, along with her former babysitter. The multigenerational class and their professor engage in heated discussions about pop culture, as well as the works of feminist activists Nancy Friday and Betty Friedan, and conservative activist Phyllis Schlafly. These discussions are joined by Alice, Catherine's mother, who, having survived a bad marriage in the 1950s, savors witnessing and participating in the results of feminist work.

As Catherine and Gwen reconnect, they see in one another what their own lives might have been and eventually decide to put this idea to a test:

Don and Catherine reunite romantically, and Gwen and her son depart for New York, where they live in Catherine's apartment. But eventually the separated spouses decide the arrangement is unsustainable and return to the lives they found unfulfilling but comfortable.

Don informs Catherine their relationship can't continue, and as she struggles to understand why, he tells her, "It's not worth your time in analysis. I'm not worth it. You should just curse me and move on." Devastated, she asks him, "I don't want to curse you. I want to understand why is this happening? I gave you everything you said you wanted," to which Don responds, "You did . . . if I actually articulate this stuff, my low self-esteem will sink to subterranean levels."[29]

In Catherine, Gionfriddo offers a blunt portrayal of a woman who was tired of trying to have it all. She wasn't aiming for "it all" anymore. She wants enough and shares this to Don, saying, "I want a flawed, tired marriage to cushion my falls. I am ready and willing to embrace mediocrity and ambivalence, you're just not letting me."[30]

Rapture, Blister, Burn opened Off-Broadway as a rush of articles examining the state of marriage in the United States exploring the idea that ultimate passion and fulfillment could be found in one relationship flooded publications. *Marry Him! The Case for Settling for Mr. Good Enough*, by Lori Gottlieb, was published in 2010, urging women to not miss out on a partner who is decent.[31] The *Atlantic* published a piece in 2012 titled "The Marriage Problem: Why Many Are Choosing Cohabitation Instead."[32] Reports on people marrying later in life, if at all, packed the news.

An academic woman, unfulfilled in her personal life, questioning where feminism has left her—the parallells between *The Heidi Chronicles* and *Rapture, Blister, Burn* were plentiful. Heidi's story concluded in 1989, and *Rapture, Blister, Burn* began in 2012, but the same questions that hovered in the air as the curtain fell on Heidi contentedly rocking her baby persisted and hovered in the air before the opening of *Rapture, Blister, Burn*. The relevance was not lost on Gionfriddo, who addressed it in an essay for the *New York Times*, saying, "I did not set out to rewrite *Heidi* or to talk back to *Heidi*, but no one is ever going to believe that. Both plays depict a female academic just over forty with a successful career as an author." She continued,

Both women, Wasserstein's Heidi and my Cathy, regard their personal lives as lacking (neither has a romantic partner or children) and find themselves reexamining the feminist movement to sort out how they could have come so far and still wound up unsatisfied. Both women mourn the loss of a relationship they perceive to be a casualty of their ambitions. (It's not just perception, actually; each play contains a scene in which the man in question confirms our heroine's fears.) And both plays force our fortysomething doubters to confront bold, confident women in their early 20s who believe they have figured out how to have it all by observing the older women's mistakes. [33]

Gionfriddo's play didn't attempt to provide any answers to the questions it posed. Instead, it reinforced that there were no answers. As Avery, a student at the local college, says after listening to Catherine and Gwen discuss their choices, "So is the message that women are fucked up either way? You either have a career and wind up lonely and sad, or you have a family and wind up lonely and sad?" Catherine responds, "Maybe you have both and you wind up fulfilled," but Gwen replies, "I don't know anyone who has that." [34]

Rapture, Blister, Burn, a finalist for the 2013 Pulitzer Prize in Drama, received critical praise. Joe Dziemianowicz wrote in the *Daily News*,

Gina Gionfriddo's new play *Rapture, Blister, Burn* is a smart, funny, and lightning-paced look at feminism—past and present. Can women have it all? The show's title alludes to a lyric from a Courtney Love song that speaks of, among other things, "emptiness" and "awful truths." That's your first clue. [35]

Calling it a "searing and rueful play," Alexis Soloski addressed the show's demographics in *Politico*, writing,

Since Playwrights debuted Wendy Wasserstein's *The Heidi Chronicles* in 1988, few Broadway or Off-Broadway scripts have charted a similarly head-on approach to the subject of contemporary American feminism. (Well, the straight, white, middle-class version at any rate.) But whereas Wasserstein's play concludes, in a scene as sweet as it is saccharine, with the heroine's cuddling of an adopted baby girl, Rapture doesn't offer any such soothing, rock-a-bye answers. [36]

Charles Isherwood of the *New York Times* opined,

You might wonder what fresh insights are to be found by tilling such well-covered ground. . . . *Rapture* more largely illuminates how hard it can be to forge both a satisfying career and a fulfilling personal life in an era that seems to demand superhuman achievement from everyone.[37]

Rapture, Blister, Burn does not conclude with a happy ending. But, in portraying the questions that plague present-day feminism, the play offers an honest look at how and why people are shaping their lives, struggling to incorporate their ideals with the demands of everyday existence.

"That real life catches up with all three characters is part of Gionfriddo's nuanced understanding of twenty-first-century women," Jill Dolan wrote.

Feminism might provide a certain kind of woman, situated in certain ways, with certain choices and advantages. But, ultimately, we make our own choices, which have less to do with politics or dogma than with who we are and how we're hard wired to interact with a culture that keeps switching out the screensaver on gendered options for a living.[38]

Despite the obvious similarities between Gionfriddo's script and Wasserstein's, the most obvious was just how similar the characters' problems and challenges were. "I wish Wasserstein were here to weigh in on all this," Gionfriddo wrote in the *Times*. "I wonder if she would be bummed out. We were supposed to have resolved all of this, right?"[39]

THE EVOLUTION OF HAPPILY EVER AFTER

Modern-day fairy tale heroine Elphaba was joined on Broadway ten years later by another political activist when *Rogers and Hammerstein's Cinderella* opened in 2013. Adapted from the 1957 TV broadcast starring Julie Andrews, and featuring additional songs by Rogers and Hammerstein, the musical featured a new book by four-time Tony nominee Douglas Carter Beane, an obvious attempt to update the story/eliminate the problematic elements familiar to fairy tales.

In Charles Perrault's *Cendrillon*, which inspired the 1950 Disney animated feature, the title character is a beautiful, submissive, mild-mannered woman who works as a maid to a wicked stepmother and stepsisters. It's only with the aid of a fairy godmother that she attends a royal ball and wins the coveted hand in marriage of the village's prince. *Cinderella*, by the Brothers Grimm, differs greatly. The story begins with the death of Cinderella's mother, who swears to watch over her daughter from Heaven. Cinderella visits her mother's grave daily and weeps over her life, in a marked contrast to Perrault's Cendrillon, who serves her stepmother and sisters with kindness. While Perrault's Cendrillon is aided by fairy godmothers, the magic for Grimm's Cinderella comes from a tree that grew watered by Cinderella's tears. Cendrillon does not seek help to change her life, but Cinderella does: When ordered to sort lentils from the ashes, she calls upon the birds to help her. When she needs a gown for the ball, she asks the tree that she grew to give it to her. There is no fairy godmother in this story, and her gown does not disappear at midnight; she manages to hide and disguise herself.

The story of Cinderella has inspired operas, ballets, books, and films, often with themes of independence and feminism weaved into their plots. In the 1997 novel *Ella Enchanted*, the title character is cursed to behave obediently, but her personality remains rebellious. Seeking loopholes in the curse, Ella strives to maintain her agency, and her romance with the Prince grows throughout time, as the two exchange letters, rather than love at first sight and marriage after one dance. In the 1998 film *Ever After*, the fiery young woman Danielle saves the Prince from a band of gypsies before a growing intellectual connection between the two begins. In 2015, Disney released a live-action film of *Cinderella*, in which Ella and Kit (the prince), meet before the ball, while riding horses in the woods, and he tells her he is an apprentice at the palace rather than revealing his true identity. Ella doesn't want to go to the ball to meet the Prince; she only wants to see her friend. She often repeats a phrase spoken by her mother on her deathbed, "Have courage and be kind," which director Kenneth Branagh described as the source of her empowerment.

The story of Cinderella has long epitomized many of the problematic elements of fairy tales that have been analyzed and criticized throughout the years. Women were divided with the labels of "good" or "evil," determinations that also dictated their physical appearance, with beauty as the equivalent of goodness and ugliness being equated with power. The villains in fairy tales often seek a life beyond the one they are currently living, and for women, it involves obtaining power—often accessible through involvement with a man. The desire for power is associated with ugliness, reinforcing traditional gendered expectations that women remain kind, grateful, and passive—stereotypically feminine qualities that necessitate a woman being saved rather than saving herself. The beautiful, passive Cinderella lacks agency, relying on her fairy godmother, and then the Prince, to free her from her unhappy existence.

"Cinderella is an object acted upon," professor Linda Parsons wrote.

> This Cinderella cannot speak for herself, she cannot act on her own behalf, and she cannot function autonomously: Yet she is rewarded with the ultimate prize. After meek submission, humble acceptance of her fate, being good to those who abused her, and becoming beautiful, she is rewarded with the Prince, yet she did nothing. [40]

Douglas Carter Beane agreed with these assessments, initially declining the offer to write the 2013 musical's book. He told the *Tampa Bay Times*, "I thought Cinderella was just a feminist nightmare. I have a daughter now and didn't like perpetuating that. Just leave behind an article of clothing and it'll be good." [41] Bringing *Cinderella* to a modern audience would be a weighty task, as fairy tales' impact on culture and the development of young children, and their perception of gender roles, is obvious, furthered by toy production and marketing. "Fairy tales contribute to formation of the boundaries of agency, subjectivity, and anticipated rewards," Parsons wrote of fairy tales' influence. "They are powerful cultural agents that tell us how *to be*. Yet it is impossible to know the exact role stories play in shaping the unconscious and in creating positions for us to take up." [42]

Beane attempted to eliminate these problematic elements while simultaneously maintaining the fairy tale's appeal of romance, magic, and "happily ever after." *Cinderella* clearly attempted to tell a feminist story, but achieving that goal was complicated: Parsons wrote in "Ella Evolving," "A feminist text deals with issues of freedom, choice, and expanding the subject positions available to women and men, and it makes visible the fact that the tales have functioned historically to reproduce social values." [43]

The 2013 production of *Cinderella* was an ambitious show; along with challenging the expectations of heteronormative relationships, it also included political and economic inequities in its story. This Cinderella is an activist determined to help the downtrodden of her village alongside her friend Jean-Michel, and her motivations for meeting the Prince are far from romantic. Instead, she wants to talk politics, because the Prince's aide de camp had been enforcing inequities in his name and robbing people of their land. When her friend "Crazy Marie" teases her for longing to go to the ball with her stepsisters and stepmother, Ella responds, "So what if I do have a dream to see the Prince again? And tell him what life in his kingdom is really like? And what it could be."[44] She wants the Prince to fall in love with her as well, she admits, but this Cinderella is not motivated merely by romance.

Cinderella is a selfless heroine; her good-hearted motivations function in service of others, including the men in the play and especially the Prince. Prince Topher is first introduced to the audience as a lost young man struggling to define himself, a man with good intentions but who is unsure of his ability to rule and his place on the throne. It is quickly established that the well-intentioned but naïve Topher is being manipulated by Sebastian, the Lord Chancellor who helped to raise the Prince after his family's death and cares little for the welfare of the kingdom's subjects.

The purity of both Topher and Cinderella's hearts, and the fact that they are meant for one another, is apparent from their first meeting. Her kindness extends to her stepmother and stepsisters, all of whom are written sympathetically, as Beane takes pains in his book to establish strong female relationships. Neither of the stepsisters are truly wicked; instead they are weak and misguided by their mother. Quietly empathetic and passionate, Gabrielle secretly longs for the rebel activist Jean-Michel, while Charlotte is self-centered and narcissistic. Neither of the stepsisters comes across as vicious or spiteful, and sporadic moments reveal the latent affection in their relationship with Cinderella. When they return from the ball and they unwittingly reminisce with Cinderella about the evening, the women unite in a joyful song, laughing and dancing, class differences forgotten for the moment. Gabrielle's rebellion against her mother further advances when she forfeits her invitation to the following night's banquet so Cinderella can go in her place and reunite with the Prince. Strong female relationships are crucial to feminist stories, but it is worth noting that in Beane's book, the women only come together when talking about men. These fairy-tale characters do not pass the Bechdel Test.

Topher is swept away by Cinderella, but even after they share a romantic waltz and passionate kiss at the ball, she remains grounded. Instead, just before fleeing at midnight, as he pleads for her to stay, Cinderella tells the Prince, "You need to open your eyes to what's happening in your kingdom. The poor are having their land taken. You must help them. You must."[45] By engaging with the Prince about his government and policies, Cinderella is intended to be seen as Topher's peer, equal, and partner, rather than the beautiful but silent woman at his side.

At first glance, Beane's *Cinderella* is significantly more empowered than one would expect in a fairy-tale musical based on a centuries-old story. Rather than waiting for true love's kiss, this Cinderella possesses enough autonomy and strength, as well as generosity of spirit, to care for not only herself, but also others who are less fortunate than her, and believes in her own voice and ability to speak on their behalf.

Ironically, Cinderella's strength does a disservice to Beane's story, at times contradicting the Rodgers and Hammerstein score that first enchanted audiences in 1957. Beane's Cinderella is such a strong and self-sufficient woman that her first solo—her "I Want" song, "In My Own Little Corner"—contradicts the rest of the character that we see throughout the play. How can audiences believe that this woman declaring, "I'm as mild and as meek as a mouse. When I hear a command, I obey," can also boldly confront the ruler of her village without fear of reparation or consequences?[46]

In a nod to the Grimm's fairy tale, and further empowering Cinderella as an independent woman, she chooses to leave her shoe behind as a clue for the Prince to find her rather than simply lose it in her rush to flee the castle. And instead of being released from a locked attic, she willingly presents herself to the Prince, declaring that she had not yet tried on the slipper. But much of Cinderella's story follows her helping, assisting, and encouraging Prince Topher. She guides him to become a more thoughtful and benevolent leader, assisting him in establishing his identity as a good man and a just king. By the end of the show, the Prince's identity crisis has been resolved, and he has newfound confidence in his ability to rule, joyfully telling Cinderella, "I think I know who I am now! I know the king that I can be. Just, fair. Kindhearted. I've found myself, and you showed me the way."[47] Cinderella's actions, selflessly made to help her fellow citizens, establish Topher as the protagonist of the story—a story that is supposed to revolve around and is named after her.

A (SOMEWHAT) MODERN WORLD FOR A (SOMEWHAT) MODERN PRINCESS

The year 2013 was a contradictory setting for an empowered princess heroine to bow on Broadway. Barack Obama was serving his second term and had already helped to enact significant progress for girls and women in the United States. By *Cinderella*'s opening the president had appointed Sonia Sotomayor and Elena Kagan to serve on the Supreme Court; signed an executive order to form the White House Council on Women and Girls; and signed into law his first federal statute, the Lilly Ledbetter Fair Pay Act, allowing individuals facing pay discrimination to seek rectification according to federal antidiscrimination laws, in 2009. First Lady Michelle Obama shaped her agenda to focus on obesity, arts education, and fitness, as well as launching "Let Girls Learn," an initiative to improve access to secondary schools. Determined to avoid a passive role in the government, the first lady carefully selected the areas she would focus on and was determined to produce results—telling her aides, "Don't just put me on a plane, send me somewhere, and have me smile."[48]

Feminists hotly debated whether the first lady's platform was actually progressive. The Ivy League–educated woman was criticized for declaring herself to be "mom in chief" and focusing on causes that were perceived as feminine and maternal, rather than hard policy issues in which she was qualified to participate. Michelle Cottle opined in *Politico*,

> Here [higher education], finally, was an issue worthy of the Ivy-educated, blue-chip, law firm–trained first lady, a departure from the safely, soothingly domestic causes she had previously embraced. Gardening? Tending wounded soldiers? Reading to children? "She essentially became the English lady of the manor, Tory Party, circa 1830s," feminist Linda Hirshman [said].[49]

To some, First Lady Obama's decision to focus on raising her children represented feminism's success in providing women with options on how to shape their lives. To others, it was an evasion, abandoning her responsibilities as an educated woman of color who had been handed significant power. In one writer's eyes, the first lady was responsible for the death of feminism:

Frustration flared when the first lady stumbled into the raging heart of the Mommy Wars. In her speech to the Democratic National Convention last summer, she dropped in the line that "at the end of the day, my most important title is still mom in chief." Much of the nation may have been charmed; feminist commentators, not so much. "Why does mom in chief have to be the most important thing this strong, vibrant woman tells us about herself as she flexes the strange but considerable power of the office of first lady?" Emily Bazelon lamented on *Slate*. On the feminist website *Feministing*, Lilith Dornhuber was even harsher: "Judging by Michelle Obama's speech, feminism is dead to the Democratic Party."[50]

But feminism had not died. In 2013, feminist rights activist Gloria Steinem received the Presidential Medal of Freedom, honoring her lifetime of work, much of which had been devoted to reproductive rights. Worldwide attention was inspired when Malala Yousafzai, a Pakistani activist for female education, survived an attack by the Taliban. Following her recovery, she founded the Malala Fund and authored the book *I Am Malala*. And, in 2012, a record number of women were serving in Congress, and a record number of women were the first to be elected to various positions of government.[51]

Resistance to this progress was swift and severe, as any advancements made by women were met with fear and anger. After Republicans took control of the House of Representatives in 2010, and increased their voice in the Senate, reproductive rights were one of the first items of attack: President Obama's health care reform, the Affordable Care Act, had included a mandate for contraception, which was met with horror and rage from conservative representatives. State legislatures passed many laws restricting abortion rights, and abortions funded by Medicaid faced new obstacles in various forms. The phrase "War on Women" was seen in the headlines, often when referring to the frantic opposition to contraceptive mandate and attempts to defund organizations that provided abortions.

Cinderella's bow on Broadway served as a mirror of this uneasy state of women's rights. At first glance, the musical seemed like a major step forward: a reenvisioning of a decidedly old-fashioned fairy tale in which the female protagonist's voice is heard with a story that went beyond marriage and "happily ever after." But beyond the progressive presentation was the fact that this revised, supposedly empowered story contained the subversive message that a woman would find happiness while supporting a man in finding his way. It was worth noting that in a reflection of the typical demographics of Broadway, the team that brought this story to the stage was almost entirely comprised of men, including, notably, the writer and director.

"YOU LEARN TO LIVE WITHOUT"

Those demographics, well as the continuously regressive view of modern women, were seen again one year later, when *If/Then* opened on Broadway. A new musical with a score by Tom Kitt and a book and lyrics by Brian Yorkey, *If/Then* chronicled two different paths of the same woman, Elizabeth, an urban planner who divorced her husband and moved to New York. "Liz" chooses a life that leads to love, marriage, and children, while "Beth" finds herself in a high-profile, demanding career that fulfills her professionally but leaves her single, lonely, and sad.

While exploring the different paths one's life can take due to one simple choice, *If/Then* failed to intertwine the various possibilities that exist in a modern woman's life. A more fitting title for the musical would have been *Either/Or*. Presumably intended to present a complicated, middle-aged woman exploring or celebrating the different options available to her, *If/Then*, with its two characters embarking on two drastically different paths, continued to perpetuate the idea that women must choose between a family or a career, because a life that includes both is impossible.

But *If/Then*'s regressive elements progressed even further: Elizabeth is supposed to be such a fascinating, compelling woman that everyone she meets is irresistibly drawn to her—her neighbor, the ebullient Kate; her graduate-school lover, Lucas, who still loves for her; and Josh, the handsome stranger in Madison Square Park who approaches her saying, "I feel like I know you." But, as written by Yorkey, Elizabeth is a dull, boring woman, a blank canvas upon whom everyone around her projects their own desires and agendas. Kate and Lucas both bestow on her their own choice of nicknames—"Liz" and "Beth," respectively—and she accepts either one without expressing an opinion of her own. Liz misses an opportunity for her dream job simply because she didn't answer one phone call while socializing with Kate, while Beth takes the call and is hired but is constantly berated by her friend Lucas for "selling out" by taking a job with the city government. She defends her choice to Lucas, but one question sends her into a spiral of self-doubt. And when, following a series of bad dates, she sees Josh in the park and he declares, "You have to go to dinner with me," she responds with, "I owe you that much." Liz, who acts in reaction to others, is clearly lacking in autonomy.

A truly feminist female protagonist does not merely respond to those around her. She has her own thoughts, feelings, and reactions, but few of Elizabeth's actions are organic. Even her professional accomplishments are the result of other—male—people recognizing her talent, rather than her own pursuit of professional advancement, and she resists taking a promotion until her friends urge her to do so. The group of women surrounding her onstage, singing of their encouragement and support, could be seen as a moment of feminist camaraderie, but the character of Beth herself, lacking in agency and authority, is not.

Despite being the musical's main character, Liz embodies passivity, merely responding to the wishes, actions, and desires of those around her. The musical is about her reactions, not her. Rather than pursuing the man in the park, he approaches her. When they see one another again on the train, after Liz says she is not interested, Kate—who has decided she knows what's best for her new friend (who she only met a few nights ago)—proceeds to lead the entire train car in a musical number about how Liz should take his phone number, and she does. As Josh and Liz's relationship develops and he confesses that he had been returning to the park, looking for her, she makes a weak joke about him stalking her and then sleeps with him for the first time—seemingly enamored by his devotion.

Even Liz's pregnancy and marriage are seemingly not of her own accord. When she informs Josh that she is unexpectedly pregnant, without any emotion on her part, his immediate response is to say they "should see this through" and "it feels right," without asking her what she wants to do—a reflection of the political climate in which all-male panels in Congress were debating reproductive rights.

A long-lasting and frustrating trope of romantic stories is that of the female protagonist suffering from low self-esteem and only finding self-actualization or fulfillment through a romantic relationship. *If/Then* thoroughly portrayed this through embodiments of Elizabeth. After Beth is rejected by her married boss, she laments, "Another day of saving the planet—one more night of nothing but tears," and declares, "I'm accomplished and I'm funny—I've got wisdom and wit and a taste for certain men who treat me like shit."[52] She proceeds to immediately call Lucas to comfort her, and they sleep together, presumably to validate her injured self-esteem.

Liz, who pursues romance rather than career, is seemingly also incapable of self-love. Following her first night with Josh, in an apparent fit of self-loathing, Liz wakes him up to tell him, "I'm incapable of loving." Rather than seeing herself as deserving of love and devotion from this man, Liz tells him that "this is very dangerous for you" and says, "I want to be with you. But my track record is very bad."[53] The context for her self-loathing is never provided. Other than her saying she chose to leave her husband, no details are offered about Liz's divorce and why she enters relationships with so much dread. This toxic low self-esteem, which is clearly self-destructive and dangerous, comes from nowhere. Following Liz's declaration of self-loathing, she and Josh decide to pursue a relationship despite how awful she is, as Beth declares, "I'm awkward, ungrateful, and sometimes I'm hateful—as you know. . . . Still here we go," while he quickly agrees, "You're not some romantic, you know, that's no surprise. You're no good at small talk or little loving lies."[54]

While often played for comedy, the insecure leading woman who inevitably finds validation and love from the man who sees beyond her shy or awkward exterior is dangerous for young women to witness. The psychology of romantic comedies can be destructive to their viewers, Dr. Silvia Kratzer, professor of Cinema Studies in the UCLA Department of Theater, Film, and Television, said: "Rom-coms also convey the illusion that self-fulfillment and self-worth can only be found in an idealized romantic relationship. This can redirect a woman's power towards an impossible pursuit of love rather than, say, developing a healthy relationship with *yourself*."[55]

This unhealthy dynamic continues to grow between Liz and Josh, who marry after learning she is pregnant. As the two joyfully leave the church, the first words out of her mouth are, "All the things I've messed up badly, all the hurt and all the shame"—which presumably led her to the day of her wedding. Josh quickly replies, "You'd do them all again gladly if you knew it would end up the same."[56] He's quick to agree with her but never engages by sharing anything unflattering about himself, only confirming that she is, indeed, as terrible as she repeatedly states she is, never contradicting her, even as she sings, "I'm a sorry sight to see/except the fact that you love me."[57] By declaring Josh's love her only redeeming quality, Liz perpetuates the dangers of invalidating women's worth without romantic partners.

That dynamic is further perpetuated by Beth. As Liz joyfully enters into wedded bliss, Beth walks by the church wistfully musing on her solitude while "walking by a wedding." The song does not contain one lyric that is not about her being alone, the beauty of a wedding, or the sadness of how the "world will never see so lonely as when you're walking by a wedding and waiting and watching then walking away."[58] *If/Then* determinedly presents marriage as the ideal happy ending, and, despite her professional accomplishments, Beth remains unfulfilled.

If/Then's problematic elements were hardly exclusive to Elizabeth; it also personified the problematic trope of the leading lady's best friend: the sidekick who offers endless support—which is usually ignored by the protagonist—in the form of witty one-liners and who has no discernible interests of her own other than the protagonist's love life. The best friend often contributes to the story's failing of the Bechdel test, because she discusses nothing but the main character's relationship.

If/Then's cast of supporting characters featured a racially and sexually diverse ensemble, a fact worth celebrating, but the characters themselves failed to rise above common stereotypes, as David Rooney noted in the *Hollywood Reporter*, describing them as "not with friends so much as types from the urban handbook of political correctness: Plucky, Kooky, Black Lesbian Kindergarten Teacher, Kate (LaChanze), and Earnest, White, Neurotic Gay (but Occasionally Bi-Curious) Radical College Chum, Lucas (Rapp)."[59]

Elizabeth's best friend Kate embodies many of the common tropes of romantic comedies: She is not only a thoroughly underwritten character composed of a handful of clichés, but also a person of color who, despite being in a loving relationship with another woman, seemingly has nothing to do except obsess over the characters of Liz/Beth. Kate is first introduced as a quirky free spirit happily embracing every moment of life (and demanding that everyone around her do so as well) and passionately believing in fate, destiny, and signs. After meeting Liz, the effervescent Kate immediately becomes fixated on her new friend's love life, urging her to take this complete stranger's phone number because the "universe has a message for her"[60] and leading an entire subway cart in a sing-along about how Liz should give a complete stranger a chance. Kate herself seems severely influenced by rom-com tropes: When arguing with Lucas about Elizabeth's nickname, Kate adamantly declares, "Beth lives alone with cats. Liz moves to New York City to find her one true love."[61]

Dressed in flowing shirts and dancing through subway cars, Kate appears to possess no responsibilities or concerns of her own, which leaves her free to dictate how Elizabeth should live her life. While reading to her class from a book series about American heroes, she decides there aren't enough women in the series and proceeds to tell them the story of Beth. After Kate declares Beth a hero because she divorced her husband and moved to a new city, she shows up, uninvited, at Beth's office with a cape made by her students. This is seen clearly in the song "No More Wasted Time," intended celebrate a woman's independence and accomplishments, but it hardly inspires feminist pride; it contains the pedestrian lyrics, "We gonna run the whole damn place/but with some class and with some grace/and we'll do fine," an exaggerated attempt to affirm that the women on the stage are, indeed, strong and powerful.[62]

In description, Kate's character appears be a progressive addition to the musical theater canon of supporting roles. She is a person of color and a lesbian in a committed interracial relationship who proposes marriage to her partner before it is ruled a federally protected right. And Elizabeth's other best friend, Lucas, is bisexual and, in one of the plots, becomes involved with David, played by Chinese, Hawaiian, and Caucasian actor Jason Tam. Both characters are seemingly obsessed with Elizabeth—Kate and Lucas as friends, Lucas (in Beth's plot) as a lover who engages in a physical relationship with her even though she cannot reciprocate his feelings. When Beth, unexpectedly pregnant, ends the pregnancy, he is furious with her and ends their friendship—even though the word "abortion" is never said onstage (despite the musical featuring a song titled "What the Fuck?" demonstrating the ongoing hypocrisy regarding the portrayal of reproductive justice in entertainment).

Although never deliberately articulated, Beth's decision seems to doom her to further unhappiness. She loses her best friend and, despite her professional success, seems unbearably lonely. After being offered a new job opportunity, her response is not to take pride in her accomplishments or revel in her success, but to begin singing a pensive melody titled "You Learn to Live Without." This song, more than any other, embodies the disempowering tropes of romantic comedies and further establishes the musical's message that professional and personal happiness are mutually exclusive and choosing professional happiness will lead to loneliness and misery, as she muses on telling herself she is free and liberated but immediately describes drinking and going to bed alone.

For a musical to be feminist, it needs to be more than simply about a woman. That woman needs to be an actual character, not a canvas on which every other character projects their wishes and desires. A feminist text, according to professor Roberta Seelinger Trites, is "one in which the protagonist is empowered *regardless* of gender, and she discusses several characteristics that distinguish feminist texts." She added, "Thus, writers of feminist texts seek to empower women, conceive a new vision of the world, value what has been devalued, and give voice to the silenced."[63] *If/Then*, with its lack of empowerement and autonomy, and its regressive message about working women, was not a feminist musical.

AWARDS, STUDIES, AND PROGRAMS

More steps were taken, more groups were formed, and more accountability was demanded. The Lilly Awards were founded in 2010, dedicated to honoring works by women. Named after Lillian Hellman, who famously said, "You need to write like the devil and act like one when necessary," the awards were founded by playwrights Julia Jordan, Marsha Norman, and Theresa Rebeck, to recognize women writers, directors, designers, and composers, and challenge the assumption that works by women are not as profitable as those by men. The idea came, Norman recalled, when she, Jordan, and Rebeck were on the phone, furious that one of the most acclaimed plays of the year, written by Melissa James Gibson, didn't receive a single nomination. "And so we were all bitching and carrying on, and I finally said, 'We should just do our own damn awards.' And that's all it took."[64]

"It had never been done. No one had ever thought of doing that. They weren't mad enough to say we're going to do our own awards," Norman recalled. "Now we're at a place where if someone does a season with no women they get more shit from people than they've ever heard of, writing to them saying, 'What are you doing?'"[65]

The Lilly Awards have also focused on activism; beginning in 2015, the awards partnered with the Dramatists Guild to release the annual report "The Count," a study of theatrical works' demographics, including race, gender, genre, and nationality.

The first publication of "The Count," which drew data from 2,508 publications, encompassed three consecutive years—2011–2012, 2012–2013, and 2013–2014. The first publication revealed a large discrepancy between not only gender, but also race, with 78 percent of the productions by men and 22 percent by women, and an examination of racial data revealed 88 percent of the productions by white people and 12 percent by people of color.[66]

"The Count" reported an increase from a 2002 report from the New York State Council on the Arts when female playwrights throughout the country totaled 17 percent, with a 5 percent increase throughout the years.[67] But numbers were low: Only 12 percent of productions were authored by writers of color during those three years, and more than half—62.6 percent of plays—were by white men from the United States, with only 14 percent by American white females. Less than a half-percent—.4—were by foreign males or females of color.[68]

The second installment of "The Count" was released in October 2018, reporting on the 2016–2017 season. There was an increase, but it was a small one: The data revealed a small uptick in the number of productions by female writers and writers of color. Despite women making up 51 percent of the American population, female writers wrote only 28.8 percent of the plays. And writers of color authored 15.1 percent of productions.[69] More than 80 percent of writers produced on American stages were white and male.

"It seemed clear that there weren't good figures anywhere on how many Off-Broadway companies were achieving anything close to parity with their hiring of theatrical offstage workers (playwrights, directors, designers, stage managers, etc.)," Catherine Porter, copresident of the League of Professional Theatre Women, said. "We now have four reports in the series. It's brought a lot of attention to the issue—surprising a number of people who, anecdotally, thought they were at or near parity."[70]

In the first release of "The Count," when studying unique writers of color by gender, 63 percent were men of color and 37 percent were women of color, and unique productions by race and gender totaled 62 percent by men of color and 38 percent by women of color.[71] Intersectionality, which was first introduced into mainstream conversation in 1992, still seemed far away.

THE MOTHERHOOD PENALTY

Lack of child care has consistently been a major contributor to the low numbers of female artists in the industry. It was even more apparent during the summer, the season of intensive programs and workshops, during which new works are often cultivated, allowing authors to see their writing performed for audiences for the first time.

Child care became another focus of the Lilly Awards in 2015, when, in collaboration with the nonprofit residency program Ryder Farm, Space on Ryder Farm was launched. The weeklong residency offered on-site child care for children between the ages of six and twelve, eliminating the need for parent artists to choose between developing their work and caring for their children. In the following years, Space on Ryder Farm had expanded, inviting children as young as three and offering two separate weeklong sessions. The new model was working to bring theaters and arts organizations out of archaic structures from a time when men were exclusively considered serous artists and able to leave their families to pursue their work. Women were and continue to be the primary caregivers, despite also creating their own art.

"Mothers do not want or need to be fully removed from their parental responsibilities in order to create theater," Julia Jordan told *Playbill* in 2015.

> And often they simply cannot leave their children behind for economic reasons. And so they opt out or simply do not apply for opportunities, especially those in the summer, that give the childless (or those with a spouse who assumes the primary caretaker role) crucial development of their work, relationships with collaborators, and visibility. [72]

The challenges of child care are hardly restricted to the summer. While various high-end extensive contracts have some maternity leave structures in place, there is no consistent child-care policy in the theater industry that is not already included within the FMLA requirements and location coverage. As a result, regional theaters, tours, and production houses that fall outside the government requirement for provision are left without any established parental leave for employees and contributing artists, which often results in artists and performers retreating from their careers to raise families, delaying or halting creative and professional advancement, as well as income.

"A woman just getting her start, historically, is difficult," Rachel Spencer-Hewitt, founder of the Parent-Artist Advocacy League, said.

> Then you get some opportunities and recognition, and your opportunities to fail are much lower. Midlife hits, and if you are at the point in your life where you want to expand to a family, you have to do that—likely at a time when you have to double down on your career, while extending your work–life balance and entering into an environment that is without empathy, because many of it is male without caregiver responsibilities.

Viewing career and family within the framework of one or the other can often cause a woman to choose a different career path and remove herself from possibilities of advancement to prioritize her family. Spencer-Hewitt added, "We have fewer women on this path, because the path has made it impossible to continue."[73]

With no established maternity leave in the United States—the only developed country that does not offer paid parental leave—and the theater industry requiring irregular hours and contract lengths, while employing artists who are working as freelancers or self-employed, the systems theaters use, if any, can be ill-suited for present-day parenting, with the archaic expectation of the mother as the primary caregiver. "There are a lot of reasons we don't have parity in the American theater, and it's not all bias," Jordan told *Playbill.* "It's culture. Systemic bias. And this is a big one. Lillian Hellman didn't have kids. You just didn't participate. You were a raiser of the society and you were a director of the society, and you had to choose. And it's just a completely bad idea."[74]

The Parent Artist Advocacy League for Performing Arts (PAAL) was founded in 2017, following the establishment of Mothers Artists Makers (MAM) in Ireland, and Parents and Careers in the Performing Arts (PIPA) in the United Kindgom. PAAL launched with a three-year plan: breaking the silence; actional solutions, initiatives, and opportunities; and parent-friendly policy and protocols.

Spencer-Hewitt had been examining the circumstances of working mothers since the birth of her own child. While chroncling her experiences on AuditioningMommy.com, parents began contacting her, sharing their own stories of micoraggressions and discrimination. Some were told they wouldn't be hired because they might go into labor or that having two children was a liability. The stories were infuriating, Spencer-Hewitt said, but they were also exposing the fact that theaters and their employees were breaking the law. The established structures and systems of the theater, which had been put in place decades ago, were not supportive of working parents.

"There's a misogynist mindset that goes into the industrialization of our artistic structure," Spencer-Hewitt commented, listing some of the accepted norms that are harmful to working parents, for example, the perception that parents aren't committed if they can't work late and that even the possibility that someone might one day have children has prevented them from being hired—a mindset known as the "motherhood penalty/fatherhood bonus." She continued,

> There are actual laws being broken, and federally protected classes of pregnant women are not being respected and our artistic structures. I believe because we have this idea that because we are artistic platform, we have a natural, inherent sense of progress, they think they couldn't possibly be doing something wrong or breaking a law that's discriminatory. . . . When an institution does not have an intentional understanding of socioeconomic responsibility, they have the potential to either discriminate on a level they can anticipate or be inconsistent where they let some moms get help and other moms they completely leave out.[75]

Along with providing information on which theaters are supportive of working parents and helping to faciliate support, the organization offers need-based grants to provide child care for parent artists in need of help.

"While the theater prides itself on being a progressive institution, it cannot say we respect a woman's choice on when she wants to have a family and you say you cannot have a family and work in this career at the same time because it's an obligation or choice for her to say either/ or," Spencer-Hewitt said.

> It's not really a choice at all. The choice is being made by the structure as opposed to by the individual. . . . I would say that true feminist theater is about finding access points for everyone, by restructuring the

practice of theater into more of a form of power sharing, as opposed to power holding.[76]

These awards, organizations, and instutions were working to establish and create change, as the demographics on Broadway remained steady. The 2017–2018 Broadway season, according to a study by the entertainment technology company ProductionPro, featured only 37 percent of female principal roles. Offstage, the numbers were no better. Only 20 percent of set designers were women, 19 percent worked in lighting, and only 4 percent were employed as sound designers. Women were the majority only in wardrobe and makeup, where 65 and 67 percent of the employees, respectively, were women, and in the category of hair and makeup, they comprised 71 percent of the employees. The numbers were especially low with regards to leadership positions on the shows: Women made up only 16 percent of writers, 19 percent of directors, and 18 percent of choreographers.[77]

Third Wave feminism, and enacting equality and intersectionality in the theater industry, had come a long way. But it still had a long way to go.

8

BROADWAY COMES TO THE *FUN HOME*

"**Y**ou have to see it to be it." Acclaimed composer Jeanine Tesori made history when she spoke those words on June 7, 2015. Tesori, along with playwright and lyricist Lisa Kron, had just become the first all-female writing team to win Best Score at the Tony Awards for the new musical *Fun Home*. Tesori and Kron's victory was only one of the historic moments the musical adaptation of Alison Bechdel's graphic memoir achieved throughout its journey to Broadway. *Fun Home*'s success marked benchmarks for both women and gay culture in an industry largely dominated by men.

"Is America ready for a musical about a middle-aged butch lesbian?" asked *Slate* before *Fun Home* began performances Off-Broadway at the Public Theater in 2013.[1] Gay men had prominently been featured on Broadway throughout the years, both as characters and creators, but gay women were largely absent—and as protagonists, let alone characters, they were almost completely absent. *Spring Awakening* featured a kiss between two gay teenagers, and *A Chorus Line*, *Falsettos*, *La Cage Aux Folles*, and *Kiss of the Spider Woman*, among many others, told the stories of gay men. But before Bechdel's story of reconciling with the memory of her father, a closeted gay man who died, ostensibly by suicide, just months after she came out to her family, lesbian protagonists were few and far between in mainstream commercial theater.

"Even musicals about women, where women are the central characters and not just a romantic lead and really have a story of their own, [are rare]," Bechdel told *Playbill* during the musical's Off-Broadway run.

"The moment with Small Alison singing about the butch delivery woman feels *huge*. To have a child sing about desire and identification; it's brilliant."[2]

THE WRITERS

Tesori and Kron were a fitting team to bring this boundary-breaking work of art to the stage. Both women had explored memories in their work, and both women had told the stories of outsiders.

Kron, the author of the critically acclaimed autobiographical plays *2.5 Minute Ride* and *Well*, was eagerly received by Bechdel to adapt her book.

"When this whole project began, the only reason I proceeded with it was because Lisa Kron would get it right," Bechdel told the *Atlantic* following *Fun Home*'s Off-Broadway opening. "I think I would have felt more trepidation if it had been anyone else, certainly if it had been a man. I knew Lisa was a lesbian. I know her work. I trusted her to get this right. I trusted that she understood the importance of representing a lesbian accurately."[3]

Bechdel's faith in Kron was well-founded. She was a founding member of the Five Lesbian Brothers, along with Maureen Angelos, Babs Davy, Dominique Dibbell, and Peg Healey, which presented works about lesbian and feminist topics. The Brothers first performed at the WOW Café in Manhattan's East Village, a venue for lesbian performing art dedicated to artistic freedom that welcomed the satirical performances that examined and mocked gender and sexual conventions.

"At the WOW Café I was in this world—this artistic world—it was a lesbian world," she told *Playbill*. "It was taken for granted. Then we went on and made all this theater based on that. We didn't have to keep coming out or explaining or justifying."[4]

Kron also wrote and performed in solo performances, two of which explored memories of her parents: *2.5 Minute Ride* and *Well*. Integrating two drastically different trips—with her family to an amusement park in Ohio and with her father to Auschwitz, where his parents, her grandparents, were killed—into a single narrative, *2.5 Minute Ride* was lauded for its harmonious composition, fusing such different stories into a single, deeply personal experience.

Ben Brantley of the *New York Times* praised it, saying, "Though any-thing but linear in its chronology it is as carefully plotted as a historian's time chart." He also commented, "That these shards of history coalesce into an illuminating whole has much to do with the accumulation of seemingly incongruous details, which come to echo off and enhance one another."[5] A "slide show" in which all the slides are blank, *2.5 Minute Ride* explored, rather than simply narrated, Kron's memories. The play-wright explained her work, saying, "Humor and horror are juxtaposed, and you might not know for a second whether you are at Auschwitz or at the amusement park. The show does not tell you when to laugh and when to be solemn. The response is up to you."[6]

Kron's mother was brought to the stage in *Well*, a self-described "play in progress" exploring the subjects of mothers and daughters, as well as physical illness as a metaphor for societal "illnesses." It's not actually a play, Kron stated, it's a "multicharacter theatrical exploration of issues of health and illness both in the individual and in a community."[7]

Declaring, "This play is not about my mother and me," the character of Lisa discusses her chronically unwell mother and recounts her past, while her mother interjects her own commentary involving her devotion to racial integration, as well as her chronic ailments. Despite almost uni-versal critical acclaim, *Well*'s Broadway run was cut short, closing after twenty-three previews and fifty-three performances. Along with Kron and her costar Jayne Houdyshell's performances, which earned both women Tony nominations, the play was praised for its unique approach to an autobiograpical performance, with the *New York Times* writing,

> *Well*, directed by Leigh Silverman, turns out to be about the mystery of human personalities, even and especially those of the people you think you know intimately. What makes *Well* much more than a clever, deconstructed theatrical riff is the way it keeps surprising itself with glimpses of an emotional depth, both murky and luminous, that goes beyond any tidy narrative.[8]

Joining Kron to bring *Fun Home* to the stage was Jeanine Tesori, a composer with a widely varied resume who created some of the most unique musicals to play Broadway, encompassing everything from a physically disfigured woman on a spiritual quest, to a black single mother in the 1960s, to a musical adaptation of an animated Hollywood block-buster.

Tesori began her composing career after years of conducting with the Off-Broadway musical *Violet*, based on Doris Betts's short story "The Ugliest Pilgrim." Following a young woman with a large scar on her face from a tragic childhood accident who embarks on a journey by bus to see a TV evangelist faith healer, *Violet* features a variety of musical styles, notably bluegrass and gospel. Tesori and lyricist and bookwriter Brian Crawley's musical daringly explored the themes of physical beauty, self-esteem, racism, faith, and forgiveness.

Premiering Off-Broadway at Playwrights Horizons in 1997, *Violet* was praised by *Variety* as "one of the most impressive small-scale tuners in recent memory,"[9] while the *New York Times* faulted it for lack of character development and depth.[10] Nevertheless, it received the Obie Award, the New York Drama Critics Circle Award for Best Musical, and the Lucille Lortel Award for Outstanding Musical. Following a critically acclaimed one-night-only concert in 2013, *Violet* opened on Broadway in 2014, seventeen years after its Off-Broadway bow.

After *Violet*'s Off-Broadway opening, Tesori served as a music arranger for several musicals and earned her first Tony nomination for Best Original Score in a 1998 revival of Shakespeare's *Twelfth Night*. Her remarkable diversity was exemplified when she returned to Broadway in 2002, having composed the music for *Thoroughly Modern Millie*. Adapted from the movie starring Julie Andrews, the musical's score featured works by Tesori and lyricist Dick Scanlan. With a book by Scanlan and Richard Morris, *Millie* followed the title character's move from a small town to 1920s New York City and her determined efforts to land a wealthy husband.

Millie's definition of modern womanhood was questionable. While defying the social norms of her small-town life by moving to New York on her own, she intended to marry a wealthy man and enjoy a life of luxury funded by her husband's paycheck. She proudly viewed herself as a modern woman, wedding for practical comfort rather than sentimental love—before she met a charming ne'er-do-well who forced her to reconsider her plan.

The lightly satiric tone of *Millie*, which won six Tony Awards, notably Best Musical and Best Actress for its leading lady, Sutton Foster, was grounded in Tesori's satiric and mischievous musical score. Packed with comic pastiche numbers with nostalgic nods to the Jazz Age–era flappers, *Millie* earned the composer her second nomination for Best Original

Score. With sly nods to classical compositions, operas, and even Gilbert and Sullivan, the score evoked thoughts of playful irony, as well as old-fashioned romance—the first hints of the chameleonic career Tesori had established for herself where she could write in almost any genre or style.

Tesori's versatility was on full display when she took a drastically different turn with her next musical, collaborating with acclaimed playwright Tony Kushner. *Caroline, or Change* opened in 2004, Off-Broadway, at the Public Theater, before transferring to Broadway just three months later, where it received five Tony nominations. Tesori's sung-through score consisted of a tapestry of different musical fabrics, fusing Motown, blues, classical music, spirituals, and Jewish Klezmer and folk music, as it follows Caroline, a single mother working as maid for a Jewish family in 1963, in Louisiana.

Caroline develops a friendship with her recently widowed employer's young son. Both political and economically driven, the musical Caroline's financial troubles, the political turmoil of the growing civil rights movement, and the assassination of John F. Kennedy. Caroline, who is instructed by Noah's stepmother to pocket the coins Noah left in his pants pockets so he will learn the value of money, voices her thoughts through songs performed by the appliances around her.

Caroline's unique story and method of telling it, which defied traditional conventions of musical theater, was praised by critics. Adam Feldman of *Time Out New York* wrote,

> The things we have come to expect in a Broadway musical—a perky heroine looking for love, a sexy young chorus, extravagant costumes and sets—are not to be found in Kushner and Tesori's ravishing and surreal examination of race, loneliness, and economics in 1963 Louisiana. The show does not try to save face with an ironic wink at musical-theater conventions; it simply ignores them and starts fresh.[11]

"In truth, it is almost too good to be good," the *New York Times* wrote of *Caroline, or Change*, which, despite critical acclaim, had a brief Broadway run of 132 performances.[12]

Feldman opined about the show's quality, asking,

> Why hasn't the theater community united behind this groundbreaking work? Half of the show's reviews at the Public were raves; the other half seemed puzzled or dismissive. . . . If Broadway theater is to

remain a force of any artistic consequence, it needs more producers like these—and an equally courageous audience. *Caroline, or Change* may not be for everyone, but it deserves to be seen by full houses of open minds. Because the show is indeed too good to be good—it's great. And there should be room for greatness, every once in a while, on the street still known as the Great White Way.[13]

Tesori also composed music for Tony Kushner's translation of Bertolt Brecht's *Mother Courage and Her Children* and the 2008 Broadway musical *Shrek the Musical*, which earned her both Tony and Drama Desk award nominations for her music. *Shrek*, adapted from the hit Dream-Works film by Tesori and Pulitzer Prize winner David Lindsay Abaire, outwardly and proudly placed the outsiders center stage, giving them the triumphant song "Let Your Freak Flag Fly," while championing the characters who were not the title characters of the classic storybooks. A departure from Tesori's previously less commercial shows, *Shrek the Musical*, with a rumored budget of approximately $25 million, was one of the most expensive musicals to open on Broadway.[14]

Tesori had built a reputation for writing strong female characters—often viewed as The Other in mainstream culture—bringing their stories to the forefront. Daryl H. Miller wrote in the *Los Angeles Times*, "Outsiders figure prominently in all of Tesori's shows, whether she initiated the project, as with *Violet*, or was asked aboard. She describes the characters as 'the people who are deemed invisible, are outside the power structure in some way.'"[15] So the pairing of Tesori and Kron to bring a boundary-breaking, genre-defying musical like *Fun Home* to New York stages seemed natural. While Bechdel was a fan of Kron's work, she was not familiar with Tesori, as she told *After Ellen*:

> I was approached with this idea to do a musical, and part of that plan was that Lisa Kron would write the book. I was like, "Hell yeah." I'll do anything Lisa Kron is involved with. That being said, I still felt a little skeptical. Like, a musical? What would that look like? I really had no idea. I didn't know Jeanine. In the original proposal Jeanine's name wasn't mentioned. She came in a little bit later. I'm trying to remember how this all happened. I said yes, and then for many years I didn't even really see anything. I didn't know what was happening. Then one day, in December of 2010, I got a CD and a script, and I was totally blown away. I had signed a contract in 2007, so, three years before I saw anything. I did meet with Lisa and talk a little bit with her,

Tonya Pinkins and Harrison Chad in *Caroline, or Change.* **Photofest (Photographer:** *Michal Daniel)*

but I didn't have any direct involvement in the process. Then they introduced me to Jeanine, and they both had lots of questions for me. Like what my process writing had been like, which was really fun to talk about with them, but I wasn't sure what they were going to do with it. When I finally saw what they had been doing, I was completely blown away. [16]

"A FAMILY TRAGICOMIC"

Published in 2006, *Fun Home: A Family Tragicomic*, received critical acclaim and landed on the *New York Times* bestseller list soon after its publication. Lauded as the best nonfiction book of the year by *Entertainment Weekly* and the best book of 2006 by *Time*, *Fun Home* was listed as one of the "1,000 novels everyone must read" by the *Guardian*. [17] Bechdel's graphic memoir, which chronicles her childhood in nonlinear style, recounting her growing up in rural Pennsylvania in her family's elegant house, to which her father devoted much of his time restoring to its Victoria aesthetic. It details her youth as a curious tomboy who rebels against the traditional feminine expectations of being a young girl, as well as her coming out as a college student.

The book illustrates the emotional distance of Bruce, Bechdel's father, from his children, devoting much of his energy to restoring the house, teaching at the local high school, and running the titular family funeral home. Bruce was often a cold, distant parent prone to outbursts of rage. After coming out to her parents in a letter mailed from college, Alison learns from her mother that her father is a closeted homosexual who has been in relationships with younger boys throughout their marriage.

Bechdel attempts to understand her father's sudden death, which was presumed by many to be a suicide and took place just months after she came out to her family and learned the truth about her father—and two weeks after his wife asked for a divorce.

Unflinchingly honest, *Fun Home* offers a blunt look into Bechdel's life. Panels are illustrated with quotes from her childhood diary in blunt, childish narrative. It also illustrates a frank examination of Alison's developing sexuality, memories of masturbation, and a unabashed recounting of her first sexual experience.

The musical's tone matched the book's, its opening scene ending with Alison stating, "Caption: Dad and I both grew up in the same small

Pennsylvania town. And he was gay, and I was gay, and he killed himself, and I became a lesbian cartoonist."

"CAPTION"

By diving into Alison's memories and chronicling her coming-of-age, *Fun Home* simulatenously narrates Alison's childhood, her teenage years and coming out in college, and her adulthood, where she attempts to reconcile with her father's death, with three different performers bringing her to life.

Fun Home was directed by Sam Gold, marking the first traditional musical directed by the iconoclastic artist. Gold had directed a number of new plays by Will Eno and Annie Baker, and revivals of Tom Stoppard's *The Real Thing* and William Inge's *Picnic*. He first directed *Fun Home* at the Public Theater's Lab in 2012, followed by its Off-Broadway run in 2013, and he approached directing with a focus on the acting ensemble, an approach that was apparent in *Fun Home*'s performance.

Adult Alison, played by Beth Malone, is the narrator of this story, revisiting and witnessing her life as scenes from her childhood played out in front of her. She remembers herself as a tomboyish ten-year-old, rebelling when her father insists she wear a dress and deliberately losing a barette he insists remain in her hair. Played by Sydney Lucas, Small Alison, a fiesty young girl, doesn't hide her love for her father, opening the show with the chlidish command, "Daddy, hey, daddy, come here, okay? I need you."[18]

As a freshman at Oberlin College, Medium Alison is more withdrawn as she comes to terms with her sexuality, falling in love with her classmate, Joan, and coming out to her family in a letter. Played by Emily Skeggs, Medium Alison declares her newfound passion in the song "I'm Changing My Major to Joan," after her first sexual experience. The heartfelt ballad, which she sings in its entirety while dressed in a polo shirt and underwear, as Joan lies asleep in her bed, joyously declares the first feelings of love. Alison witnesses her youth, at times shuddering with embarassment or with a sarcastic remove, but at moments her removed demeanor breaks as she reveals, with desperation, how much pain from her father lingers within her as an adult.

As Alison tells her own story while witnessing her past—an omnipresent figure, watching, walking through, and commenting on her history—*Fun Home* establishes her as the narrator, the main character and not The Other. Kron and Tesori ensured their musical would not attempt to fit into a heternormative world or contain an atmosphere of guilt or embarasment, like many shows they had seen:

> The characters are dealing with coming out, but the show is comfortable in its skin. And I think it's hard for people who have these issues around coming out. It's hard for women dealing with ambition who think one thing as being feminine and one thing as being masculine. I see women who can't even picture that they don't need to become men to be artists. There is a holistic way of women being integrated. The show has built into its DNA that sense of integration. If there are people who are only comfortable seeing what they've seen before, they're like, "This is in the round. I heard the word lesbian. I'm freaked out"—there's nothing we can do about that. We're not doing something that looks like other things. That being said, this has traditional theater values and bones. This works as a piece of theater. [19]

Fun Home opened in October 2013, to critical acclaim. Described as a "beautiful heartbreaker" by Ben Brantley of the *New York Times*,[20] the musical was extended four times and swept the season's Off-Broadway awards.

It was groundbreaking in more ways than one. Unlike traditional musicals centered on a leading man and an ingenue, *Fun Home*'s central relationship was between a father and daughter, and there was no joyful reconciliation at the conclusion of the show. Instead, *Fun Home* portrayed a woman attempting to make peace with her past—peace that she could only make on her own, because the man whose mysteries haunted her was dead. Instead, audiences were invited into Alison's memories, seeing the events through Alison's eyes. And while romance was a part of the story, it wasn't the driving conflict.

Along with its groundbreaking content, the musical's structure defied classic conventions of musical theater. Rather than an "I Want" song, in which the musical's protagonist establishes expectations for the story, one of the first few songs in *Fun Home* is "He Wants," depicting Bruce's wife and children scrambling to meet his exacting standards as they nervously clean the house.

Tesori and Kron's score used period-appropriate musical stylings to evoke the atmosphere of the different times the show captured. When Small Alison, overhearing her parents bitterly scream at one another, attempts to escape her unhappy home, her living room transforms into a stage of a musical variety show strongly resembling *The Partridge Family*. The entire family happily sings the lyrics, "Everything's all right, babe, when we're togethah/'Cuz you are like a raincoat made out of love."[21] But the song's ebulliently fizzy happiness quickly fades; as the other characters dance offstage, Bruce remains onstage, singing alone.

Bruce fuels his obsession with apperance with his obsessive maintenance of his house, with its orderly and precise appearance masking the tumultuous unhappiness within its walls—and within him. It is then projected onto Alison, as he expects her to dress in feminine clothing. She stubbornly refuses, failing to maintain his carefully cultivated image of a perfect family.

Alison's resistance to appearing as a typically feminine child enrages her father, demonstrated in a moving scene in which, preparing for a party, she rebels against his demand that she put on a pale pink dress, declaring, "I despise this dress. What's the matter with boy's shirts and pants?" Her father's only reply is, "You're a girl," before intimidating her into obeying by threatening that people at the party will talk about how she is not dressed like everyone else.

In a moment of melancholy foreshadowing, after hearing her father's burst of temper, Small Alison, chastened and grasping for her father's approval, replies by singing, "Maybe not right now"—the same melody her mother sang earlier in the show, resigned to pretending to be someone she is not to please the overbearing man in the house. Another painful scene depicts Bruce adomishing Small Alison as she draws a cartoon, roughly instructing her how to "make it better" and angrily dismissing her, even after she, fearful of his angry reaction, desperately says, "No, I like the one you did, Daddy."[22]

Alison is only ten years old when she receives her first glimpse of identity—while sitting with her father in a diner. She sees a woman, described by herself as "old-school butch," and immediately recognizes something of herself in her.[23]

"I was spellbound," Bechdel recalled of the moment to NPR.

My jaw dropped. My father saw me looking at this woman, and he whipped his head around and said, "Is that how you want to look?" And there was so much going [on] in that exchange. In that moment, I recognized that woman: I identified with her; I wanted her; I wanted to be her. And I knew that that was completely unacceptable.[24]

That moment is crystalized in *Fun Home*, captured in the moving song "Ring of Keys." Gazing upon the woman, the young girl attempts to describe her emotions, struggling to find the words that articulate her feelings of identity. As her confusion evolves into clarity, she sings, at first in a state of confusion, in a way that escalates into rapturous declaration, "Your swagger and your bearing and the just-right clothes you're wearing/Your short hair and your dungarees and your lace-up boots/And your keys, oh, your ring of keys!" The song concludes with her slowly declaring, with growing awareness and wonder, "I know you."[25]

It's in college that Alison truly establishes her own identity, but she is unable to escape thoughts of her father. She announces early in the show, "Caption: My dad and I were exactly alike." After a pause she adds, "Caption: My dad and I were *nothing* alike." As an adult, she wonders, "I can't find my way through. Just like you. Am I just like you?"[26]

Both statements are clearly, painfully true: While both Alison and Bruce were gay, their reactions to their sexuality could not be more different. Bruce lived a painfully closeted, outwardly traditional life as a husband and father to three children. But his desires led him to pursue local boys, including young, underage ones. One particularly painful scene shows Bruce seducing a local handyman and former student in his parlor, while his children play nearby and his wife sits in another room. Playing a melancholy melody on the piano, Helen is achingly aware of what is happening under her roof while their three children watch television, happily ignorant. Every member of the family is singing in this scene, but each melody is separate. The house is loud, but no one is in harmony.

"ONE OF THE PREVIOUSLY MOST INVISIBLE CREATURES IN THE CULTURAL WORLD"

Alison was a character unlike many had seen onstage before, and her presence was welcome. Following the show's Off-Broadway opening,

Adam Feldman, of *Time Out New York*, declared, "As gay men increasingly claim pride of place in musical theater, gay women remain largely invisible there."[27] Charles McNulty of the *Los Angeles Times* added,

> How many musicals have you seen with a lesbian protagonist? This is pioneering territory. . . . These are characters you may not have encountered before on stage, but you've seen them on campuses and in shopping malls—something in their dress and demeanor marking them as unconventional, as "other."[28]

Many members of the queer community responded with happiness, with professor and author Jill Dolan writing in the *Feminist Spectator*,

> Isn't it something that such a character can be *played* on stage now? So many of us have truly never seen anything like our lives being embodied on stage in front of our eyes. What a miracle to see this show performed last week. What a miracle to have same-sex marriage legalized in New Jersey last week, so LGBT people can marry if they wish. I left the theater a week ago feeling strangely *seen* and not quite sure how to think about that: I've spent so many years watching for lesbian subtext and trying to read queerness underneath protestations of heterosexuality. To see lesbian desire as the *text* felt almost startling—and more wonderful than I can even begin to describe.[29]

The way in which *Fun Home* presented Alison was a deliberate and careful approach by its creators. Kron told *Slate* that, in recent musicals, "there was a moment where someone would say the word *lesbian* as a non sequitur because it was funny." She continued, "I'd be so on board, and then I'd be slapped in the face by it. It was just like, *This character's a joke. This is not a person.*" Instead, in *Fun Home*, Kron and Tesori humanized Alison—and introduced audiences to a character they likely had never encountered in a musical and, as Kron described a butch lesbian, "one of the previously most invisible creatures in the cultural world."[30]

Representation was equally as important to Tesori, who told *Slate*, "I wanted to see a woman who was close to my age on stage. And I wanted to see a gay character at eight years old—I wanted to reveal the things in musical theater that I haven't seen yet."[31] Praised as "miraculous" by *New York Magazine*, *Fun Home* was recognized for its unconventional structure and the powerful impact it carried:

Much will be out of place before the evening is over, and the question of who is the actual protagonist will form an important part of the drama. But this sideways approach to introducing unusual characters and issues is more than just an effective way to set up an unusual story; it also signals the show's radical formal intentions. That *Fun Home* carries them out so thoroughly, while retaining the musical theater's unparalleled capability for expressing emotion and color, is something of a miracle. [32]

Tesori's chameleonic composing abilities resulted in a score that included an exuberant children's number in the style of the Jackson 5, a joyful aria of first love, and a climactic emotional collapse that culminates in Bruce's death. This wide range of emotions resulted in an unconventional and deeply emotional musical. Describing the score, Linda Winer of *Newsday* wrote, "Tesori . . . finds just the right internal voices for conflicted moods, with unpredictable melodies over a strong back and repeated rythms." [33]

A previously unheard voice *Fun Home* amplified is that of Helen, Alison's mother. Played by Judy Kuhn in the Off-Broadway and Broadway productions, Helen is an at times peripherial character, sometimes anxiously and most times sadly existing in the background of Alison's memories.

Helen is seen in Alison's memories, returning from local theater rehearsals, attempting to practice the piano while Small Alison distracts her with her chatter, and reluctantly informing Medium Alison that her father is gay. It's when Medium Alison visits her family from college after learning the truth about her father that her mother finally erupts in an outpouring of emotion. "Days and Days" serves as a somber and melancholy look at her life and everything that was sacrificed in her devotion to being a wife and mother, her devotion to her marriage to a brilliant but tormented man. And when looking back, Helen realizes her own life was lost in an endless series of tasks while taking care of other people.

The audience has learned little about Helen throughout the musical— she formerly aspired to be an actress but now performs in local theater productions, she plays the piano, and she and Bruce lived in Germany after getting married before returning to Pennsylvania to continue the family business. The audience witnesses angry scenes between Helen and Bruce, seeing his explosive temper erupting. After Alison comes out, Helen describes herself as being "really at odds" with the news and warning her daughter against "romanticizing this path" before abruptly saying, "Alison, your father has had affairs with men."[34] In a seemingly short phone call, Helen informs Alison that Bruce's relationships have been ongoing throughout their entire marriage. Alison tells Joan she doesn't want to talk or think about it.

When Alison returns to Pennsylvania from college to visit her parents, Helen finally gives voice to her anger, saying, "I'm sick of it. I'm sick of cooking for him, and I'm sick of cleaning this museum," and sharing a memory of Bruce losing his temper due to his repressed sexuality.[35] Seemingly stunned, Alison says, "I don't know how you've done it," to which her mother responds with the song "Days and Days," an outpouring of grief concerning the opportunities she missed, listing the daily obligations of a mother—"lunches and car rides and shirts and socks and grades and piano," before expressing years of grief in the single line, "and no one clocks the day you disappear."[36]

Reflecting on the societal obligations that trapped her, Helen laments, "Days made of bargains I made because I thought as a wife I was meant to and now my life is shattered and laid bare." The music crescendos as she repeats, "Days and days and days and days," before erupting in the same refrain Alison sang as the show opened: "Welcome to our house on Maple Avenue. See how we polish and we shine."[37] While adult Alison sang the refrain in a distanced, even sarcastic, manner, Helen erupts in trembling soprano. To Alison, the house is a memory viewed from a distance, but to Helen it is her life, a thankless symbol of everything to which she has devoted her life and from which she has received so little.

In many musicals, the wife is a secondary character, if she is a character at all. Stories are often driven by the romantic pursuit of a leading man and a female ingenue, the dramatic tension driven by the question of whether they will find one another and seemingly live a heteronormative life together. At times, both partners are leading roles, for example, the Baker's Wife in *Into the Woods*, but oftentimes wives are firmly established as supporting characters, for instance, Abigail Adams in *1776*, Mrs. MacAfee in *Bye Bye Birdie*, and Golde in *Fiddler on the Roof*.

"For us, it was very important that this wife not remain invisible," Kron told the *New York Times* of Helen. "We were also addressing this character as she has largely been portrayed in the theater—the long-suffering wife, in the background, some kind of satellite. It's just absurd how little we have expected from our female characters onstage."[38]

Helen's song, a single number performed late in the show, offers piercing insight into the woman, fully illuminating the impassioned emotions that were glimpsed throughout the show—anger, disappointment, and regret. In a moment of subtle foreshadowing as the musical begins, the family scrambles to make the house meet Bruce's standards, singing together, "We're a typical family quintet," and Helen quietly adds, "And yet—."[39]

In marked contrast to musicals in which a character finally experiences a climactic breakthrough, Helen's song does not conclude with a declaration of change or a triumphant expression of independence. Instead, she ends by addressing her daughter, commanding, quietly but powerfully, "Don't you come back here. I didn't raise you to give up your days like me."[40] One song, "Days and Days," was one of the most feminist moments in an already extraordinarily feminist show, revealing in just a few words how societal restrictions led a talented woman to abandon a promising career to raise children in a small town and offering hope to the next generation. Helen's command to her daughter attempts to free her from repeating what she saw while growing up. While inspiring as Helen tries to protect her daughter from repeating what she views as her mistakes, her declaration is also devastating, as she makes no mention of reclaiming her own life.

Continuing one family's cycle is a clear theme in *Fun Home*, a spectre hovering over Adult Alison as she watches her life unfold, at times standing directly behind her younger self as she interacts with Bruce. When Alison goes on a drive with her father, nervously anticipating that they will talk about their sexualities and foster a new connection, she is greatly disappointed; her father remains remote and closed off, refusing to discuss it with her. When Bruce reflects on his youth, saying, "Lots of boys messed around, but I always knew," Alison eagerly jumps at the chance to relate, chiming in with, "Dad, me too! . . . I was like you," but he doesn't seem to hear her.[41]

Father–daughter relationships frequently drive a subplot of a musical. In *Sweeney Todd*, *Fiddler on the Roof*, *110 in the Shade*, *Violet*, *Carousel*, and *Ragtime*, among many others, daughters are supporting characters, but rarely outside of Shakespeare's canon do the relationships between a father and daughter drive the plot of a musical. In *Fun Home*, Alison and Bruce's relationship is the story, and the musical dives into the complex and painful emotions that come with it.

Tesori and Kron musicalize the familiarities between Bruce and Alison, with different characters echoing the same melody: Along with Small Alison repeating her mother's expression, "Maybe not right now . . ." after Medium Alison's first sexual experience at college, she asks herself, "Am I falling into nothingness or flying into something so sublime?"[42] —the same phrase Bruce himself utters—"And I'm falling into nothingness or flying into something so sublime" in "Edges of the World," his final song before his death.[43]

NATIONAL ATTENTION

After four extensions, *Fun Home* closed at the Public Theater. Rumors of a Broadway transfer circled. The musical was named a finalist for the Pulitzer Prize for Drama, along with Annie Baker's *The Flick* and Madeleine George's *The (Curious Case of the) Watson Intelligence*. *Fun Home* did not win, but it did transfer to Broadway. As befitted the daring, groundbreaking show, as it moved to Broadway, it was reenvisioned and restaged from its performance in the proscenium theater at the Public for the Circle in the Square, a theater in the round. This change excited Sam Gold, who told *Slant*,

> As soon as I was presented with the idea of moving the show uptown, I immediately thought of Circle in the Square. I knew the strength of the show had to do with a kind of intimacy. I didn't want to sit in the back of one of those old Shubert houses and feel so far away. So I said to the producers, "I want to do this so that people can come see it on Broadway and the show is more intimate than it was before." People should think, "I'm getting the experience of *Fun Home* more now."[44]

Before its opening at the Circle in the Square Theatre, *Fun Home* received nationwide attention when the graphic novel inspired controversy in Charleston, South Carolina. Bechdel's book had been included in the College of Charleston's College Reads! program, in which one book was selected and students were encouraged but not required to read the book with the intention of fostering conversation on campus. Following the book's selection, state representative Garry Smith said a constituent's daughter attending the college complained about the book—specifically, its addressing of gay and lesbian themes. Smith then proposed cutting

$52,000 from the College of Charleston and $17,142 from the University of South Carolina Upstate, where the book *Out Loud: The Best of Rainbow Radio* had been assigned, from the state's budget.[45]

Smith justified his actions, saying, "I think the university has to be reasonable and sensible to the feelings and beliefs of their students. That was totally ignored here."[46] Tweeting that Bechdel's memoir could be considered "pornography," Smith told the *New York Times*, "I was trying to hold the university accountable. Their stance is 'Even if you don't want to read it, we'll shove it down your throat.' It's not academic freedom—it's academic totalitarianism."[47] On Twitter, he claimed the book referred to Christians as terrorists, also saying, "Because I I [*sic*] were to give this book to a seventeen-year-old I would be arrested." Moreover, he asserted that two pages of the book, depicting women engaged in a sexual act, constituted "pornography" and declared that the College Reads! program was "purely about promotion, not debate or critical thinking."[48]

In response, the entire cast, as well as Tesori, Kron, and Bechdel herself, traveled to Charleston, where they performed a concert production of the play at an off-campus theater and participated in question-and-answer sessions. Both performances were sold out, and Bechdel told Out.com that audiences responded strongly to "Changing My Major to Joan," sung by Medium Alison after her first sexual experience with a woman. The soaring ballad described her wish for a major in "sex with Joan" and a "foreign study to Joan's inner thighs, a seminar in Joan's ass in her Levi's."

"The audience so wanted to see that," Bechdel told *Slate* while reflecting on her own personal reaction as well, adding, "especially the students who are having this very difficult time with their college. . . . I think I've gotten quite complacent in my old age, seeing how much progress has been made in terms of gay stuff. It was a wake-up call. There's still a lot of work to be done."[49]

While Kron and Tesori's musical was far from typical Broadway entertainment, the strong reviews and the story's relevance facilitated the transfer, establishing the groundbreaking *Fun Home* on Broadway—the first musical on Broadway to feature a butch lesbian protagonist and the fifth Tony-nominated musical to be written entirely by women.

The statistics for women on Broadway were bleak and had been for a long time. The only Tony Award for Best Score to go to a musical without a male writing partner had gone to a woman just two years prior, when Cyndi Lauper won for composing *Kinky Boots*.

Inequality in the theater has been credited to a variety of circumstances, notably conscious and unconscious bias. Tesori and Kron weighed in, telling *Playbill*, "Men are often given opportunities based on their potential, and women are given opportunities based on their accomplishments. The only way to learn how to do theater is to do theater. And, if you don't give young women chances, if you don't let women develop their work."

"Failures are not celebrated the way they should be," Tesori added. "And we know that failure, not in context, is 'They failed' instead of 'What are they after? What are they going for? What in their careers have they been searching for?'"[50]

While often discussed, the number of female creatives being produced on Broadway had not seen a significant shift in recent years. Kron told *Playbill* she thought that diversity, while crucial to theater, was possible but not always welcomed. "If someone wanted to change [it], they could change it," she said.

> They would bring more vibrance into the theater. I'm also not interested in the argument in terms of fairness. I'm interested in why it's important in terms of the quality of art and what theater is about. I think theater is not actually about looking at people who are like you. Theater is about what happens when people unlike each other [collide]—that's what happens on a stage. That's what drama is made of—when people unlike you reach across that divide. And when that can happen on the stage, the play is better. When that can happen in the audience, the experience of the theater is better.[51]

"LESBIANS JUST AREN'T SEXY"

Restaged in the round at the Circle in the Square Theatre, *Fun Home* opened on April 19, 2015, just a few days before the U.S. Supreme Court began hearing oral arguments on whether gay marriage is a constitutional right and whether marriages performed in states where it had been legalized must be recognized in states where it had not. *Fun Home*'s timing was fortuitous.

Skepticism pervaded *Fun Home*'s transfer, with many wondering how a musical featuring young children gyrating on coffins and exploring the memory of a possible suicide would find an audience. But it opened to strong reviews, with the *New York Times* stating that it "pumps oxygenating fresh air into the cultural recycling center that is Broadway."[52] *Variety* wrote, "This show (a finalist for the Pulitzer) could be staged on the back of a truck and still break your heart."[53]

The question of how to market the show, however, weighed on the producers. Should *Fun Home* be advertised as a lesbian musical? How could it reach as many people as possible without abandoning the essence of the show or perpetuating the idea that queer characters do not belong on a Broadway stage? In *Fun Home*, the main character—played by three different actors, nonetheless—was a lesbian. How could *Fun Home*'s history-making achievement in representation be celebrated without alienating potential audience members who could be moved and educated by its story? And, at the same time, how could it honor being a "lesbian musical" without being reductive?

"Lesbians just aren't sexy!" Bechdel told *Rolling Stone* shortly after *Fun Home*'s Tony victory. "Not in the conventional theatrical or popular-cultural sense. Lesbians go against every traditional notion of romance. How to make that character appealing to people who aren't lesbians was a challenge."[54]

The producers hired SpotCo, an advertising agency that worked on numerous hit Broadway shows. *Fun Home* had hardly shied away from its subject matter, with the cast performing at LGBT centers and partnering with businesses that supported LGBT rights, but its logo—the outline of a house with a child leaning against an adult—hardly advertised its specific content. In attempting to advertise the story's universal themes of family, loss, and grief, the team ran the risk of downplaying the themes that made the show so unique.

Unlike many other shows about homosexuality, *Fun Home* did not feature a triumphant anthem of pride—a common act-one closing number in musicals. The show did not advocate for inclusion of a group on behalf of a large social change; instead, it offered a deeply personal look at two people whose lives were affected by their sexuality.

Tom Greenwald, SpotCo's cofounder and chief strategy officer, said the marketing team had called *Fun Home* a "lesbian suicide musical" in jest. When explaining his strategy to the *Atlantic*, he said the main goal was to "make sure that it's never ever associated specifically with the plot or subject matter. . . . And make sure that people realize that it's a beautiful, universal family story of self-identification, reflection, and, ultimately, hope."[55]

A "RING OF KEYS" MOMENT

The 2015 Tony Awards were different from pervious years in many ways. Unlike many previous years, the Best Muscial category was a toss-up. Four shows were nominated: the Shakespearean send-up of musical theater *Something Rotten!*, the Gerswhin movie-to-musical *An American in Paris*, the macabre murderous love story *The Visit*, and *Fun Home*. There was no clear winner in sight, and the race between *Fun Home* and *An American in Paris* was surprisingly tight in the weeks leading up to the Tonys.

Fun Home was nominated for a total of twelve Tony Awards: Best Book, Best Score, Best Director, Best Leading Actor, Best Leading Actress, Best Supporting Actress (three times), Best Scenic Design, Best Lighting Design, Best Orchestrations, and Best Musical. With six female nominees—four for acting, one for book, and one for score—*Fun Home* set a Tony record. When the nominations were announced, ticket sales for *Fun Home* hit $392,450—the first musical to reach that amount at the Circle in the Square Theatre.[56]

If *Fun Home* took home Best Musical, the win would not only be momentous for the LGBTQ community, but also history-making for female and female-identifying people in the industry. Winning Best Musical almost inevitably spikes ticket sales for a show, ensuring a longer run on Broadway, and, for the scrappy, small musical that had defied the odds, the award would mark a victorious end to a long journey.

But *Fun Home* had some stiff competition: *An American in Paris*, the stage adaptation of Vincente Minnelli's Oscar-winning 1951 film, packed with songs by George and Ira Gershwin, had opened nine days before *Fun Home* and also received twelve Tony nominations. Adapted from the Gene Kelly vehicle, the lush romantic musical was described as "rhapsodic" and "just plain gorgeous" by the *New York Times*[57] and a "dazzling achievement" by *USA Today*.[58]

It was a critical darling among the nominators, receiving twelve Drama Desk Award nominations and eight from the Outer Critics Circle—awards that *Fun Home* had swept in 2014, following its Off-Broadway run at the Public Theater. But the popularity of *An American in Paris* proved effective: Speculation that the old-fashioned, traditional, big-budget $11.5 million show would defeat the small, edgy musical swept the community.

The two presumed front-runners couldn't have been more different: *Fun Home*'s Broadway production budget was $5.2 million, while *An American in Paris* came in at $11.5 million.[59] *Fun Home* was performed by a cast of nine, while *An American in Paris* featured more than twenty performers onstage. The protagonist of *Fun Home* was a butch lesbian, while the romance driving the plot of *An American in Paris* was a traditional heterosexual pairing between a leading man and an ingenue.

Predictions for the big night flooded the message boards, with many predicting that *An American in Paris* would win Best Musical, while Best Book and Best Score would go to *Fun Home*. A nationwide tour of *An American in Paris* was expected, while *Fun Home*'s appeal outside of New York was questionable, demonstrated by the protests against Bechdel's book in South Carolina, as well as at Duke University.[60]

Early in the night, *Fun Home* won Best Book and Best Score. Accepting their awards, Tesori and Kron made history as the first all-female writing team to take home Tony Awards for those categories. But the joy felt by many women in the theater community was dampened because those acceptance speeches—along with other creative awards—were not included in the broadcast.

This had been a subject of conversation prior to the awards, when a petition circulated requesting that the awards be included in the broadcast, stressing the importance of representation and young girls seeing women accept these awards, and highlighting the fact that so few female composers had won Best Original Score and just four musicals written by women have been nominated for Best Musical, adding, "This year there is a chance to show girls that someone who composes and writes a Broadway musical can look like them."[61]

The online petition received 2,276 supporters before the awards, but the acceptance speeches were not included on the broadcast in full, instead being announced during the commercial breaks, and snippets totaling about ten seconds aired later in the night.

Both Tesori and Kron's speeches included calls to action that *Fun Home*'s history-making accomplishments not be one-hit wonders and that gender diversity/parity continue to increase on Broadway. When accepting the award for Best Book, Kron cited a dream in which she discovered that her apartment had rooms she didn't know were there, saying,

> We all live in this big house. And we've all been sitting in the same one or two main rooms, thinking that this was the whole house. And this season, some lights got turned on in some other rooms. And we're all like, "Oh my God, this house is so much bigger than I thought! . . . All those other rooms have always been there, and there have always been really interesting people in them, doing ravishing things. And wouldn't it be so great if, after this season, we didn't all just go back to the living room?" This has been the most successful season in Broadway history because all of us have been going into these amazing rooms in our house where we live together that we haven't been before. Our house is so big. Please let's don't go back into the living room.[62]

"I didn't realize that a career in music was available to women until 1981," Tesori said when accepting the award for Best Score.

> I saw the magnificent Linda Twine conduct "The Lady and Her Music," Lena Horne. And that was my "Ring of Keys" moment, which, by the way, is not a song of love, it's a song of identification. Because for girls, you have to see it to be it. And I'm so proud to be standing here with Lisa Kron. We stand on the shoulders of other women who've come before us: Mary Rogers, Tania Leon, Linda Twine.[63]

Fun Home won five of the twelve Tony Awards for which it had been nominated. Along with Best Book and Best Score, Best Director went to Sam Gold, Best Actor in a Musical went to Michael Cerveris for his performance as Bruce, and it won Best Musical.

An especially powerful moment at that year's Tonys took place when Sydney Lucas sang "Ring of Keys." Songs about gay identity had been performed before at the Tonys, but never before had a song about a woman identifying with another woman been seen on the major network broadcast. A crucial opportunity to advertise a show, the selected musical number for the Tonys is typically a large ensemble performance or features a high-profile star, demonstrating the high performance value of the production. But *Fun Home* performed a simple, meaningful ballad sung by a child.

Jesse Green of *New York Magazine*/Vulture wrote of the decision,

> Instead of misrepresenting the musical with one of its funny, catchy numbers or freaking everyone out with one of its dark, regretful arias, they sent 11-year-old Sydney Lucas onto the stage of Radio City Music Hall, into the homes of however many million were watching on CBS, to sing "Ring of Keys." That's the song in which Lucas's character, the prepubescent Alison Bechdel, life-changingly identifies with a butch deliverywoman she sees at a diner. Socking it directly into the eyes of whatever slice of America actually follows the awards, she was part of something unquestionably new, not so much because of the moment's proto-lesbian content as because of its joy. Take that, dancing cats![64]

It was an evening of victory for women at the Beacon Theatre, where 33 percent of the Tony-eligible shows were directed by women—a 20 percent increase from 2014.[65] Along with *Fun Home*'s wins, women won Best Direction of a Play (Marianne Elliott for *The Curious Incident of the Dog in the Night-Time*), Best Scenic Design of a Play (Bunny Christie for *The Curious Incident of the Dog in the Night-Time*, along with Finn Ross), Best Costume Design of a Musical (Catherine Zuber for the revival of *The King and I*), Best Scenic Design for a Play (Bunny Christie for *The Curious Incident of the Dog in the Night-Time*, along with Finn Ross), and Best Lighting Design (Natasha Katz for *An American in Paris*).

In the press room, Tesori reflected on the night's achievements, expressing her hope that it would motivate more women to pursue working in the theater. "We just hope that it will inspire other people," she said.

> We need to enlist women to write music for musicals as a career—to start when they're teenagers. You [Kron] said something that was so smart: You need to . . . do it again and again. And again. And again. That's the way you learn. You can't learn just by studying it. You have to do it. And live theater is expensive. It's not a novel. You can't do it by yourself. You have to have other people with you.[66]

"A HUGE CULTURAL WAVE"

Change was sweeping the streets outside of the theater. A few weeks after the Tony Awards, on June 26, 2015, the U.S. Supreme Court ruled on *Obergefell v. Hodges*, declaring that the fundamental right to marry is guaranteed to same-sex couples in all fifty states. The Broadway community burst into celebration, and for the *Fun Home* cast, the moment was especially joyful.

"It's all just been about trying to be seen," *Fun Home* star Beth Malone said of the ruling. "Just see us, see us as we are right in front of you, as these couples who are going to live their lives side by side; that is who we are, that's what this is. Now everyone will see that we are married just like you are married."[67]

"I guess there are moments in history where the tide of change can't be stopped, and this feels like one of those moments that people's hearts and minds are opening up to each other and focus on the right things for once," Cerveris told *Playbill*.

> When you feel like you're on the right side of history with your colleagues and friends and audiences it's a great place to work. I think in most ways our play is the most eloquent speech we could give. Alison's story that she was courageous enough to give the world and loan to us in the hands of Jeanine and Lisa makes an extraordinarily strong argument for seeing each other and learning to love each other and ourselves and our differences. And that's the message we would most want to put into the world anyway.[68]

Following that night's performance, a rainbow flag was walked onto the set during the curtain call, and Beth Malone ran the perimeter of the stage, wearing it as a cape, declaring it was an "amazing time to be an American." She continued, "We owe this night to the people who came before us."[69]

Sydney Lucas's understudy, twelve-year-old Gabby Pizzolo, also reflected on the night, saying, "Ever since I knew anything about this show, I was waiting for that day to happen. It was an amazing feeling to be alive on that night."[70]

Fun Home's impact on young people was not lost on Malone, who reflected on it as follows:

If I had been exposed to this material at age eleven, I think that I would have felt an inner strength and pride grow inside of me that, instead, I had to manifest way later in my life. I feel like there was a hidden part of me as I grew up that I definitely didn't give honor to. It was a coating of shame around this part of me that was a true part of me that was something to explore, unearth, and celebrate. [71]

In 2015, it seemed like the perfect time for *Fun Home* to be playing on Broadway and celebrating its victory, as progressive events were sweeping the country. President Obama declared that "playing like a girl means you're a badass" when congratulating the U.S. women's national soccer team on their World Cup victory, leading tech companies to begin offering parental leave for both men and women, and the portrayal of trans characters in entertainment saw significant progress—Caitlyn Jenner was featured on the cover of *Vanity Fair*, transgender activist Laverne Cox was featured in *Orange Is the New Black* and produced and starred in the documentary *Free CeCe*, and the series *Transparent* swept the Emmys.

"*Fun Home* absolutely rode the crest of this huge, cultural wave," Malone said.

People made pilgrimages to see it from all over the world. One night we played to ambassadors from fifteen different countries where homosexuality is a crime punishable by law. It felt like hearts and minds were changing that night. Not just in the United States, but internationally . . . I feel like the world was ready for *Fun Home* when it happened. [72]

Fun Home continued to infuse popular culture, a significant moment taking place when Medium Alison's love anthem, "Changing My Major," was performed on *Late Night with Seth Meyers*. Emily Skeggs, who played Medium Alison, Colindrez, and Malone gave a six-minute performance, with a full scene introducing the moment, including a preamble and kiss between the two women before Skeggs sang the song. *Fun Home* was the first Broadway musical to perform on Meyers's show, and Bechdel was interviewed by Meyers following the performance.

The publicity translated into ticket sales: *Fun Home*, playing in a theater with just 730 seats—Broadway's second-smallest theater—was predicted to bring in more than $600,000 in sales by June 8. [73] It played at the Circle in the Square Theatre until September 2016, after twenty-six previews and 582 regular performances.[74]

A national tour of the show launched in October 2016, recouping its investment in just seven months. The little show that few thought could succeed on Broadway had exceeded expectations. As Shoshana Greenberg wrote in *Women and Hollywood* when reflecting on the show's closing,

> *Fun Home* proved that musicals can tell complex stories about women not often represented in our culture and that those musicals can be written by women and be successful on Broadway, a risk-averse place where audiences are assumed to gravitate toward the mainstream. *Fun Home* may be a small chamber musical, but the implications of this are huge.[75]

9

REVIVALS ECLIPSED BY MILESTONES

Change had actually happened, and all signs pointed toward more to come. At the 2015 Tonys, an all-female writing team had won the highest honors in the American theater community, and they did it by writing a show about a butch lesbian protagonist. Seven women were awarded trophies that night. There were only two categories in which women had been nominated and did not win, and the evening's victories marked the highest number of women to win Tonys in the history of the awards.[1] With this monumental victory, the future for women in theater looked bright—at first glance.

The question was, Would this change continue? Would *Fun Home*'s achievements actually get more women produced?

"I AM HEIDI"

The same season of *Fun Home*'s remarkable achievements, a notable disappointment also took place. A highly anticipated revival of Wendy Wasserstein's *The Heidi Chronicles* opened on Broadway, with *Mad Men* star Elisabeth Moss in the title role. It seemed the perfect time to revive the famously feminist play. *Girls*, Lena Dunham's exploration of millenial female life, was in its fifth season, and Sheryl Sandberg's 2013 treatise *Lean In* had sparked heated dialogue about women's careers and the elusive work–life balance.

Slated to direct was Pam MacKinnon, a Tony winner who had risen to Broadway prominence by infusing classic revivals with present-day relevance. To her, the play was not dated at all—"in any way, shape, or form," she told *Playbill*.

> I wish it were dated more than it is, but it does feel like the issues of today and fulfilling your potential and having it all—there's this complicated psychology of being a woman, as well as the sociology of making your way in your own career and thoughts of family—are still very, very current in our country.[2]

"Having it all," a phrase spoken frequently in Wasserstein's script, had, in modern colloqueal terms, become a shorthand for having both a career and a family. Its roots can be traced to Helen Gurley Brown's bestselling 1982 book *Having It All: Love, Success, Sex, Money . . . Even If You're Starting with Nothing*, guiding women who seek more in life—love, money, sex—to fullfil their desires. Ironically, the book rarely mentions children, and Brown was strongly opposed to its title. But rather than empowering women to seek more from life, since the book's publication the idea of "having it all" has become both an onus and a chestnut.[3]

The phrase continued to persist, but, in 2014, a revision was suggested. In 2014, New York senator Kirsten Gillibrand, a former lawyer and mother of two, said the following about the phrase "having it all": "I think it's insulting. What are you 'having'? A party? Another slice of pie? 'All' implies that a woman staying home with her kids is somehow living a life half-full. What we're really talking about is doing it all. How do we help women do all the things they want to do?"[4]

Heidi's return to Broadway, chronicling the decades of her life, inspired reflection on what had and hadn't changed since the play's first production, and one of the most notable differences was the economic circumstances that either propelled women forward or prevented them from "having it all." When Heidi was attending college and graduate school, and then writing a book, her job prospects differed greatly and her student loan debt—two frequently cited reasons for postponing marriage and family—would have been significantly less than that of a woman in 2015.

During the years leading up to *Heidi*'s premiere, the United States saw a consistent growth of economic activity, with 18.7 million new jobs generated from 1982 to 1989. The number of women in professional roles increased 5 percent, from 44 to 49 percent, between 1972 and 1985, and women in managerial roles increased from 20 to 36 percent.[5] The United States was one of the top employers of women in 1990, but in 2014, the *New York Times* reported that women in the workforce were declining, with more than half—61 percent—of women who were not working saying they were leaving because of family responsibilities.[6]

The choice between work and family—which often wasn't a choice at all—was examined in the *Atlantic*, where Anne-Marie Slaughter penned a lengthy essay titled "Why Women Still Can't Have It All." Scrutinizing the social, political, economic, and even technical contributions to the challenges of managing both a career and a family, Slaughter concluded that the current systems make the elusive balance impossible. Recalling a lecture, she wrote of the many young women who were already weighing the sacrifices they expected to make to pursue professional and personal fulfillment. Before they had the jobs or partners, they were thinking about what they would have to compromise to keep both:

> Women of my generation have clung to the feminist credo we were raised with, even as our ranks have been steadily thinned by unresolvable tensions between family and career, because we are determined not to drop the flag for the next generation. But when many members of the younger generation have stopped listening, on the grounds that glibly repeating "you can have it all" is simply airbrushing reality, it is time to talk. . . . I still strongly believe that women can "have it all" (and that men can too). I believe that we can "have it all at the same time." But not today, not with the way America's economy and society are currently structured.[7]

Women had found themselves in a world that had changed but hadn't changed its expectations for the women in it. Rising education costs, lessening job security, and fewer professional and practical benefits had left many women overextended, trying to succeed while questioning what role they wanted, or were supposed, to play.

"Many women do not have careers or children. And this is not always by choice," wrote Tina Rodia in the *Washington Post*, in an article featuring the subhead, "I'm not a high-powered, corporate mother. Have I failed as a woman?" She continued, "Not all women can have or want to have children. Having married in my late thirties, I may be too old and economically disadvantaged to have a baby. Having no career, and no baby, am I arguably even a woman at all? Or am I a woman who has nothing at all?"[8]

Similar feelings had been articulated by Heidi, who, rather than writing an op-ed, shared her thoughts in a speech. When asked to speak on the subject, "Women, Where Are We Going?" at Miss Crain's East Coast girls' high school, Heidi gave voice to the fatigue with which modern-day women struggled and confessed to feeling "stranded" by the feminist movement and left behind by her friends, and saying, "I thought the point was we were all in this together."[9]

Why wouldn't Heidi's troubles resonate with audiences in 2015? Like Heidi, women were struggling to find fulfillment. Economists Betsey Stevenson and Justin Wolfers examined the trends of happiness for U.S. citizens between 1970 and 2005. and learned that while men's scores had remained stable, women's scores had decreased—despite advancements made in education, professional accomplishments, and legal protections against discrimination and harassment.[10]

Despite, or perhaps because of, its relevance, *The Heidi Chronicles* divided critics. To some, it was a poignant reminder of how little had changed for women in the past thirty years, while others viewed Wasserstein's play as outdated, clouded by privilege, and irrelevant to present-day feminists, who were focused on more than simply balancing a career and a family. Charles Isherwood of the *New York Times* wrote that the play's questions "are being posed once again, with the same bright humor and reflective intelligence. . . . And the immense popularity of *Lean In* and books about the motherhood-vs.-career debate attest to how germane the play's questions remain, notwithstanding the strides women have made since its premiere."[11] Describing the play as "smart and funny, tender and big-hearted," David Rooney of the *Hollywood Reporter* declared the pertinence of the "imperfect but nonetheless illuminating work," while writing that the "influential play's themes and the author's distinctive voice have inevitably been diluted by imitation."[12]

But after its opening on March 18, *Heidi* failed to find an audience, never filling more than 75 percent of the seats in the Music Box Theater. Originally scheduled to run through August 9, the show closed early, on May 30, after eighty performances.

The low ticket sales were difficult to explain; the demographics had all matched up. The majority of Broadway tickets are purchased by wom-

REVIVALS ECLIPSED BY MILESTONES

en, most of whom are college-educated and in their forties—seemingly the ideal audience for *Heidi*. But they didn't go to see her story.

Some blamed the marketing strategy. While Wasserstein's script revolved around a woman's search for personal and professional fulfillment in a turbulent culture, those unfamiliar with the show might have perceived it as a romantic comedy. A commercial for the play featured Moss, dressed in a brightly colored, form-fitting dresses, laughing confidently and dancing with her two male costars as Betty Everett's "It's in His Kiss" played. There was little to no indication that the play was a comedy, let alone a comedy about feminism.

Others said *The Heidi Chronicles* was simply outdated and irrelevant to feminism in 2015, when intersectionality was a heightened focus and the loneliness of a well-off white art professor might not resonate. "It represents a moment in feminism that has passed," professor and author Jill Dolan told the *New York Times* after the closing notice was posted. "The question 'Can we have it all?' is just not the main question that American feminism is asking right now."[13]

It was Heidi herself who others struggled to relate to. The title character is an internal woman, an observer of the world around her, and the overstimulated audiences of 2015 may have struggled to invest in her. And Moss's performance personified detachment; whether at a consciousness-raising group, a wedding, or a baby shower, she was often standing to the side, looking slightly uncomfortable and watching everyone else rather than engaging in the actual event. Alisa Solomon wrote in the *Nation*,

> Heidi's predicament, rather, is that for most of the play she doesn't take charge of her life. "LEAN IN!" one wants to shout at her—not as a strategy to advance at work, but as basic dramaturgy. Heidi is a passive protagonist. What fortysomething, overworked, second-shifting Broadway ticket-buyer has patience for that?[14]

It appeared that Broadway audiences didn't, but Wasserstein's play continues to be frequently produced in community and academic theaters, as well as professional venues.

If *Heidi* was considered outdated, then perhaps it was time for another woman's voice to be heard on Broadway. And women were already working to make that happen.

THE KILROYS COME TOGETHER

In 2013, a group of playwrights and producers formed the Kilroys. Named after a graffiti tag World War II soldiers left to alert people to their presence, the activist group, devoted to promoting works by women, soon released the List, a gender parity initiative inspired by Franklin Leonard's Black List, a collection of popular, unproduced screenplays in Hollywood. A selection of plays ready for production that were written by women, the List was served as a response to the repeated claim that theaters and artistic directors wanted to produce new works by women but just didn't know of any.

"I've been working in the professional theater for about ten years, and during that time I have consistently heard artistic directors, when asked why they don't have more women in their season, say, 'We just choose the best plays,'" founding member Joy Meads told *HowlRound*. "I know this isn't intended, but the logical analog to that, the next unsaid sentence is, 'And the best plays are written by men.' I know from ten-plus years of reading, a lifetime of reading plays, I know for a fact that isn't true."[15]

After seeking recommendations for female-authored plays that had been produced only once or not at all, the Kilroys received more than three hundred play titles from 127 playwrights, dramaturgs, and artistic directors, and the June 2014 premiere of the List featured the forty-six most-recommended works.

"Systemic, institutional, and unconscious bias" were contributors to the persistent lack of female playwrights being produced. They materialize in various forms, one of the most popular being money. A frequent claim made regarding works by women is that plays by women make less money than plays by men, but a 2009 study authored by Princeton graduate Emily Sands examining gender parity in theater found that, among all the plays and musicals produced on Broadway between 1999 and 2009, even though women wrote only 11 percent of the works, their works sold 16 percent more tickets on a weekly basis and earned an average of 18 percent increased earnings.[16]

"A lot of it is perception," playwright and director Emily Mann said of the belief that works by women make less money. She continued,

> A work by a woman is going to be softer, the men will feel left out, they're not going to come, which is not true. It's also not true that you have fewer people coming to the theater if it's written by a person of

Founding members of the Kilroys. From left: Meg Miroshnik, Sheila Callaghan, Tanya Saracho, Laura Jacqmin, Annah Feinberg, Zakiyyah Alexander, Daria Polatin, Marisa Wegrzyn, Kelly Miller, Sarah Gubbins, Carla Ching, Joy Meads, and Bekah Brunstetter. *Photo by Elisabeth Caren at the Wallis Annenberg Center*

color. Actually, you have more. You also have that niche market added on to your base. None of this is true. It just perpetuates, and the question is why. No matter how much you tell the truth and back it up with data, it's hard to change people's entrenched perceptions and biases.[17]

"GENDER PARITY AND ALL"

The movement for parity was happening throughout the country; in 2015 came the premiere of the Women's Voices Theater Festival in Washington, D.C. The creation of seven artistic directors from prominent D.C. theaters—Arena, Ford's Theater, the Shakespeare Theater Company, the Signature Theater, the Round House Theater, Studio Theater, and the Woolly Mammoth Theater Company—the festival saw fifty-one participating theaters commit to producing new works by women. Smith, who had worked at Arena Stage for seventeen years, was the only woman at that brunch.

Women made up 68 percent of the Broadway audience from 2012 to 2013 and 61 percent of the theatergoing audience in Washington, D.C., in 2000,[18] but only 22 percent of the plays being produced in the country were written by women. The previous year on Broadway, not one new play by a woman was produced, and the most recent new Broadway play that was written by a woman was *Lucky Guy*, by Nora Ephron, which ran in April 2013. The highest percentage of plays written by women was found in Chicago, peaking at 36 percent.[19]

The eight-week event saw fifty-six world-premiere productions by fifty-eight female playwrights, marking the largest collaboration in the history of theater companies simultaneously producing original works by female writers. The festival's achievements were celebrated, but the need for such an event in 2015 was clearly frustrating for many. Arena Stage director Molly Smith told *Playbill*,

> We live in a sexist society. Only one play in five is written by a woman playwright in the U.S. as far as plays produced in our country. This is a festival that will shine a spotlight on over fifty-fice women writing today. . . . We want to make sure this moment is not just a blip on the screen. . . . The theater reflects the society we live in. Women still don't make as much money as men. Fewer plays by women are being produced. Fewer women run large theaters. Fewer women run major organizations—sexism is at every level of our society. This is a moment where we've chosen to focus on women to open the eyes of our audiences, the field, and the press.[20]

Accountability was a crucial theme of the festival—both for the consumers and the artistic directors. Ryan Rilette, artistic director for Round House, admitted to *Playbill* that he had always considered himself a supporter of women's writing, but when he looked at his own seasonal lineups, he realized that wasn't quite true. He then created a structure to ensure parity in future seasons.

Women's Voices returned in 2018, but with fewer productions and a different focus. It didn't focus only on world-premiere productions; plays that had already enjoyed successful runs were featured in the lineup. The need for more festivals in the future was apparent in the coverage of the festival, much of which was written by men. One boasted the headline, "The Women's Voices Theater Festival is a winner. But it could use some work."[21]

SUCCESS AND SETBACKS

The 2015–2016 Broadway season looked promising: Along with Lin-Manuel Miranda's groundbreaking rap musical *Hamilton*, the musical *Waitress* boasted a creative team with women in the four principal roles, and the play *Eclipsed* was brought to the stage by an all-female and all-black cast and creative team. Also slated for Broadway was a revival of *The Color Purple* and the new play *Therese Raquin*, Emile Zola's story of adultery and murder; however, the season got off to a bumpy start when the Manhattan Theatre Club announced its 2015–2016 season. Eight plays were slated for production, and seven had been announced—all written by white men.

Following this announcement, the internet erupted with rage. This lack of diversity was unusual for the Manhattan Theatre Club, which had established a record of producing female playwrights. Responding to the backlash, the club's artistic director, Lynne Meadow, cited the fact that the facility had commissioned forty-nine plays in the past four years, with twenty-eight going to women and minorities. A total of 43 percent of directors and playwrights at the Manhattan Theatre Club were women and minorities,[22] and, in the 2014–2015 season, three out of eight of the programmed plays were written by women.

Meadow's explanation for the season echoed the excuses often made regarding works by women: "I don't deny the fact that this season is anomalous in terms of the percentages of diversity on our stages. It's just how the season came together."

Following the outcry, Meadow announced the final play of the season—prior to all of the arrangements being finalized—was written by a woman: Penelope Skinner's *The Ruins of Civilization*, playing Off-Broadway.

The numbers were low; only 21 percent of the plays from 2015–2016 were written by women, but they were higher than some previous seasons. Of the thirty-nine shows that opened on Broadway during the 2015–2016 season, three plays were written by women. These included *Therese Raquin*, by Helen Edmundson; *Eclipsed*, by Danai Gurira; and *Fully Committed*, by Becky Mode. Of the three musicals that season that included women on their writing teams—*The Color Purple*, *Bright Star*, and *Tuck Everlasting*—one was a revival and the other two were written by or in collaboration with a man. The number of female directors was also low—Pam MacKinnon directed David Mamet's *China Doll*, Lynne Meadow helmed Richard Greenberg's *Our Mother's Brief Affair*, Liesl Tommy directed *Eclipsed*, and Diane Paulus led the quartet of women behind *Waitress*.

With deception, sex, and murder driving its plot, *Therese Raquin* seemed a dramatic start to the season. Adapted from Emile Zola's novel, the play told the story of an orphaned woman trapped in a loveless marriage with her sickly and narcissistic cousin, Camille. After moving to Paris, Therese begins a passionate affair with Camille's childhood friend, Laurent. The two conspire to murder Camille to ensure their future together, and they succeed, but rather than rejoicing about spending their life together, Therese and Camille are so haunted by guilt that they plot to murder one another and, in the process, take their own lives.

First published in 1868, Zola's novel was considered scandalous, and he was accused of immorality and "putrid" obscenity. The author published a preface to the second edition, describing the book as a scientific study of "human animals."[23]

Zola's tale of sex, lies, and death has inspired many adaptations. The author himself wrote a play that was first performed in 1873, but it was not performed in London until 1891, because Lord Chamberlain's Office would not license the show. An opera and two musical adaptations were also written, and it was no less popular onscreen, inspiring an Italian silent film, a BBC series, and TV movies telling the story, as well as a star-studded movie titled *In Secret*, appearing in theaters one year before the Broadway opening.

Keira Knightley, known in the United States for her star turns in *The Pirates of the Caribbean* series, as well as many period dramas, made her Broadway debut playing the title character. She had been offered the role of Therese two other times before accepting, but the third time, she accepted.

"It's very rare that I get offered interesting roles; there are very, very few out there for women," Knightley told the *Hollywood Reporter* on opening night. "And when something like this comes along, you go, 'I can sink my teeth into it and not just be the supportive girlfriend or wife,' which can get rather boring."[24]

The claustrophobic nature of Therese's life is clear from the opening moments of the playwright's production. She fantasizes about the river washing her away—"I would let it take me wherever it goes. Moving.

Always moving," and after her first encounter with Laurent, she declares, "There is blood in my veins. Thank God there is still some blood in my veins. I thought they had bled me dry. Drained me. Emptied me. Flattened me, until I was nothing. A pressed flower."[25]

Therese longed for passion, and so did the audiences of this production, which was staged in a bleak, naturalistic aesthetic. Knightley's graceful demeanor was nowhere to be seen in her Expressionist performance, her appearance muted by her dull wardrobe and bleak hair and makeup. Therese's restless nature, and the miserable conditions of her life, were not depicted with enough desperation, and the lover's affair did not contain enough passion to drive the story and justify Camille's murder, according to many critics who lamented the lack of sexual heat in the play. The play was described by the *Wall Street Journal* as "once shocking but now quaint,"[26] and the *Daily News* called it a "wannabe erotic thriller."[27] Jeremy Gerard, of *Deadline*, declared it, "DOA," a "victim of its own literal dark-mindedness."[28] In his review for the *New York Times*, Ben Brantley belittled Therese's melancholy desperation with the comment, "I kept thinking that surely Therese's disposition would improve if she were ever allowed to change that mouse-brown dress she wears for the first act."[29] The play's limited run at the nonprofit Roundabout Theater Company concluded on January 6, and it received only one Tony Award nomination, for its set.

"THERE ALWAYS HAS TO BE A FIRST"

When *Eclipsed* opened on Broadway, it marked two major moments in theater history: the first time a major Broadway play featured an all-female cast, a female writer, and a female director, and the first time all of the women were black. Written by Danai Gurira, who describes herself as "Zimerican," having been born in America but raised in Zimbabwe, *Eclipsed*, directed by South African Liesl Tommy, was performed by cast female actors, all of whom were African.[30]

Set in Liberia toward the end of its second civil war, *Eclipsed* offers an unflinching look at the lives of women during that time. Gurira, who was first inspired to write the play after seeing a photograph of female Liberian freedom fighter Black Diamond in a *New York Times* article, interviewed more than thirty women affected by the fourteen years of civil war while on a trip to Liberia.

In *Eclipsed*, a trio of women—known as Wife 1 and Wife 3, and the Girl, live as the imprisoned sex slaves of a man they call the C.O. Wives 1 and 3 attempt to shield the Girl, who is much younger than them, from the C.O., but they are unable to do so. The Girl's youthful enthusiasm is evident as she tells the other women, "I want to do sometin' wit' myself, be a doctor or member of Parliament or sometin'," but this is quickly subdued as she returns to their shelter after being discovered and raped by the C.O.

When the C.O. enters the women's shelter, the women line up silently as he selects who he wants. Their identities, and their humanities, are erased in his presence; for him, they serve a single purpose. The danger that haunts these women's lives is spoken of, but they exist in a small domestic sphere, cooking, cleaning, styling each other's hair, and gossiping. Of the three "wives" of the C.O., Wife 1 acts as the matriarch. Wife 3 is pregnant with the C.O.'s baby, and Wife 2 has fled the base and become a rebel fighter.

Along with the four wives, *Eclipsed* featured one other character, Rita, a member of a female-led peace organization who meets with the Wife 1 and Wife 3 at the compound. When Rita meets with the C.O.'s wives, she makes a point of asking them their names, offering them a moment of the individual identity that had been taken from them.

The idea of a world beyond the compound is introduced to the Girl when Wife 2 returns and attempts to recruit the young woman into battle. Her choices are clear and limited—be a victim of violence at the hand of a man or be a part of it.

Gurira had frequently explored female identities in her writing throughout the years. Women living with HIV in both Los Angeles and Africa were chronicled *In the Continuum*, a performance piece cowritten with Nikkole Salter. *The Convert* follows a young woman in Rhodesia who, in the late nineteenth century, converts to Catholicism, examining British colonialism in Southern Africa.

Eclipsed opened Off-Broadway at the Public Theater in October 2015, and transferred to Broadway in March 2016. As previews began for the show, another play by Gurira—*Familiar*, a comedy about an American-born Zimbabwean daughter preparing for her wedding—was performed Off-Broadway.

Danai Gurira. *MediaPunch Inc./Alamy Stock Photo*

"That's a very significant thing to do on the Great White Way," TV host Stephen Colbert said to Gurira on *The Late Show with Stephen Colbert*, about the all-female and all-black cast and writer and director spots. "Now when this is eventually made into a Hollywood movie, what white man would you like to play the lead?" Colbert joked.[31]

Eclipsed's creative team, groundbreaking in both gender and race, was noted and praised by the media. But to the women on the team, it was much too late for them to be the first. For Tommy, it was an "outrage." Tommy added, "People keep saying it's amazing, and I don't think it's amazing—I think it's shocking. And what's shocking is that there have been all-female plays, there have been female plays written by women, but there hasn't been a female director. There hasn't been a woman in the lead, in the position of power, guiding the show."[32]

When it opened at the Golden Theater in 2016, *Eclipsed*, which marked Gurira's Broadway playwriting debut, received rapturous reviews praising the writing and directing, as well as the performances, by the all-female cast. Described as a "major achievement" by *Deadline*'s Jeremy Gerard, *Eclipsed* was praised as a "scorching work about women and war whose humor burnishes rather than undermines its seriousness of purpose."[33] Charles Isherwood, of the *New York Times*, wrote, "Under the bright lights of Broadway, where escapist fare or genteel revivals most often thrive, Ms. Gurira's play, directed with clarity and force by Liesl Tommy, reminds us of something profoundly important, and perhaps too easily forgotten amid our own country's continuing racial troubles: African lives matter."[34]

It was impossible to ignore *Eclipsed*'s feminine and feminist message. "It's no accident that all three options, if they are options, are represented in *Eclipsed* by women," Jesse Green wrote for *New York Magazine/Vulture* in his review of the Off-Broadway production. "This is not just a political play, but a feminist play, in theme and execution. Though the wives live in fear of an always imminent and male-identified evil, no men are depicted."[35]

The diverse, feminist play's road to Broadway had been a lengthy one. Following its premiere at the Wooly Mammoth theater in Washington, D.C., in 2009, Gurira's play was performed at the Yale Repertory Theater in London, and two productions were put on in South Africa. It wasn't until recent Oscar winner Lupita Nyong'o was in conversation with the Public Theater's artistic director, Oskar Eustis, about her next project, that the play's New York production was discussed. Nyong'o was already familiar with Gurira's script; as a student at the Yale School of Drama, she was the understudy for the Girl.

Eclipsed's opening Off-Broadway reunited the play with its first director, Liesl Tommy. For a play by a woman, about a woman, in which no men were visible onstage, Gurira wanted a woman to lead the team. "This is a play I wanted a woman director for," Gurira told the *Cut* at *Eclipsed*'s Broadway opening. "I wanted a play where you took out the male voice and the male face, and said we're going to extract, in this case, the antagonist and just make it about these women."[36] She elaborated further to *Vogue*, saying that women's stories of war are often overlooked and explaining the meaning of the play's title:

> We are used to women's narratives being defined through the male perspective. I challenge that as a concept. In this narrative, the essential voices on that stage were not male. They were female. It was about illuminating those that often get obscured by war. We always hear about the men who are perpetuating the war, the ones who come in and stop the war. But we never hear about the women who are at the mercy of a war. It's about that light that gets obscured. The title, it's about the eclipsing—the obscuring and blocking of those who have power and potential and who've been robbed of their own self-determination.[37]

Eclipsed's focus on women was not praised by everyone; the lack of male characters was the focus of criticism by some, with Green even suggesting that making the play solely focused on women was a detriment to its storytelling, implying that women could not carry the story alone. "At some point—the first act is overlong—what was gripping starts to feel a little desperate dramatically, as if, having chosen to represent the moral universe of Liberia's civil war entirely through women, Gurira found she could no longer make them bear all the dramatic weight of a situation that also, of course, involved men."[38]

Eclipsed had made history, but it wasn't something to celebrate. Tommy, who said she had been "very adamant" that she wanted to cast African actresses in the play, told the *New York Times* she had encountered a lack of representation, without people who looked like her, in her own career, adding,

> When I was starting out, there were no black women directors that I could look at and say, "That's the career I want." That I'm able to be in a position of leadership with this much support, to tell this story, isn't something I take for granted. None of us take these positions for granted, because they still don't always trust us with [stuff]. That

we're able to forge ahead with a story that matters so much to us is amazing.[39]

Broadway's lack of diversity could have contributed to the long delay of *Eclipsed*'s New York debut. *Ruined*, by Lynn Nottage, opened Off-Broadway to rave reviews in 2009, winning the Pulitzer Prize. *Eclipsed* may have been too similar to *Ruined*, Green opined in his review of the play, perpetuating the idea that there was only room for one story of African women on New York's stages.[40] *Eclipsed* had been performed in South Africa and London, but it hadn't made it to New York. Tommy recalled when, promoting the play, she got the impression that, with *Ruined*, audiences did not want to see another play about women in Africa.

The play received six Tony nominations, two of which were for Best Play and Best Director, which made Tommy the first black woman to earn a nomination in that category. But New York isn't the measure of success for Gurira. Instead, she said, if her plays are not received well in Africa (where they have been performed to sold-out audiences), that's when she feels they have not succeeded.

"It has to be something that works on the continent—it can't just work here," she told *American Theatre Magazine*. "Otherwise it's failed."[41]

SUGAR, BUTTER, WOMEN

Two blocks north of *Eclipsed*, even more history was being made. The musical *Waitress*, written by Sara Bareilles and Jessie Nelson, had already established itself as a proudly women-centric show. The musical staging of Adrienne Shelley's indie film told the story of a small-town baker with a gift for making pies who is trapped in an abusive marriage. *Waitress* boasted a female book writer, Jessie Nelson; a female composer, Sara Bareilles; a female choreographer, Lorin Latarro; and a female director, Tony Award winner Diane Paulus. With four women filling the principal creative slots, *Waitress* made history.

Female-led musicals were rare on Broadway, only occurring twice before and both times with one woman wearing many hats: Elizabeth Swados's 1978 musical *Runaways*, for which she crafted a book, score, choreography and direction, and 1984's *Quilters*, led by Molly Newman, who wrote the book, and Barbara Damashek, who wrote the book, music, and lyrics, and directed and contributed to the orchestrations. Paulus's directing *Waitress* marked the second year in a row, and the third time in your years, that she was the only woman directing a musical on Broadway.[42]

Paulus acknowledged the rarity of a team like the one assembled for *Waitress*, but she said she did not deliberately build a team of women. Instead, she said she sought the best people for the job—the same explanation frequently often offered by men for largely or entirely male teams.

"I'm glad it was pointed out, and it *is* a moment we are acknowledging," Paulus told *Time*. "But what's important to me is that every woman is in the position on this team because they're the best person for the job. So what does that mean? It means that women are on the top of their game."[43]

The women were already under scrutiny, and the subject material of *Waitress* only invited more of it. Despite the cheerful advertising campaign and heartwarming images (and smells) of pie permeating its theater, the story of *Waitress* involved domestic abuse, infidelity, and an unexpected pregnancy. Jenna, the star baker at the local diner, is married to her high school sweetheart, Earl, an abusive man who she longs to divorce. Forbidden to own a car or even handle her own money, handing her tips over to Earl every day after work, Jenna is trapped. After learning Jenna is pregnant, Earl demands that she promise to not love the baby more than she loves him. Fearful of what kind of father her husband will be, Jenna plots an escape by entering a national pie-baking contest that boasts a prize of $20,000—and begins an affair with her married gynecologist.

Jenna is flanked by her two friends, Dawn and Becky, who work with her at the diner. They force her to take the pregnancy test and urge her to think about her marriage and actually leaving Earl. It is the women of *Waitress* who drive the show; the men are the supporting characters, and, in an echoing of the criticism lobbed at *Eclipsed*, some reviewers did not approve of the omission.

Chris Jones, of the *Chicago Tribune*, described the underwritten male roles as "such a missed opportunity," adding, "Gehling's Dr. Pomatter feels like a sitcom doc rather than a serious love interest for a serious young woman, and thus you don't pull for them as you should." Jones continued, "I had the same issue with Nick Cordero's Earl (Jenna's husband), played as a standard-issue man-spreader when the show would be better if you saw deeper into his anger and depression."[44]

Peter Marks, of the *Washington Post*, had similar criticisms, writing,

> It's surprising that *Waitress*'s director, the resourceful Diane Paulus . . . would not have required the softening of at least one of Earl's monstrous edges, because he's a villain so transparently designed to provoke a specific response that—no disrespect to the highly competent, physically imposing Cordero—the character comes across as an inane contrivance.[45]

But *Waitress*'s female focus wasn't seen as a failure by everyone. Danielle Feder of *HowlRound* relished the reversing of the audience's expectations regarding the main characters:

> Reviews, while never identifying this switch in specific terms, have criticized the male characters—primarily Earl—as one-note, thankless, standard-issue, even inane. Some have suggested the show could have been improved if only we had been able to "see deeper into [Earl's] anger and depression," or have come to the conclusion that because Earl reads transparently as a villain, he "isn't even abusive." . . . In a world filled with female characters who exist only in relation to the men on stage, I'm shocked more critics have not found that a musical in which the *men* exist only in relation to the *women* does not constitute a failure, but a subversive and exciting choice.[46]

The criticism of Earl also encompassed the show's portrayal of domestic violence. He was considered a caricature by some, with *Variety* describing him as "selfish and dreadfully overbearing, but so spineless, he isn't even abusive."[47] Earl is never seen hitting Jenna—he comes close to and only stops when she tells him she's pregnant—but his abuse is alluded to in conversation and song. Whether the suggestion of violence heightened or lessened its impact was debatable.

The question of whether *Waitress* was, in fact, feminist plagued audience members and reviewers alike. Some claimed that simply telling Jenna's story established the musical as a feminist show. Others said that the deliberate portrayal of the strong friendship between the three women was a feminist approach. And others praised the show's portrayal of women as sexual beings, enjoying casual relationships, allowing them to be flawed characters rather than examples of morality, without seeking a traditional "happily ever after."

Waitress was criticized for its depiction of motherhood, which was disparaged as being out of place in a show that strove to be progressive. Jenna fervently hopes she is not pregnant, and her immediate reaction to learning she is is to utter, "Shit," but she is adament she will have the baby. Her reasoning for this, be it religious, moral, or political, is never explained, nor is the word "abortion" said onstage. Jenna, ambivalent at first about her pregnancy and increasingly fearful as the story progresses, radically transforms when her daughter is placed in her arms. She begins singing a song titled "Everything Changes." This drew criticism for presenting the cliched idea that becoming a mother completely and instantly changes people. Jenna never had the motivation to leave her husband on her own, but moments after her daughter is placed in her arms, she informs Earl she is leaving him. And the fact that her financial well-being is saved by an old man did not go unnoticed.

Nor did the portrayal of Ogie, Dawn's all-too-eager suitor, who appears at her job the day after their first date. Despite Dawn's pleading with him to leave, he informs her in a sprightly song that he has fallen in love and will not leave without her. Performed by comedic character actor Christopher Fitzgerald, the song evoked much laugther, despite lyrics that stated, "I'm not going, if it seems like I did/I'm probably waiting outside. . . . I love you means you're never, ever, ever getting rid of me."

Such sentiments evoke thoughts of stalking, but such severity is lessened by the comedy of the moment, a common problem in romantic comedies. And Dawn, rather than repeating her request for Earl to leave, is encouraged by her friends to give him a chance. After learning of their common passion for historic war reenactments, she falls for Ogie, even marrying him before the musical ends—just a few months later, if one was clocking the time by Jenna's pregnancy.

With Dawn and Ogie, *Waitress* presents the trope of the determined suitor helping the withdrawn love interest come out of her shell. Despite its intended message of empowerment, with Jenna finding her voice and leaving her husband, *Waitress* communicated another message about relationships—that ones with problematic elements were not dangerous if the abuser is goofy, nonthreatening, and seemingly well-intentioned. Instead, the abuse is thus forgiven and even rewarded. (Fitzgerald earned a Tony nomination for his performance.)

Paulus, a Tony winner for directing *Pippin* and a two-time nominee for revivals of *Hair* and *The Gerswhin's Porgy and Bess*, was scrutinized for her approach to *Waitress*. Seemingly encroaching on the boy's club of Broadway, the creative team of *Waitress* was held to an extremely high standard, higher, perhaps, than other productions. Paulus was patroniz-

Diane Paulus. *PACIFIC PRESS/Alamy Stock Photo*

ingly described as a "Very Serious Artist" by the *New York Post*'s Michael Riedel, who scoffed at "Paulus and her band of feminists'" portrayal of domestic violence, reporting, "The first act is 'very dark,' says a source, which jars with what is, at heart, an optimistic show about female empowerment: The waitress breaks free of her husband by starting her own pie-making company." He further reinforced the smug male superiority that permeated the industry by concluding his column with, "Let's leave domestic violence to Tennessee Williams and David Mamet."[48]

Studies have consistently shown that women have been held to higher standards than men, both professionally and artistically. Art by women sells at auctions for 47.6 percent less than art by men, further demonstrating the systemic sexist bias that women face in many industries.[49] Along with financial worth, women are consistently held to higher ethical standards than men in professional settings,[50] which, given *Waitress*'s story of adultery, could also contribute to the male critics' dismissal of the musical's artistic merits. Feder considered this in *HowlRound*, writing,

> I hesitate to think the response to *Waitress* would have been the same had its creative team been primarily male; why are we harder on female creators, especially when it comes to a feminist reading of their work? If women were given the same freedom to fail—or if we stopped giving men pats on the back for effort—I am confident we would end up with a more feminist theater.[51]

Both *Eclipsed* and *Waitress* accomplished celebratory landmarks, but the actual stories they brought to the stage warranted skepticism rather than celebration. A disturbing commonality between these two shows existed: They were both about women in tragic situations. In *Eclipsed*, the women are trapped as sex slaves. In *Waitress*, Jenna is abused by her husband. Another popular show that season was a revival of *The Color Purple*, in which Celie overcomes years of abuse and suffering. This begged the question, Why did women need to suffer to be the subject of commercially successful entertainment?

Both *Waitress* and *Eclipsed* appeared to be a dramatic improvement for the industry, but they were decidedly outliers. The previous forty-one seasons of Broadway had seen more than half—a total of 52 percent—of musicals with their top four creative roles filled by men. Approximately *one* out of every four choreographers were women, and the numbers of female writers, composers, and directors were even more stark, averaging one out of every ten.[52] These productions marked landmark firsts in the industry, and another soon followed when in 2018 director Leigh Silverman assembled an all-female design team for the play *The Lifespan of a Fact*.

"PLOT POINTS IN SILK"

The most commercially successful show of the season—and one of the most successful in Broadway history—was Lin-Manuel Miranda's *Hamilton*, the musical telling of the life of the Founding Father. Transferring to Broadway after a sold-out, extended run at the Public Theater, *Hamilton* was celebrated for the abundance of diversity it brought to the Great White Way. White actors made up 74 percent of the casts in musicals in the previous Broadway, with black actors coming in next, at 17.7 percent, and Asian and Hispanic making up 4.5 and 3.5 of casting, respectively.[53] The twenty-one-person cast (not including swings) consisted primarily of people of color, who performed the roles of the Founding Fathers; George Washington, the first president of the United States, was played by a black man.

"Groundbreaking," declared review after review, following *Hamilton*'s Off-Broadway opening. After three extensions, the show closed and prepared for a transfer to Broadway's Richard Rodgers Theatre—the same theater where, seven years prior, Miranda's first musical, *In the Heights*, opened. *Hamilton*'s move uptown did nothing to deter the critics. "Yes, it really is that good," declared the *New York Times*, before adding, "*Hamilton* is making its own resonant history by changing the language of musicals."[54] "*Hamilton* not only incorporates newish-to-Broadway song forms; it requires and advances them, in the process opening up new territory for exploitation. It's the musical theater, not just American history, that gets refurbished," wrote Jesse Green for Vulture.[55] Miranda, wrote Leah Greenblatt in *Entertainment Weekly*, "has turned a Founding Father's largely forgotten narrative into one of the most joyful, kinetic, and extravagantly original musicals ever imagined for the stage."[56]

But for all of its achievements, in the eyes of some, *Hamilton*'s portrayal of women was not to be celebrated. Of the fourteen principal characters, only four were women, and primary vocals had been written for only three of them. And despite powerhouse performances, two of which were nominated for Tony Awards and one of which won, the women in *Hamilton* existed on the periphery of Miranda's musical, in relation to the title character. (The musical's creative team was almost entirely male—men were credited with book, music, lyrics, direction, choreography, scenic design, costume design, lighting design, sound design, and hair and wig design.)

Hamilton was a decidedly masculine musical. Its leading men sang and danced about fighting in battle, commanding other men in war, crafting legislation for the country, and establishing financial systems. What they expressed through song was power—over other people, determining the shape of their lives—masculine power.

This power is masculine, exclusive only to men. And with power driving a musical about war and forming a new country, the women in *Hamilton* were often quiet. In Hamilton's forty-six songs, one is sung by three women ("The Schuyler Sisters"), two are solos ("Helpless" and "Satisfied"), two are a duet ("That Would Be Enough" and "Say No to This"), and one is a trio ("Take a Break").

"The treatment of the story's women—Eliza Schuyler, who becomes Hamilton's wife; her sister Angelica, who becomes his romantic friend; and Maria Reynolds, a mistress who betrays him—particularly invites questions," noted Jesse Green, "even though Miranda has clearly taken pains to at least acknowledge the way history (and his story) have sidelined them. (Eliza gets *Hamilton*'s moving, final word.)"[57]

In *Hamilton*'s opening number, men strode about the stage, singing of Hamilton's trials, tribulations, achievements, and tragedy before sharing how they knew the man: "Me, I fought with him/Me, I died for him/Me, I trusted him," but, aside from one line sung by Eliza, the women only say, together in unison, "Me, I loved him."

Hamilton's first song is representative of the entire show: Of the spoken lines in the musical, the title character speaks or sings the most, followed by Aaron Burr. Eliza, the female lead, was written almost one-third of the lines of the male lead, with Angelica following and Maria Reynolds far behind both other women.

After the opening number, the women in *Hamilton* aren't seen until the middle of the first act, striding onto the stage in the exuberantly upbeat song "The Schuyler Sisters." Angelica, the oldest, is immediately introduced as a passionately bright and independent woman: She defies their father's rules forbidding the daughters to go into the city, and when approached by Aaron Burr, she dismisses his romantic advances but engages with him politically and demonstrates her intelligence by citing the Declaration of Independence and envisioning a political future that involves women.

Throughout the song, the sisters repeatedly declare, "Look around, look around/How lucky we are to be alive right now. . . . History is happening in Manhattan, and we just happen to live in the greatest city in the world!" But despite their joy, the history that is happening does not include these women. It is being made by men, and the women are only on the outside looking in. Angelica and Eliza, Angelica's younger sister, only witness it firsthand because of their relationship to Hamilton.

Both Angelica and Eliza immediately fall in love with the young revolutionary moments after meeting him. An intellectual spark, described by Angelica as "like Ben Franklin with a key and a kite," brings him and Angelica together, as he recognizes her as a "woman who will never be satisfied." Hamilton adds, "You're like me." But Angelica, the oldest daughter and intended to marry for money, suspects Hamilton only desires her for her social status and introduces him to her sister Eliza—a decision she explains with heartbreaking regret in a stunning rap solo that illustrates her despair and grief.

Angelica's narration establishes Eliza as sweet and naïve, a devoted younger sister guided by Angelica's leadership. The seemingly more demure and traditional Eliza immediately wins the heart of Hamilton, as she chronicles in the song "Helpless." Firmly establishing Eliza as the ingenue of the show, the song tells of the whirlwind romance between the revolutionary and the revolutionary's daughter, as Eliza blissfully describes herself as "down for the count."

By introducing Hamilton to Eliza, Angelica breaks her own heart. While giving a toast at their wedding, she relives the last few weeks, offering her own point of view on the seemingly happy event and revealing the truth: that she also had fallen in love with Hamilton that night and desperately found a little solace in the fact that Hamilton would remain in her life—even though he had married her sister.

Angelica, depicted as Hamilton's intellectual equal and perhaps his intellectual soulmate, was referred to by Miranda as the smartest person in the show,[58] and the two continue their relationship through intense, flirtatious letters, with Angelica even querying if he meant to write, "My dearest, Angelica" or "My dearest Angelica" and confessing, "One stroke and you've consumed my waking days." In writing, Angelica advises Hamilton on his political pursuits, offering glimpses of how she affected American history from across the Atlantic Ocean while living the life of a wealthy woman. Renee Elise Goldsberry reflected on the moment's significance in an interview with *Playbill*, praising Miranda for his ability to fit so much into a single scene. "She spins a parasol, but she basically solves his problem and changes the world. It's so subtle, but he was able to give her that power," she said. "[Miranda] makes Angelica the reason why he gets his debt plan through."[59]

Angelica's brilliance is on display throughout the musical, but aside from advising Hamilton, she is unable to use it. The societal limits of the time are acknowledged; when asked what Angelica would have done if she had been a man, Goldsberry replied, "I'm saying George Washington. As much as Angelica accomplished with as little as she could . . . I believe it's comparable to Washington the levels she could go in terms of leadership."[60]

Angelica's intellectual superiority is even demonstrated in the way in which she expresses herself. The men in *Hamilton* rap while the women sing, with Angelica as the only exception. She is the only woman in the show who performs the rapid-fire complex rhythms of rapping, further establishing her as a unique and exceptional woman. Despite her ability to literally speak the same language as the men building the new world, Angelica remains on the sidelines, restricted by her gender and existing on the periphery rather than a part of the action.

Eliza, although a decidedly different character, faces a similar fate in the musical. First introduced as a giddy, lovestruck girl, she evolves into a devoted, loving wife who, in her attempt to build a happy home, urges her husband to appreciate his life and curb his restless obsession with accomplishment. After surprising him with news of her pregnancy, Eliza sweetly urges him in song to find happiness and joy in his life at home.

Eliza's communication with her husband can be seen as an empowered declaration of articulating what she wants out of life with the man she chose to marry. But it can also be seen as the pattern of a domestic woman failing to understand the needs of a great man and thus limiting him—in contrast to his true nature and that of Angelica, who, one wonders, might have understood how Hamilton's need to work comes at the cost of time with his family. A loyal and loving wife, Eliza's character remains steady until her husband's public admission of infidelity, when the audience witnesses her pain and anger, as well as her declaration that she will erase herself from his narrative. Eventually, she does forgive him.

The woman with whom Hamilton cheats receives significantly less attention: The sultry Mariah Reynolds seduces him in a sensual song punctuated with breathy vowels and suggestive moans. A pawn in her husband's plot to blackmail Hamilton, she possesses even less agency than Angelica or Eliza, existing only to function for her husband in relation to Hamilton. And his succumbing to her temptation is portrayed with sympathy: He appears more as a good man who lost his way than a lusty, unfaithful husband. The affair shifts the musical away from its unique plot and closer to a typical narrative. Hilton Als wrote,

> The later scenes of Miranda's work [are] just another backdrop to the standard narrative of a man being undone by a lady. . . . Reynolds's desperation is not grating or awful; it's a force of nature, and Jones conveys it with real understanding. But Miranda keeps her mainly in the background. He doesn't have much feeling for his female characters; for the most part, they're plot points in silk. [61]

Hamilton's depictions of women place them in the slots of the wife, the muse, and the whore—reductive categories such a groundbreaking musical should have avoided. It is only when Eliza takes her story into her own hands, first following Hamilton's confession and then in the final moments of the show, that narrative agency is ceded to women. As the ensemble sings a choral echoing of, "Who lives, who dies, who tells your story?" Eliza steps to center stage and narrates the rest of her life following her husband's death. She lived for fifty more years, becoming a political activist speaking out against slavery and working to preserve the memory of her husband and his fellow revolutionaries' work by raising funds for the Washington Monument and founding the first private orphanage in memory of her husband. She and Angelica read everything Hamilton wrote, helping to protect and craft his story. The final moment shows Eliza, center stage, rapt, looking beyond the audience, presumably toward her husband's spirit, as it slowly appears to the audience that the story they just witnessed was because of her.

It's a powerful moment and a tribute to a remarkable woman. But held off until the last moments of the show, it is debatable if this final moment holds greater impact because it is so late in the show or if it is too little, too late.

Considering what *Hamilton* was—entertainment based on history—begs the question, Was it actually necessary for women to get equal time to men in this show? How much of an obligation to historic accuracy did Miranda actually have, and how much duty did he have to giving women equal time onstage? When writing a musical about historic events, how much creative liberty could the author take? Miranda did take liberties with *Hamilton*, omitting certain characters, and his portrayal of Hamilton's stance on slavery received criticism[62]—neglecting to mention that the Schuyler family, Hamilton's in-laws, owned slaves or his own stance on abolition and slavery.[63] So where did the women fit in? Should Miranda have extended his creative liberties to the women's roles? In the *Common Reader*, Kelsey Klotz said yes:

> It is striking that the few women of Hamilton receive no such development through musical genre and are nearly entirely excluded in rap performances. While Miranda's revisionist history turns traditional musical historical values on their head by not only privileging popular music, but by allowing hip-hop and rap to be valued in terms of rhythm and flow, his history is inclusive only for male characters; this leaves significant room for the development and growth of his female characters.[64]

The story of Hamilton the man shows him wrestling with not only his personal demons—being orphaned, insecure, always himself—but also the questions of the country, delegating power, deciding the shape and future of politics, and determining the rights of the men who lived there. But in *Hamilton*, the women talk and sing about men. It's striking to note that just one year after *Fun Home*'s victories on Broadway, the most notable musical to follow it fails the Bechdel test.

Miranda owed the women more, James McMaster wrote in *HowlRound*. The musical asked, "Who lives, who dies, who tells your story?" McMaster thought the author should have told the women's stories more fully. If Miranda could creatively adapt facts about men, why were women excluded? Wrote McMaster,

> One could rationalize Miranda's gender-related creative choices with ye olde historical accuracy argument: "Well, this is just how things

were back then! Can't argue with history!" But it's hard to accept such an explanation when black and brown men populate the stage, a historically *in*accurate depiction of our founding fathers. Given all of the cross-racial casting, why was gender-bent casting beyond the musical's imagination? Though Miranda does offer an admirable amplification of Eliza Schuyler's historical contributions, this move is both too little and too late for this male-dominated musical. Where were the duets between women about women? Why choose to tell this story?[65]

10

CRITICAL PROGRESS?

One step forward, two steps back. Or sideways. That seemed to be the pattern of progress for women in the industry. For every major step forward, there seemed to be subtle or not so subtle biases, prejudices, and setbacks.

Activist work continued to push forward. In 2016, Parity Productions, a company dedicated to promoting equality by producing work with a behind-the-scenes team that is 50 percent female and transgender, was formed. Founded by artistic director Ludovica Villar-Hauser, the company maintains a database of female and transgender artists, including directors, choreographers, makeup artists, and puppetry and projection artists, among others. Its efforts also include funding and financing: Parity also runs an online store, selling work by female artists to fund its commissioning program, and releases a list of qualifying productions that execute or surpass parity. It furthers its mission with a commissioning program, awarding a cash prize and readings of the winning work, along with the other productions Parity mounts each year. In 2018, the company partnered with the website Show-Score, which began promoting the productions that qualified, listed on the company's website and in its monthly newsletter.

EVERYONE'S A CRITIC—EXCEPT WOMEN

The power that theater critics hold in the industry is undeniable. A review in a major publication can determine a show's future, with the critic determining the show's value and appeal. And, more often than not, the person with the power is a man.

The *New York Times* is widely considered the most powerful publication in arts criticism. And throughout history, theater critics have largely been white and male. Before Ben Brantley and Jesse Green, there was Charles Isherwood. And before them there was Frank Rich, the infamous "Butcher of Broadway," preceded by Mel Gussow, Brooks Atkinson, and Walter Kerr, among others.

The *Times* was far from alone in its male-dominated cultural coverage: The chief critic of the *Los Angeles Times* critic is Charles McNulty. Peter Marks and Nelson Pressley cover theater for the *Washington Post*. The *Chicago Tribune* publishes Chris Jones, and the *Boston Globe*'s critic is Don Aucoin.

An opportunity for major change came about in February 2017, when the *New York Times* began searching for a new theater critic. The publication's longtime second-string reviewer, Charles Isherwood, was no longer writing for the paper, and a new critic was needed. Asking applicants to describe how they would approach the job, the *Times*' job listing read, in part:

> We are seeking a critic with a deep appreciation for plays, musicals, and theater history, but it is equally important that this person is able to connect the themes and issues on stage to those of the wider world. The writer must be gifted at assessing performances and stagecraft, but also eager to help readers understand the ideas that drive the work. While a background writing about theater is a plus, it is not a prerequisite.[1]

People immediately began voicing their hope that the *Times* would choose a new voice—a woman, a person of color, a transgender person—for the job. A petition was posted on Change.org by playwright Winter Miller that read,

> Dear New York Times Masthead and Culture Desk,

With the vacancy of Charles Isherwood as 2nd string theater critic, an extremely powerful post, we invite you take this opportunity to hire a POC who is female and/or transgender. It's a brave new world we're all writing; we'd like you to witness it a bit more from the inside.

With Urgency,
Winter Miller + Friends aka
More Playwrights (and Theatergoers) Than You Can Shake a Stick At[2]

The petition garnered 908 signatures, and the subject was discussed on various message boards and social media platforms. But the *Times* did not fulfill these hopes: In March 2017, it announced that Jesse Green would join the staff as cochief theater critic. Formerly of *New York Magazine*, Green is white, male, and gay—just like the *Times'* resident chief theater critic, Ben Brantley.

The disappointment wasn't lost on Green. He told *American Theatre* that when he was offered the job, for which he did not apply, his first response was, "Don't you want someone who brings more diversity to the table?"

When I spoke to Dean Baquet, the *Times'* executive editor, I raised the issue. I'm a trifecta of nondiversity: I'm a gay white Jew, and that's almost the entry requirement to the theater in New York. He said something quite interesting—and he should know—he said, "It's wrong to try to solve all of an institution's diversity problems in one hire." I have to believe that they wanted me for things that took priority. I wasn't going to turn down the offer; I'm not a saint. But I share the critique that the theater would be better served by more diversity.[3]

The news sparked conversation about diversity in the critics' pool, including speculation on if the *Times* had been sincere in its search for a new voice. In a roundtable for *Exeunt*, Nicole Serratore asked,

Even where there is diversity in the ranks of critics, how do people get seen and promoted? Is there an element of implicit bias in place to prevent female, trans, and POC candidates from being seen as "lead" critic material? At what point will the *New York Times'* staff theater critics reflect the theater world around them?[4]

"In picking this particular symbol, the *Times* has sent a number of messages," Loren Noveck told *Exeunt*.

> That they don't value the voices of their own nonstaff critics (who are a more diverse pool) as much as the voice another institution has accredited; that they're not interested in bringing in a voice who might do something surprising; and that they're not really interested in broadening or complicating the conversation.[5]

Looking at the major publications in New York, women were reviewing theater but often as freelancers or third-string critics, rather than the staff-approved kingmakers.

Linda Winer was one of the few staff critics, writing for *Newsday* from 1987 to 2017, until she announced her retirement. Her reason for leaving, she said, was because she didn't want to go in the new direction of arts criticism, writing listicles and clickbait. Winer, who began writing for the *Chicago Tribune* in 1969, before moving to the *New York Daily News* and then *USA Today*, was the only female first-string critic in New York for decades and the only woman in the New York Drama Critics' Circle for years.

Comparing Chicago to New York revealed a difference in parity, one she attributed to money and the bias women face regarding authority and money. She told *American Theatre*,

> At the *Tribune*, there was no problem being a woman; Chicago had a great tradition of strong women critics. Which is why I was so surprised when I came to New York and saw all the men on the aisle. I thought, "What's going on here?" . . . I do think that in terms of women, things are getting better. But it's slow, very slow. It's that, "Don't move too fast," which is ridiculous—we've always been here. There have been a lot of Off-Broadway critics who are women. The general feeling has been, "It's arty, so the girls can do it." And there are a lot of female dance critics, because it's men in tights and girls en pointe; that's okay. But when it's an $8 million musical on Broadway? That's about money, so just send the men. That's my theory, anyway.[6]

Was it unconscious bias that factored into the hiring? Or was the lack of women at major publications a product of long-term systemic failures that resulted in women being considered unqualified to write for major publications?

One major change was made at *New York Magazine*, when it was announced that the successor to Jesse Green would be Sara Holdren. Following Winer's departure, Holdren was one of the few female theater critics at a major publication in New York. Websites, blogs, and social media amplified women's voices, but the power of a review from the *Times* persisted, and the repercussions of lack of diversity were apparent when, in his review of *Head over Heels*, Brantley lamented the use of the word "binary," writing, "And its dichotomous nature matches the didactic thrust of a show that celebrates the importance of not being (and pardon me, for trotting out what's starting to feel like the decade's most overused word) binary." Referring to Pythio, Brantley later wrote of Dametas as finding someone who "finds himself strangely drawn to her—I mean them."[7] Outrage ensued and an apology was issued, but the need for a more varied roster of critics was clear.

The need for diversity was crucial, playwright Emily Mann, when discussing criticism, said:

> I think there should be more than two white gay males. I think you need diverse points of view looking at the work. . . . There are fantastic writers all over the country who can, in fact, look at the work from different options of view, and it is essential because careers are made and broken, often unjustly. And certain people are anointed and others are disgraced, and often it's not right. . . . There needs to be another point of view.[8]

WORKING TO BREAK THE BINARY

Progress and representation seemed slow at times, but 2018 saw significant advances with trans performers on Broadway. In the span of three months, four trans-identified artists made their Broadway debuts in three hotly anticipated shows. Jess Barbagallo, a trans actor and playwright, was cast in the ensemble of the blockbuster hit *Harry Potter and the Cursed Child*. And Young Jean Lee's subversive comic drama *Straight White Men*, the first Broadway production of a play by an Asian American female playwright, also featured as its Persons in Charge writer and interdisciplinary artist Ty Defoe, who identifies as two-spirit, and nonbinary author and activist Kate Bornstein. After welcoming the audience members into the theater prior to the show beginning, as loud hip-hop music played, Defoe and Bornstein took the stage and greeted the audience while slyly apologizing for the music, saying they hoped no one felt uncomfortable. The two shared their own stories, presenting themselves as the opposite of the titular characters in Lee's play and serving as tour guides throughout the show, leading the actors onstage, or moving set pieces between scenes.

Straight White Men marked both Bornstein and Defoe's Broadway debuts. "We're two trans people framing this show," Bornstein told *Slant*. "Young takes two different forms of theater—performance art and traditional theater—and breaks a binary that, as far as I know, hasn't been broken to this degree on Broadway."[9]

Performing in *Straight White Men* marked a step forward, Defoe told the National Endowment for the Arts.

> I wanted to be a part of this play because I feel like it is, I feel like it's a step that is heading towards the future where the theater is meant for everybody. . . . We can afford right now to take more risks leaning in that direction. I am talking about culture, race, religion, class, sexual orientation, gender. That we get to experience stories that we couldn't even imagine that we would be seeing on stages. Whoever comes to see that show, they should be able to see themselves portrayed on the stage in some capacity.[10]

Just a few avenues east of *Straight White Men, RuPaul's Drag Race* alum Peppermint was performing in the new musical *Head over Heels*. The first openly trans contestant on *Drag Race*, Peppermint was also the first openly trans actress to originate a principle role on Broadway. She played Pythio, a nonbinary oracle who is referred to as "neither he nor she, but . . . they . . . Pythio the Oracle is *they*."[11]

Loosely adapted from Philip Sidney's sixteenth-century romance *The Arcadia*, with a score of hit Go-Go songs, *Head over Heels* was one of the most inclusive shows on Broadway. The *New Yorker* called it a "trans-positive spin on a sixteenth-century romance,"[12] and *Buzzfeed* hailed it as the "most radically queer show on Broadway."[13] Along with a nonbinary principal character played by a transgender performer, *Head over Heels'* plot concluded with a man who had been disguised as a woman choosing to embrace the female identity as crucial to his own and a king promising to pay more respect to the matriarchy.

The casting of Peppermint as Pythio was cause for celebration. While *Kinky Boots* and *La Cage aux Folles* featured characters dressing in drag, they were cis men donning the clothes of women. The opportunity to play such a role was unique to Peppermint, who told *GQ*,

> When I was auditioning, the only trans roles that existed were *the prostitute who gets killed at some point or gets arrested*. Those are valid existences, but it's not all we have. That's all we had in entertainment. That's all people think about trans women: prostitutes and porn. They have no other context to our existence. [14]

Expanding the perception and depiction of trans characters is a goal of Pooya Mohseni, an actor, writer, filmmaker, consultant, and trans activist. "The powers that be—the big writers, big producers, big studios—haven't quite gotten past the idea that a trans person can be a mother, a coworker, a sibling, a lover, a parent. . . . They just haven't quite gotten there," said Mohseni, who is on the advisory council for the Ackerman Institute's Gender and Family Project and also acts as a trans inclusivity consultant for the Casting Society of America and the Actors' Equity Association. Mohseni continued,

> And even within that frame, I believe when they do bring a trans character in, they have an idea of what a trans person is supposed to look like and sound like. For the most part, it kind of follows the old stereotype: This is what a trans person sounds like and looks like and their background. Using trans as a type, which it's not. [15]

The casting of trans actors in trans roles had been the subject of heightened focus in film and TV, as well as theater, with some previously announced cis actors withdrawing from projects in which they would play trans characters—a decision many in the trans community have voiced support of.

"Trans roles, roles specifically for trans people, should be played by trans actors. That's pretty simple," Barbagallo told the *New York Times*, and playwright MJ Kaufman added,

> Definitely. Though I am trying to push the conversation away from this authenticity bias of who can do the role most realistically and toward a labor justice question of who's getting cast and who's not.

Trans actors have a harder time getting cast even in trans roles, and this shouldn't be true.[16]

In 2018, it was a breakthrough year for trans artists on Broadway, with a long history of trans performance artists preceding it. In 2017, Mx. Justin Vivian Bond played the role of Anna Madrigal in a benefit performance of *Tales of the City*, the first actor who identifies as transgender to play a transgender role on Broadway. Taylor Mac's *Hir* played Playwrights Horizons in 2015, and Bianca Leigh's autobiographical show *Busted* was performed in 2012. In 2008, Luster, a Midwinter Trans-Fest, was held. The first trans artist to star on the Great White Way was Bond, who costarred in *Kiki & Herb: Alive on Broadway* in 2006. The previous year, Bradford Louryk created and starred in the solo show *Christine Jorgenson Reveals*.

In 1998, audiences met Hedwig, John Cameron Mitchell's "girly-boy who became the internationally ignored song-stylist barely standing here," who underwent a "botched sex-change operation" and was left with the titular "angry inch." Mitchell has said he views Hedwig as not trans, "because he is kind of forced into this gender reassignment, with this absurd operation forced upon her by a mendacious boyfriend—and as a drag character instead."[17] *Hedwig* soon became a commercial success, inspiring tours, a film adaptation, and a revival on Broadway in 2014.

Years earlier, in 1988, David Henry Hwang's *M. Butterfly* opened on Broadway. Inspired by the affair between French diplomat Bernard Boursicot and Peking opera singer Shi Pei Pu, Hwang's play chronicled a relationship between French diplomat Rene Gallimard and an opera star he believes to be a woman but is a man pretending to be a woman to work as a spy for the Communist Party. Hwang's play, which examined and dissected gender roles, race relations, and international politics, was a critical hit and received seven Tony Award nominations.

Trans characters in mainstream theater were few and far between, and often written by cisgender writers. In 2018, Kit Yan and MJ Kaufman formed Trans Lab, a fellowship for trans and gender nonconforming artists. The Lab, which is supported by the Public Theater and the Women's Project Theater, offers fellowships to help facilitate professional development. Trans characters being written by cis writers were a source of frustration for Kaufman, who told the *New York Times*, "I don't see very many cis writers writing about trans experience responsibly. I would love to see that. There's an unfortunate compounding problem that theaters would rather produce work about us, not by us, right now. We should get to tell our own stories first."[18]

Inclusivity is often an inherent part of activism, and including the trans community in feminist activism was a crucial part of intersectionality, Mohseni said. "I think I understand [intersectionality] more as an actual concept than just a word," Mohseni commented.

> I personally would like to think that trans feminism . . . could be a more inclusive term for feminism and something that also includes trans women and their experiences and a part of the larger umbrella of feminism. What I understand trans feminism to be is feminism that is also trans inclusive. I would like to take a step further and say trans feminism is essentially what true feminism is which has space for women of all journeys and backgrounds.[19]

"HAVE I GOT A GIRL FOR YOU"

One theatrical moment in 2018 that inspired hope for a more equitable future was a revival of a musical, from decades ago, written by men. Award-winning director Marianne Elliott helmed a revival of Stephen Sondheim's 1970 musical examination of marriage, *Company*, with one radical change. Originally centered on Bobby, a 35-year-old single man evaluating his life as a bachelor, surrounded by his "good and crazy people, my married friends," the musical shows Bobby's relationships with his urban family through a series of vignettes, offering glimpses of loving matrimony, as well domestic dysfunction.

Company was considered groundbreaking in its time for both its concept and structure. Inspired by George Furth's one-act plays, Sondheim and Furth crafted a musical that daringly followed a nonlinear narrative structure and didn't revolve around a romantic pairing finding their happily ever after. Robert, defiantly ambivalent about marriage, is the only single person in his social circle, the subject of his friends' pity, envy, and fascination. Rather than seeking and finding a love interest, Bobby goes deep within himself to examine his life but does not conclude the musical with a partner. The decision shocked audiences in the 1970s—a rapidly changing culture following the sexual revolution—along with the musical's frank discussion of sex, relationships, sexual politics, and societal norms.

In 2018, Bobby became Bobbie. Produced by Elliott's company, which was founded with Chris Harper, with the intention of putting up dramatic works with a female focus and strong female protagonists, this revival of *Company* was about a woman. Bobbie, played by Rosalie Craig, was a successful, sexually active, modern woman who, on her thirty-fifth birthday, finds herself thinking about a future that includes marriage and children, and if it was what she wanted for her life.

One of the crucial differences, noted in the reviews, was the idea that Bobbie's stakes are higher because of her ticking "biological clock," exemplified in the "Tick Tock" dance routine, which depicted Bobbie watching four versions of herself in different stages of pregnancy and motherhood.

Timing is everything, the critics agreed, saying Bobbie's age and concerns about reproductive health brought new weight to her new reflection on marriage. This decidedly female approach to the material was noted. Elliott's production also flipped stereotypes regarding sex. Nothing was scandalous or unexpected about Bobby the man man dating several women at once, but judgment was inevitably passed on a woman with an active sex life. This Bobbie dates several men, who admonish her in song for her refusal to commit—a drastic change from the expected norms of relationships. And when Bobbie enjoys a passionate night with a chiseled flight attendant, the man spends much of his time onstage in his underwear, a defiant flipping of the countless times women spend their time onstage clad in nothing but lingerie. Elliott's approach to the material was what drew in one of its stars, Tony winner Patti LuPone. After starring in *War Paint* on Broadway, LuPone had said she was finished performing in musicals, but Elliott's work drew her in, and, as she noted, she had never done a musical with a female director before.[20]

The production opened to glowing reviews, praised as "wonderfully fresh" by the *Evening Standard*.[21] The *Atlantic* raved, "The fact that a director can find so much new resonance in a forty-eight-year-old work just by inverting the gender of an unmarried character points to both the richness of *Company* and the complexity of a culture that still can't agree on what women should actually want."[22]

Company was unusual when it first opened, but Elliott's revival was considered unusually timely in 2018. With marriage rates declining and education, economics, and reproductive independence establishing women more independent than ever, Sondheim's musical observation and introspection resonated strongly with audiences in a society in which being single and childless at a certain age still carries a stigma. With a woman center stage who is successful, single, and sexually active, rejecting the expected societal norms of marriage and motherhood, *Company* is for women in 2018 what it was for men in 1970: forty-eight years later—a revolutionary—and feminist—piece of theater.

50/50 BY . . .

The fight continued. In the 2018–2019 season, a play about Gloria Steinem, by Emily Mann, opened Off-Broadway. Opening two years after Donald Trump's election and immediately after Brett Kavanaugh was confirmed to serve on the Supreme Court, Mann's play was especially poignant. Women and young students flooded the audience, and post-show talkbacks featuring activists, notably Steinem herself, were frequent.

Disney's *Frozen* opened in April 2018, bringing the story of feminist empowerment to the stage, and Disney presented its second annual Women's Day on Broadway, hosting conversations about gender equality in the industry. A surge of female music directors worked during the 2018–2019 season. With *Ain't Too Proud*, a new musical about the Temptations, Dominique Morisseau was the third woman of color to write a book for a Broadway musical, and the first in twenty years, the last book coming in 1997, when Cheryl L. West wrote the book for *Play On!* Twenty-five years had passed between West and Micki Grant, who wrote 1972's *Don't Bother Me, I Can't Cope.*[23]

Works by women filled Off-Broadway stages. Theater companies dedicated to producing work by women and female-identifying and trans artists were opening throughout New York. New Georges, which was founded in 1992, has produced new work for decades, and women were claiming male Shakespeare roles as their own at Spicy Witch Productions and the Queen's Company, while the Hearth produced daring new work. *The Prom*'s performance in 2018 featured the first lesbian kiss seen during the Macy's Thanksgiving Day Parade, and Heidi Schreck's *What the*

Emily Mann. *Photo by Matt Pilsner, courtesy of Emily Mann*

Constitution Means to Me offered an unapologetic portrait of how the U.S. governing document neglects to protect half the population.

Regional theaters were offering opportunities for drastic change in leadership as longtime artistic directors began resigning, and, with the opportunity of new hires, diversity seemed more possible. The people who determined each season's lineups could be women, people of color, nonbinary, or transgender. This would mark an enormous shift for an industry in which, as of 2014, white men made up 73 percent of artistic directors in the United States and 62 percent of executive directors at U.S. theaters.[24] The predominance of patriarchy in regional theater defies its roots, which trace back to Margo Jones, who launched Theatre 47, the first regional professional company, Zelda Fichandler, who led Arena Stage in Washington for forty-one years, and Nina Vance, the founder and first artistic director of the Alley Theater in Houston, Texas. But a survey conducted by two directors in California reported that eighty-five job openings had been filled with 41 percent women and 26 percent people of color.

In 2018, four women were named the top leaders of major American theaters: Rachel Fink became executive director at Chicago's Lookingglass Theatre, Jennifer Zeyl was named artistic director at Intiman Theatre in Seattle, Marcela Lorca was hired as artistic director at Ten Thousand Things Theater Company in Minneapolis, and Pam MacKinnon was named artistic director at San Francisco's American Conservatory Theater. Four out of hundreds was a small percentage that reflected the country's patterns: The American Conservatory Theater commissioned a study in 2016, which found that out of all of America's nonprofit theatres, women have never held more than 27 percent of the leadership roles.[25] In 2019, a notable number of women and people of color were hired as artistic directors of regional theaters, for example, Hana Sharif at the Repertory Theater of St. Louis, Stephanie Ybarra at Baltimore Center Stage, Maria Manuela Goyanes at Woolly Mammoth Theater Company, and Nataki Garrett at the Oregon Shakespeare Festival.

In 2018, the League of Professional Theatre Women launched the campaign #OneMoreConversation, a hiring initiative that asked those with decision-making powers in theater (directors, artistic directors, technical directors, etc.) to have one more conversation with a woman before making a hiring decision, ensuring that if the woman candidate isn't hired, the organization or production would remember her. The Count, an ongoing study that analyzes race, gender, genre, and nationality to determine who is being produced in the United States, conducted by the Lilly Awards, in partnership with the Dramatists Guild, continued to examine the data on women's employment in theater, and while 50/50 by 2020 had been the goal for the league, the Women's Project Theater, and the New Perspectives Theatre, by April 2019, it didn't look like it would be achieved on Broadway.

But the need for parity was more obvious than ever. "If you don't have plays written by women at your theater, it is as if you are only covering half of the day," Marsha Norman said.

> You're either not covering the night or not covering the daytime. It's half women and half men here. Plays by women are crucial if you want to understand the full human experience. Plays by people of color are crucial, plays by people from other countries are crucial if we want to have a chance at understanding each other.[26]

"I hope to see parity in my lifetime," Emily Mann said.

That we're not just on the hunt for women writers. What we're finding is that what comes to us on the whole, the work by women and people of color are the strongest plays being written right now. As Gloria Steinem said, "If you can't see it, you can't do it." If more women see other women writing and directing, it will start perpetuating itself. . . . I'm so happy for the new wave of women who actually have cracked it. I hope it lasts. I hope it continues. Because we cracked it and the door shut again. We cracked it, and it shut.[27]

NOTES

INTRODUCTION

1. William Missouri Downs, Erik Ramsey, and Lou Anne Wright, *The Art of Theatre: Then and Now* (Boston: Wadsworth Cengage Learning, 2011), 52.
2. Jennifer Ashley Tepper, e-mail to Carey Purcell, March 17, 2019.
3. Wendy Goldberg, e-mail to Carey Purcell, March 6, 2019.
4. Pooya Mohseni, interview by Carey Purcell, April 9, 2019.
5. Teresa Lotz, e-mail to Carey Purcell, April 4, 2019.
6. Rachel Spencer-Hewitt, e-mail to Carey Purcell, April 4, 2019.
7. Winter Miller, e-mail to Carey Purcell, February 19, 2019.
8. Mfoniso Udofia, e-mail to Carey Purcell, April 11, 2019.
9. Donna Lynne Champlin, e-mail to Carey Purcell, March 25, 2019.
10. Gina Gionfriddo, e-mail to Carey Purcell, March 29, 2019.
11. Georgia Stitt, e-mail to Carey Purcell, March 11, 2019.
12. Diep Tran, e-mail to Carey Purcell, March 7, 2019.

1. OFF STAGE

1. "Women in Theatre: A Historical Look," *NCTheatre*, March 18, 2015. Accessed March 11, 2018, https://nctheatre.com/nct/blog/women-in-theatre-a-historical-look.
2. Sue-Ellen Case, "Classic Drag: The Greek Creation of Female Parts," *Theatre Journal* 37, no. 3 (1985): 317–27.
3. Case, "Classic Drag."
4. Case, "Classic Drag."

5. Mark Cartwright, "Women in Ancient Greece," *Ancient History Encyclopedia*, July 26, 2016. Accessed March 18, 2019, https://www.ancient.eu/article/927/women-in-ancient-greece/.

6. Herman W. Haley, "The Social and Domestic Position of Women in Aristophanes," *Harvard Studies in Classical Philology* 1 (1890): 159–86.

7. K. Kapparis, "Women and Family in Athenian Law," *Center for Hellenic Studies, Harvard University*, n.d. Accessed March 31, 2019, https://chs.harvard.edu/CHS/article/display/1190 .

8. Nancy Sorkin Rabinowitz, "Politics of Inclusion/Exclusion in Attic Tragedy," in *Women's Influence on Classical Civilization*, ed. Eireann Marshall and Fiona Mchardy, pp. 450–55 (New York: Routledge, 2004).

9. Rabinowitz, "Politics of Inclusion/Exclusion in Attic Tragedy," 42.

10. Case, "Classic Drag."

11. Case, "Classic Drag."

12. "Greek Mythology," *History.com*, December 2, 2009. Accessed March 31, 2019, https://www.history.com/topics/ancient-history/greek-mythology.

13. "Greek Mythology," https://www.history.com/topics/ancient-history/greek-mythology.

14. Mary Beard, *Women and Power: A Manifesto* (New York: Liveright Publishing, 2017).

15. Paul Chrystal, "A Brief History of Sex and Sexuality in Ancient Greece," *History Extra*, n.d. Accessed March 31, 2018, https://www.historyextra.com/period/ancient-greece/a-brief-history-of-sex-and-sexuality-in-ancient-greece/.

16. Thomas R. Martin, "Aristotle on Slaves and Women," *An Overview of Classical Greek History from Mycenae to Alexander*, n.d. Accessed April 1, 2018, http://www.perseus.tufts.edu/hopper/text?doc=Perseus%3Atext%3A1999.04.0009%3Achapter%3D15%3Asection%3D14.

17. Ovid, *Metamorphoses* (Bloomington: Indiana University Press, 1983), 236.

18. Chrystal, "A Brief History of Sex and Sexuality in Ancient Greece," https://www.historyextra.com/period/ancient-greece/a-brief-history-of-sex-and-sexuality-in-ancient-greece/.

19. Case, "Classic Drag."

20. Richard Seaford, "Dionysiac Drama and the Dionysiac Mysteries," *Classical Quarterly* 31 (1981): 252–75; Charles Segal, *Dionysiac Poetics and Euripides' "Bacchae"* (Princeton, NJ: Princeton University Press, 1981), quoted in Rabinowitz, "Politics of Inclusion/Exclusion in Attic Tragedy," 45.

21. Euripides, *Alcestis* (Oxford: Clarendon Press, 1996), 3, 5.

22. Euripides, *Medea* (New York: Dover Publications, 1993), 8.

23. Euripides, *Medea*, 9.

24. Aristophanes, *Lysistrata* (New York: Samuel French, 1915), 34.

25. Case, "Classic Drag," 318.

26. Aristophanes, *Lysistrata*, 49.

27. Aristophanes, *Lysistrata*, 66.

28. Haley, "The Social and Domestic Position of Women in Aristophanes," 160–61.

29. J. Ellen Gainor, "Hrotsvit of Gandersheim," in *Norton Anthology of Drama: Volume 1: Antiquity through the Eighteenth Century*, ed. J. Ellen Gainor, Stanton B. Garner, and Martin Puchner, pp. 490–94 (New York: W. W. Norton, 2009).

30. "Hrotsvitha of Ganedrsheim (C. 935–1001)," *Encyclopiedia.com*, n.d. Accessed March 26, 2018, https://www.encyclopedia.com/women/encyclopedias-almanacs-transcripts-and-maps/hrotsvitha-gandersheim-c-935-1001.

31. Gainor, "Hrotsvit of Gandersheim," 494.

32. Hrotsvitha, *The Plays of Roswitha*, translated by Christopher St. John, with an introduction by Cardinal Gasquet and a critical preface by the translator (London: Chatto & Windus, 1923).

33. Christopher St. John, "The Plays of Roswitha: Translator's Preface," *Internet Medieval Sourcebook*, October 1999. Accessed March 26, 2018, https://sourcebooks.fordham.edu/basis/roswitha-trans_pref.asp.

34. Case, "Classic Drag."

35. Gainor, "Hrotsvit of Gandersheim," 492.

36. Howard McNaughton, "Hrosvit," in *International Dictionary of the Theatre: Playwrights*, ed. Mark Hawkins-Dady, pp. 497–500 (Farmington Hills, MI: St. James Press, 1994), 498.

37. St. John, "The Plays of Roswitha," https://sourcebooks.fordham.edu/basis/roswitha-trans_pref.asp.

38. St. John, "The Plays of Roswitha," https://sourcebooks.fordham.edu/basis/roswitha-trans_pref.asp.

39. St. John, "The Plays of Roswitha," https://sourcebooks.fordham.edu/basis/roswitha-trans_pref.asp.

40. Gainor, "Hrotsvit of Gandersheim," 490.

41. Case, "Classic Drag."

2. FIGHTING THE FEMALE WIT

1. Nick Smurthwaite, "Mary Pix Rediscovered: The Playwright Who 'Held Her Own' against Patriarchy," *Stage*, March 16, 2018. Accessed April 15, 2018, https://www.thestage.co.uk/features/2018/mary-pix-playwright-who-held-her-own-against-patriarchy/.

2. Annette Kreis-Schnick, *Women, Writing, and the Theater in the Early Modern Period: The Plays of Aphra Behn and Suzanne Centlivre* (Madison, NJ, and Teaneck, NJ: Fairleigh Dickinson University Press, 2001.

3. Kreis-Schnick, *Women, Writing, and the Theater in the Early Modern Period*, 25.

4. Kreis-Schnick, *Women, Writing, and the Theater in the Early Modern Period*, 28.

5. Kreis-Schnick, *Women, Writing, and the Theater in the Early Modern Period*, 149.

6. Smurthwaite, "Mary Pix Rediscovered," https://www.thestage.co.uk/features/2018/mary-pix-playwright-who-held-her-own-against-patriarchy/.

7. Edward C. DuBois, "Plato as a Proto-Feminist," *Transcending Silence* (Spring 2007). Accessed April 15, 2019, http://www.albany.edu/womensstudies/journal/2007/dubois.html.

8. Royal Shakespeare Company, "The Fantastivc Follies of Mrs. Rich," *RSC.org*, n.d. Accessed May 15, 2018, https://www.rsc.org.uk/the-fantastic-follies-of-mrs-rich/about-mary-pix.

9. Kreis-Schnick, *Women, Writing, and the Theater in the Early Modern Period*, 28.

10. Kreis-Schnick, *Women, Writing, and the Theater in the Early Modern Period*, 15.

11. Susan Staves, *A Literary History of Women's Writing in Britain, 1660–1789* (New York: Cambridge University Press, 2010).

12. "Susanna Centlivre," *Encyclopedia.com*, n.d. Accessed February 25, 2019, https://www.encyclopedia.com/history/encyclopedias-almanacs-transcripts-and-maps/centlivre-susanna.

13. Misty Anderson, "Susanna Centlivre: The Tina Fey of the Eighteenth Century," *Clarence Brown Theatre*, n.d. Accessed May 15, 2018, https://clarencebrowntheatre.com/susanna-centlivre-the-tina-fey-of-the-eighteenth-century/.

14. Susan Staves, "Susanna Centlivre," in *The Oxford Encyclopedia of British Literature, Volume 1*, ed. David Scott Kastan, pp. 426–30 (Oxford, UK: Oxford University Press, 2006), 426.

15. Kreis-Schnick, *Women, Writing, and the Theater in the Early Modern Period*.

16. Kreis-Schnick, *Women, Writing, and the Theater in the Early Modern Period*, 32.

17. Kreis-Schnick, *Women, Writing, and the Theater in the Early Modern Period*, 221.

18. Kreis-Schnick, *Women, Writing, and the Theater in the Early Modern Period*, 21.

19. Kreis-Schnick, *Women, Writing, and the Theater in the Early Modern Period*, 41.

20. Kreis-Schnick, *Women, Writing, and the Theater in the Early Modern Period*, 65.

21. Kreis-Schnick, *Women, Writing, and the Theater in the Early Modern Period*, 138.

22. Kreis-Schnick, *Women, Writing, and the Theater in the Early Modern Period*.

23. Kreis-Schnick, *Women, Writing, and the Theater in the Early Modern Period*.

24. Kreis-Schnick, *Women, Writing, and the Theater in the Early Modern Period*, 61.

25. Arlene Stiebel, "Aphra Behn," *Poetry Foundation*, n.d. Accessed February 25, 2019, https://www.poetryfoundation.org/poets/aphra-behn.

26. Kreis-Schnick, *Women, Writing, and the Theater in the Early Modern Period*, 23.

27. Kreis-Schnick, *Women, Writing, and the Theater in the Early Modern Period*, 109.

28. Kreis-Schnick, *Women, Writing, and the Theater in the Early Modern Period*.

29. Kreis-Schnick, *Women, Writing, and the Theater in the Early Modern Period*.

30. Sheila Stowell, *A Stage of Their Own: Feminist Playwrights of the Suffrage Era* (Ann Arbor: University of Michigan Press, 1992), 111.

31. Michael Billington, "Chains," *Guardian*, November 19, 2007. Accessed April 10, 2018, https://www.theguardian.com/stage/2007/nov/19/theatre1.

32. *Times* review, May 18, 1910, quoted in Stowell, *A Stage of Their Own*, 111.

33. Austin E. Quigley, *The Modern Stage and Other Worlds* (New York: Methuen, 1985), quoted in Stowell, *A Stage of Their Own*, 101.

34. Stowell, Shelia. 1992. *A Stage of Their Own: Feminist Playwrights of the Suffrage Era.* Ann Arbor: University of Michigan Press, 101–2.

35. Stowell, *A Stage of Their Own*.

36. Stowell, *A Stage of Their Own*.

37. Stowell, *A Stage of Their Own*.

38. Stowell, *A Stage of Their Own*, 103.

39. Mark Brown, "Githa Sowerby, the Forgotten Playwright, Returns to the Stage," *Guardian*, August 14, 2009. Accessed April 10, 2018, https://www.theguardian.com/stage/2009/aug/14/githa-sowerby-playwright-rutherford-son.

40. Harriet Blodgett, "Cicely Hamilton: Independent Feminist," *Frontiers: A Journal of Women Studies* 11, no. 2/3 (1990): 100.

41. Richard Eyre, "Ibsen: The Man Who Knew the Soul of Women," *Telegraph*, November 25, 2015. Accessed April 10, 2018, https://www.telegraph.co.uk/theatre/playwrights/ibsen-the-man-who-knew-the-soul-of-women/.

42. Stowell, *A Stage of Their Own*, 11.

43. Stowell, *A Stage of Their Own*, 13.

44. Stowell, *A Stage of Their Own*, 14.

45. Stowell, *A Stage of Their Own*, 28.

46. Stowell, *A Stage of Their Own*.

47. Stowell, *A Stage of Their Own*.

48. Stowell, *A Stage of Their Own*, 44.

49. Cicely Hamilton, *Life Errant* (London: J. M. Dent, 1935), quoted in Stowell, *A Stage of Their Own*, 74.

50. Blodgett, "Cicely Hamilton."

51. Blodgett, "Cicely Hamilton," 99.

52. Blodgett, "Cicely Hamilton."

53. Stowell, *A Stage of Their Own*, 79.

54. Stowell, *A Stage of Their Own*, 82.

55. Blodgett, "Cicely Hamilton."

56. Blodgett, "Cicely Hamilton," 103.

57. Blodgett, "Cicely Hamilton," 102.

58. Kreis-Schnick, *Women, Writing, and the Theater in the Early Modern Period*.

59. Blodgett, "Cicely Hamilton."

60. Kreis-Schnick, *Women, Writing, and the Theater in the Early Modern Period*.

61. Kreis-Schnick, *Women, Writing, and the Theater in the Early Modern Period*, 91.

62. Kreis-Schnick, *Women, Writing, and the Theater in the Early Modern Period*, 86–87.

63. Kreis-Schnick, *Women, Writing, and the Theater in the Early Modern Period*.

64. Kreis-Schnick, *Women, Writing, and the Theater in the Early Modern Period*, 149.

65. Kreis-Schnick, *Women, Writing, and the Theater in the Early Modern Period*, 135.

66. Kreis-Schnick, *Women, Writing, and the Theater in the Early Modern Period*, 136.

67. Kreis-Schnick, *Women, Writing, and the Theater in the Early Modern Period*, 63.

3. THE GROUNDBREAKING WORK OF HELLMAN AND HANSBERRY

1. Maureen Corrigan, "Lillian Hellman: A 'Difficult,' Vilified Woman," *NPR*, April 26, 2012. Accessed February 28, 2019, https://www.npr.org/2012/04/26/150727939/lillian-hellman-a-difficult-vilified-woman.

2. Harry Gilroy, "The Bigger the Lie: Drama Dealing with the Big Lie," *New York Times*, December 14, 1952. Accessed February 28, 2019, https://www.nytimes.com/1952/12/14/archives/the-bigger-the-lie-drama-dealing-with-the-big-lie.html.

3. Misha Berson, "'The Children's Hour': Sex, Lies, and Lillian Hellman," *Seattle Times*, May 27, 2015. Accessed February 28, 2019, https://www.seattletimes.com/entertainment/theater/the-childrens-hour-sex-lies-and-lillian-hellman/.

4. Eric Pace, "Herman Shumlin, 80, Dies, Leading Producer-Director," *New York Times*, June 15, 1979, p. 18.

5. Lillian Hellman, *The Children's Hour* (New York: Dramatists Play Service, 1934), 66.

6. Hellman, *The Children's Hour*, 66.

7. Sarah Churchwell, "The Scandalous Lillian Hellman," *Guardian*, January 21, 2011. Accessed February 28, 2019, https://www.theguardian.com/stage/2011/jan/22/lillian-hellman-childrens-hour-sarah-churchwell.

8. Brooks Atkinson, "'Children's Hour': Circumstantial Tragedy Set in a Girls' Boarding School—the Disputed Ending to a Swiftly Written Play," *New York Times*, December 2, 1934, p. 1.

9. Atkinson, "'Children's Hour,'" 163.

10. Pace, "Herman Shumlin, 80, Dies," 18.

11. Brooks Atkinson, "Tallulah Bankhead Appearing in Lillian Hellman's Drama of the South, 'The Little Foxes,'" *New York Times*, February 16, 1939. Accessed February 28, 2019, https://www.nytimes.com/1939/02/16/archives/the-play-tallulah-bankhead-appearing-in-lillian-hellmans-drama-of.html .

12. Hellman, Lillian, "The Little Foxes," in *Sixteen Famous American Plays*, ed. Bennett Cerf and Van H. Cartmell, pp. 842–43 (New York: Garden City Publishing, 1941).

13. Hellman, *The Little Foxes*, 73.

14. Hilton Als, "It's a Man's World," *New Yorker*, September 27, 2010. Accessed February 28, 2019, https://www.newyorker.com/magazine/2010/10/04/its-a-mans-world-2.

15. Churchwell, "The Scandalous Lillian Hellman," https://www.theguardian.com/stage/2011/jan/22/lillian-hellman-childrens-hour-sarah-churchwell.

16. Victor Navasky, "The Antagonist: On Lillian Hellman," *Nation*, August 29, 2012. Accessed February 28, 2019, https://www.thenation.com/article/antagonist-lillian-hellman/.

17. Churchwell, "The Scandalous Lillian Hellman," https://www.theguardian.com/stage/2011/jan/22/lillian-hellman-childrens-hour-sarah-churchwell.

18. "Documentary Winners: 1977 Oscars," *YouTube*, July 20, 2014. Accessed February 28, 2019, https://www.youtube.com/watch?v=owqQ10kdwk4.

19. Corrigan, "Lillian Hellman," https://www.npr.org/2012/04/26/150727939/lillian-hellman-a-difficult-vilified-woman.

20. Navasky, "The Antagonist," https://www.thenation.com/article/antagonist-lillian-hellman/.

21. Corrigan, "Lillian Hellman," https://www.npr.org/2012/04/26/150727939/lillian-hellman-a-difficult-vilified-woman.

22. Navasky, "The Antagonist," https://www.thenation.com/article/antagonist-lillian-hellman/.

23. William Wright, "Why Lillian Hellman Remains Fascinating," *New York Times*, November 3, 1996. Accessed February 28, 2019, https://www.nytimes.com/1996/11/03/theater/why-lillian-hellman-remains-fascinating.html.

24. Dick Cavett, "Lillian, Mary, and Me," *New Yorker*, December 9, 2002. Accessed February 28, 2019, https://www.newyorker.com/magazine/2002/12/16/lillian-mary-and-me .

25. Frank Rich, "Zoe Caldwell as Hellman in 'Lillian,'" *New York Times*, January 17, 1986. Accessed February 28, 2019, https://www.nytimes.com/1986/01/17/theater/the-stage-zoe-caldwell-as-hellman-in-lillian.html.

26. Rich, "Zoe Caldwell as Hellman in 'Lillian,'" https://www.nytimes.com/1986/01/17/theater/the-stage-zoe-caldwell-as-hellman-in-lillian.html.

27. Ben Brantley, "Courting Lillian Hellman, Most Carefully," *New York Times*, November 7, 1996. Accessed February 28, 2019, https://www.nytimes.com/1996/11/07/theater/courting-lillian-hellman-most-carefully.html.

28. Greg Evans, "Cakewalk," *Variety*, November 10, 1996. Accessed February 28, 2019, https://variety.com/1996/film/reviews/cakewalk-1200447758/.

29. "Lillian Hellman, Playwright, Author, and Rebel, Dies at 77," *New York Times*, July 1, 1984. Accessed February 28, 2019, http://movies2.nytimes.com/learning/general/onthisday/bday/0620.html.

30. Frederick McKissack and Pat McKissack, *Young, Black, and Determined: A Biography of Lorraine Hansberry* (New York: Holiday House, 1998), 11.

31. McKissack and McKissack, *Young, Black, and Determined*.

32. McKissack and McKissack, *Young, Black, and Determined*.

33. McKissack and McKissack, *Young, Black, and Determined*.

34. McKissack and McKissack, *Young, Black, and Determined*.

35. McKissack and McKissack, *Young, Black, and Determined*.

36. McKissack and McKissack, *Young, Black, and Determined*, 55.

37. McKissack and McKissack, *Young, Black, and Determined*, 60–61.

38. Michael Anderson, "A Landmark Lesson in Being Black," *New York Times*, March 7, 1999. Accessed July 10, 2018, https://www.nytimes.com/1999/03/07/theater/theater-a-landmark-lesson-in-being-black.html.

39. Nan Robertson, "Dramatist against Odds," *New York Times*, March 8, 1959, p. X3.

40. McKissack and McKissack, *Young, Black, and Determined*.

41. McKissack and McKissack, *Young, Black, and Determined*.

42. Samuel G. Freedman, "Yale Marking 25th Anniversary of 'Raisin in the Sun,'" *New York Times*, November 1, 1983. Accessed July 10, 2018, https://www.nytimes.com/1983/11/01/theater/yale-marking-25th-anniversary-of-raisin-in-sun.html.

43. Freedman, "Yale Marking 25th Anniversary of 'Raisin in the Sun,'" https://www.nytimes.com/1983/11/01/theater/yale-marking-25th-anniversary-of-raisin-in-sun.html.

44. Freedman, "Yale Marking 25th Anniversary of 'Raisin in the Sun,'" https://www.nytimes.com/1983/11/01/theater/yale-marking-25th-anniversary-of-raisin-in-sun.html.

45. Freedman, "Yale Marking 25th Anniversary of 'Raisin in the Sun,'" https://www.nytimes.com/1983/11/01/theater/yale-marking-25th-anniversary-of-raisin-in-sun.html.

46. McKissack and McKissack, *Young, Black, and Determined*, 77–78.

47. Robertson, "Dramatist against Odds," X3.

48. Campbell Robertson, "Lloyd Richards, Theater Director and Cultivator of Playwrights, Is Dead at 87," *New York Times*, July 1, 2006. Accessed July 10, 2018, https://www.nytimes.com/2006/07/01/theater/01richards.html.

49. McKissack and McKissack, *Young, Black, and Determined*.

50. Michael Anderson, "A Landmark Lesson in Being Black," https://www.nytimes.com/1999/03/07/theater/theater-a-landmark-lesson-in-being-black.html.

51. Brooks Atkinson, "Review of the Original 1959 Broadway Production," *Huntington Theatre*, March 12, 1959. Accessed July 8, 2018, https://www.huntingtontheatre.org/articles/A-Raisin-in-the-Sun/Review-of-the-Original-1959-Broadway-production/.

52. McKissack and McKissack, *Young, Black, and Determined*.

53. "Background and Criticism of *A Raisin in the Sun*," *Chicago Public Library*, n.d. Accessed March 2, 2019, https://www.chipublib.org/background-and-criticism-of-a-raisin-in-the-sun/.

54. McKissack and McKissack, *Young, Black, and Determined*, 83.

55. "Background and Criticism of *A Raisin in the Sun*," https://www.chipublib.org/background-and-criticism-of-a-raisin-in-the-sun/.

56. McKissack and McKissack, *Young, Black, and Determined*, 83.

57. "Lorraine Hansberry," http://www.pbs.org/wnet/americanmasters/lorraine-hansberry-sighted-eyes-feeling-heart-biography/9877/.

58. McKissack and McKissack, *Young, Black, and Determined*.

59. Salamishah Tillet, "For Lorraine Hansberry, 'A Raisin in the Sun' Was Just the Start," *New York Times*, January 12, 2018. Accessed March 2, 2019, https://www.nytimes.com/2018/01/12/arts/television/lorraine-hansberry-sighted-eyes-feeling-heart.html.

60. "Her Dream Came True," *New York Times*, April 9, 1959, p. 37.

61. Lillian Ross, "The Talk of the Town: Playwright," *New Yorker*, May 9, 1959, p. 33.

62. McKissack and McKissack, *Young, Black, and Determined*, 114.

63. Jeanne-Marie A. Miller, "Lorraine Vivian Hansberry (1930–1965)," in *Heath Anthology of American Literature*, ed. Paul Ed Lauter (Boston: Houghton Mifflin College Division, 1998). Accessed March 2, 2019, http://faculty.georgetown.edu/bassr/heath/syllabuild/iguide/hansberr.html.

64. Lewis Funke, "Along the Rialto: Miss Hansberry's Two Plays—Other Items," *New York Times*, June 23, 1963, p. 89.

65. Howard Taubman, "Theater: 'Sidney Brustein's Window'; Lorraine Hansberry's Play at Longacre," *New York Times*, October 16, 1964, p. 32.

66. William Gibson, "Audience Apathy," *New York Times*, November 8, 1964, p. 4.

67. Chris Jones, "Magnificent 'Sign in Sidney Brustein's Window' Is a Rediscovered Classic," *Chicago Trbune*, May 10, 2016. Accessed March 2, 2019, https://www.chicagotribune.com/entertainment/theater/ct-sign-in-sidney-brusteins-window-goodman-ent-0511-20160510-column.html.

68. McKissack and McKissack, *Young, Black, and Determined*.

69. McKissack and McKissack, *Young, Black, and Determined*, 120.

70. Lorraine Hansberry, *A Raisin in the Sun* (New York: Vintage Books, 1959), 51.

71. Elise Harris, "The Double Life of Lorraine Hansberry," *Out*, September 1999. Accessed March 2, 2019, https://medium.com/@girlsinmitsouko/the-double-life-of-lorraine-hansberry-out-magazine-september-1999-a60c1d471d49.

72. "Lorraine Hansberry," http://www.pbs.org/wnet/americanmasters/lorraine-hansberry-sighted-eyes-feeling-heart-biography/9877 .

73. Alvin Klein, "Celebrating Hansberry in Her Words," *New York Times*, January 29, 1995, p. 13.

74. Howard Taubman, "Lorraine Hansberry," *New York Times*, January 17, 1965, p. 3.

4. REVOLTING WOMEN

1. Barry Friedman, *The Will of the People: How Public Opinion Has Influenced the Supreme Court* (New York: Farrar, Straus and Giroux, 2009), 290.

2. Kira Cochrane, "1963: The Beginning of the Feminist Movement," *Guardian*, May 7, 2013. Accessed July 25, 2018, https://www.theguardian.com/lifeandstyle/2013/may/07/1963-beginning-feminist-movement.

3. Michelene Wandor, *Carry on Understudies: Theatre and Sexual Politics* (London and New York: Routledge & Kegan Paul, 1986).

4. Chris Megson, *Modern British Playwriting: The 1970s: Voices, Documents, New Interpretations* (London: Bloomsbury, 2012).

5. Wandor, *Carry on Understudies.*

6. Wandor, *Carry on Understudies.*

7. Wandor, *Carry on Understudies*, 26.

8. Wandor, *Carry on Understudies.*

9. Wandor, *Carry on Understudies*, 27.

10. Jenny Lyn Bader, "A Brief History of the Gender Parity Movement in Theater," *Howlround*, March 4, 2017. Accessed July 25, 2018, https://howlround.com/brief-history-gender-parity-movement-theatre.

11. Bonnie G. Smith, ed., *Oxford Encyclopedia of Women in World History, Volume 1* (Oxford, U.K.: Oxford University Press, 2008).

12. Graham Saunders, *British Theatre Companies, 1980–1994* (London: Bloomsbury, 2015), 69.

13. Clive Tempest, quoted in Saunders, *British Theatre Companies, 1980–1994*, 68.

14. Lamede, quoted in Saunders, *British Theatre Companies, 1980–1994*, 69.

15. Saunders, *British Theatre Companies, 1980–1994.*

16. Megson, *Modern British Playwriting*, 50.

17. Jozefina Komporaly, *Staging Motherhood: British Women Playwrights, 1956 to the Present* (New York: Palgrave MacMillan, 2007), 38–39.

18. Megson, *Modern British Playwriting.*

19. Megson, *Modern British Playwriting.*

20. Michelene Wandor, *Post-war British Drama: Looking Back in Gender* (New York: Routledge, 2000), 126–27.

21. Red Chidgey, "Cunning Stunts: Women's Theater in the 1970s and '80s," *F Word*, December 8, 2008. Accessed July 20, 2018, https://www.thefword.org.uk/2008/12/cunning_stunts/.

22. Michael Billington, "Margaret Thatcher Casts a Long Shadow over Theater and the Arts," *Guardian*, April 8, 2013. Accessed July 20, 2018, https://www.theguardian.com/stage/2013/apr/08/margaret-thatcher-long-shadow-theatre.

23. Marianne Novy, ed., *Cross-Cultural Performances: Differences in Women's Re-visions of Shakespeare* (Chicago: University of Illinois Press, 1993), 215.

24. Peter Hall, "Taking Stock of Creativity during the Thatcher Years," *New York Times*, January 20, 1991. Accessed July 20, 2018, https://www.nytimes.com/1991/01/20/theater/theater-taking-stock-of-creativity-during-the-thatcher-years.html.

25. Janelle Reinelt, "Resisting Thatcherism: The Monstrous Regiment and the School of Hard Knox," in *Acting Out: Feminist Performances*, ed. Lynda Hart and Peggy Phelan, pp. 161–79 (Ann Arbor: University of Michigan Press, 1993).

26. Gillian Hanna, *Monstrous Regiment: Four Plays and a Collective Celebration* (London: Nick Hern Books, 1991).

27. Kathryn Mederos Syssoyeva and Scott Proudfit, *Women, Collective Creation, and Devised Performance: The Rise of Women Theatre Artists in the Twentieth and Twenty-First Centuries* (New York: Palgrave Macmillan, 2016), 181.

28. Linda Fitzsimmons, *File on Churchill* (London: Methuen Drama, 1989).

29. Wandor, *Carry on Understudies*, 71.

30. Christopher Innes, *Modern British Drama: The Twentieth Century* (Cambridge, U.K.: Cambridge University Press, 2002).

31. Reinelt, "Resisting Thatcherism," 163.

32. Reinelt, "Resisting Thatcherism."

33. Reinelt, "Resisting Thatcherism," 179.

34. Reinelt, "Resisting Thatcherism."

35. Reinelt, "Resisting Thatcherism," 163.

36. "Monstrous Regiment," *Unfinished Histories*, n.d. Accessed July 19, 2018, http://www.unfinishedhistories.com/history/companies/monstrous-regiment/.

37. "Mrs. Worthington's Daughters," *Unfinished Histories*, n.d. Accessed August 3, 2018, http://www.unfinishedhistories.com/history/companies/mrs-worthingtons-daughters/.

38. "Mrs. Worthington's Daughters," http://www.unfinishedhistories.com/history/companies/mrs-worthingtons-daughters/.

39. "Gay Sweatshop Theatre Company," *Unfinished Histories*, n.d. Accessed July 25, 2018, http://www.unfinishedhistories.com/history/companies/gay-sweatshop/.

40. Simon Callow, "Simon Callow: In Praise of Gay Sweatshop," *Guardian*, February 15, 2015. Accessed July 25, 2018, https://www.theguardian.com/books/2015/feb/13/simon-callow-in-priase-of-gay-sweatshop.

41. "Gay Sweatshop Theatre Company," http://www.unfinishedhistories.com/history/companies/gay-sweatshop/.

42. Megson, *Modern British Playwriting*.

43. *"Any Woman Can," Unfinished Histories*, n.d. Accessed August, 5, 2018, http://www.unfinishedhistories.com/history/companies/gay-sweatshop/any-woman-can/.

44. Andrew Wyllie, *Sex on Stage: Gender and Sexuality in Postwar British Theatre* (Bristol, U.K.: Intellect, 2009).

45. *"Care and Control," Unfinished Histories*, n.d. Accessed August 1, 2018, http://www.unfinishedhistories.com/history/companies/gay-sweatshop/care-and-control .

46. The Women's Festival, n.d., http://www.unfinishedhistories.com/history/companies/gay-sweatshop/the-womens-festival/.

47. John Bull, *British Theatre Companies: 1965–1979* (London: Bloomsbury, 2017).

48. Lizbeth Goodman, *Contemporary Feminist Theatres: To Each Her Own* (London: Routledge, 1993), 72.

49. Megson, *Modern British Playwriting*.

50. Bull, *British Theatre Companies*.

51. Hilton Als, "Color Vision," *New Yorker*, November 1, 2010. Accessed August 1, 2018, https://www.newyorker.com/magazine/2010/11/08/color-vision.

52. Jill Cox-Cordova, "Shange's 'for colored girls' Has Lasting Power," *CNN Entertainment*, July 21, 2009. Accessed August 1, 2018, http://www.cnn.com/2009/SHOWBIZ/books/07/21/for.colored.girls.shange/index.html.

53. Clive Barnes, "Black Sisterhood Ntozake Shange's 'for colored girls' Opens at Papp's Anspacher Theater," *New York Times*, June 2, 1976, p. 42.

54. Kenneth Turan and Joseph Papp, *Free for All: Joe Papp, the Public, and the Greatest Theater Story Ever Told* (New York: Anchor Books, 2010), 415–16.

55. Laura Collins-Hughes, "Ntozake Shange, Who Wrote 'for colored girls,' Is Dead at 70," *New York Times*, October 28, 2018. Accessed August 1, 2018, https://www.nytimes.com/2018/10/28/obituaries/ntozake-shange-is-dead-at-70.html.

56. Turan and Papp, *Free for All*.

57. Als, "Color Vision," https://www.newyorker.com/magazine/2010/11/08/color-vision.

58. Als, "Color Vision," https://www.newyorker.com/magazine/2010/11/08/color-vision .

59. Mel Gussow, "'Colored Girls' Evolves," *New York Times*, September 16, 1976. Accessed August 1, 2018, https://www.nytimes.com/1976/09/16/archives/stage-colored-girls-evolves-play-moves-to-broadway-to-be-seen-and.html .

60. Als, "Color Vision," https://www.newyorker.com/magazine/2010/11/08/color-vision.

61. Als, "Color Vision," https://www.newyorker.com/magazine/2010/11/08/color-vision.

62. Kim F. Hall, "Finding God in Ourselves: 'for colored girls' at 40," *Ebony*, September 16, 2016. Accessed August 1, 2018, https://www.ebony.com/ entertainment/for-colored-girls-anniversary/.

63. Hilton Als, "Color Vision: Ntozake Shange's Outspoken Art," *New Yorker*, November 1, 2010. Accessed August 23, 2019, https://www.newyorker.com/ magazine/2010/11/08/color-vision.

64. Collins-Hughes, "Ntozake Shange, Who Wrote 'for colored girls,' Is Dead at 70," https://www.nytimes.com/2018/10/28/obituaries/ntozake-shange- is-dead-at-70.html.

65. Laura Collins-Hughes, "Seven Flames Kindled by the Focused Fire of Ntozake Shange," *New York Times*, November 1, 2018. Accessed August 1, 2018, https://www.nytimes.com/2018/11/01/theater/seven-flames-kindled-by- the-focused-fire-of-ntozake-shange.html.

66. Andrea Stevens, "'for colored girls' May Be for the Ages," *New York Times*, September 3, 1995. Accessed August 1, 2018, https://www.nytimes.com/ 1995/09/03/theater/theater-for-colored-girls-may-be-for-the-ages.html.

67. Jane Carr, "What 'for colored girls' Meant to Us," *CNN*, October 28, 2018. Accessed August 1, 2018, https://www.cnn.com/2018/10/28/opinions/ ntozake-shange-remembered-in-tweets/index.html.

68. Charles Wright, "Cryer and Ford: Taking the Act to City Center," *Breaking Character*, July 26, 2013. Accessed August 1, 2018, https://www. breakingcharactermagazine.com/cryer-ford-taking-the-act-to-city-center/.

69. Wright, "Cryer and Ford," https://www.breakingcharactermagazine.com/ cryer-ford-taking-the-act-to-city-center/.

70. Richard Eder, "'Getting Act Together,'" *New York Times*, June 15, 1978, p. C17.

71. Charles Isherwood, "Breaking Out of the Box (and into a Song)," *New York Times*, July 25, 2013. Accessed August 1, 2018, https://www.nytimes.com/ 2013/07/26/theater/reviews/im-getting-my-act-together-at-city-center.html.

72. David Finkle, "First Nighter: City Center's 'I'm Getting My Act Together and Taking It on the Road' Hits Bumps," *Huffington Post*, September 24, 2013. Accessed August 1, 2018, https://www.huffpost.com/entry/first-nighter-city- center_b_3654029.

73. Julie Rovner, "Twenty-two States Curb Access to Abortion in 2013," *NPR*, January 4, 2014. Accessed August 1, 2018, https://www.npr.org/sections/ health-shots/2014/01/03/259445809/22-states-curbed-access-to-abortion-in- 2013.

74. Claire Zillman, "Yes, Pregnancy Discrimination at Work Is Still a Huge Problem," *Fortune*, July 14, 2014. Accessed August 1, 2018, http://fortune.com/ 2014/07/15/pregnancy-discrimination/.

75. Chris Hedges, "A Producer with a Mission: More Plays by Women," *New York Times*, May 23, 2001. Accessed August 1, 2018, https://www.nytimes.com/2001/05/03/nyregion/public-lives-a-producer-with-a-mission-more-plays-by-women.html.

76. Mel Gussow, "'Choices,' Women's Anthology," *New York Times*, December 11, 1978. Accessed August 1, 2018, https://www.nytimes.com/1978/12/11/archives/stage-choices-womens-anthology-artistic-energy.html.

77. Alice Saville, "Bryony Lavery: 'Anger Is One of the Things That Fuels Me Wonderfully,'" *Exeunt*, February 27, 2018. Accessed August 1, 2018, http://exeuntmagazine.com/features/bryony-lavery-interview/.

78. Saville, "Bryony Lavery," http://exeuntmagazine.com/features/bryony-lavery-interview/.

79. Nick Curtis, "Playwright Bryony Lavery: 'We Have to Watch Our Backs, Particularly in This Strange Climate,'" *Guardian*, August 25, 2018. Accessed August 1, 2018, https://www.theguardian.com/stage/2018/aug/25/byrony-lavery-interview-the-lovely-bones-we-have-to-watch-our-backs.

80. Lyn Gardner, "Pam Gems Obituary: One of Britain's Leading Female Playwrights, Known for *Piaf*, *Queen Christina*, and *Stanley*," *Guardian*, May 16, 2011. Accessed August 1, 2018, https://www.theguardian.com/stage/2011/may/16/pam-gems-obituary.

81. Jozefina Komporaly, *Staging Motherhood: British Women Playwrights, 1956 to the Present* (New York: Palgrave Macmillan, 2006), 38.

82. Komporaly, *Staging Motherhood*, 38.

83. William Grimes, "Pam Gems, 85; Playwright Explored Feminist Themes," *New York Times*, May 19, 2011. Accessed August 1, 2018, http://archive.boston.com/bostonglobe/obituaries/articles/2011/05/19/pam_gems_85_playwright_explored_feminist_themes/.

84. Ted Whitehead, "Love Bite," *Spectator*, December 18, 1976. Accessed August 1, 2018, http://archive.spectator.co.uk/article/18th-december-1976/27/theatre.

85. Gardner, "Pam Gems Obituary," https://www.theguardian.com/stage/2011/may/16/pam-gems-obituary.

86. Komporaly, *Staging Motherhood*, 39.

87. Megson, *Modern British Playwriting*.

88. M. Remnant, ed., "Queen Christina," *Plays by Women*, vol. 5 (London: Methuen, 1986), 29.

89. Komporaly, *Staging Motherhood*.

90. Cliff Jahr, "Paif's Life and Loves Make a Musical," *New York Times*, February 1, 1981. Accessed August 1, 2018, https://www.nytimes.com/1981/02/01/theater/piaf-s-life-and-loves-make-a-musical.html.

91. Simon, John. 1981. "Fallen Sparrow." *New York Magazine*, February 16: 64.

92. Benedict Nightingale, "In London, Two Actresses Shine," *New York Times*, December 1, 1985, p. 65.

93. Mel Gussow, "Kathleen Turner Returns to Stage as Camille," *New York Times*, December 13, 1986. Accessed August 1, 2018, https://www.nytimes.com/1986/12/13/theater/theater-kathleen-turner-returns-to-stage-as-camille.html.

94. Gussow, "Kathleen Turner Returns to Stage as Camille," https://www.nytimes.com/1986/12/13/theater/theater-kathleen-turner-returns-to-stage-as-camille.html.

95. Mel Gussow, "How One Woman Goes to the Mat with a Harsh World," *New York Times*, August 27, 1982. Accessed August 1, 2018, https://www.nytimes.com/1982/08/27/theater/broadway-how-one-woman-goes-to-the-mat-with-a-harsh-world.html.

96. Frank Rich, "'Teaneck Tanzi,' Comedy from Britain," *New York Times*, April 21, 1983. Accessed August 1, 2018, https://www.nytimes.com/1983/04/21/theater/stage-teaneck-tanzi-comedy-from-britain.html.

97. Glenne Currie, "Life Is a Wrestling Ring in New Broadway Play," *United Press International*, April 20, 1983. Accessed August 1, 2018, https://www.upi.com/Archives/1983/04/20/Life-is-a-wrestling-ring-in-new-Broadway-play/7080062495016/.

98. Frank Rich, "'Real Estate,' by Author of 'Salonika,'" *New York Times*, December 2, 1987. Accessed August 1, 2018, https://www.nytimes.com/1987/12/02/theater/stage-real-estate-by-author-of-salonika.html.

99. Stephen Holden, "Theater in Review," *New York Times*, May 6, 1992. Accessed August 1, 2018, https://www.nytimes.com/1992/05/13/theater/theater-in-review-343592.html.

100. Clive Barnes, "Caryl Churchill's 'Owners,'" *New York Times*, June 2, 1973, p. 29.

101. Frank Rich, "Sexual Confusion on 'Cloud 9,'" *New York Times*, May 20, 1981. Accessed August 1, 2018, https://www.nytimes.com/1981/05/20/theater/stage-sexual-confusion-on-cloud-9.html.

102. Jennifer Dunning, "'Cloud 9,' as Viewed by Those on It," *New York Times*, November 6, 1981, p. 86.

103. Frank Rich, "Caryl Churchill's 'Top Girls' at the Public," *New York Times*, December 29, 1982. Accessed August 1, 2018, https://www.nytimes.com/1982/12/29/theater/stage-caryl-churchill-s-top-girls-at-the-public.html.

5. VOICES, NEW AND NOW

1. George Guilder, "Women in the Work Force," *Atlantic*, September 1986. Accessed October 24, 2018, https://www.theatlantic.com/magazine/archive/1986/09/women-in-the-work-force/304924/.

2. Nancy Gibbs, "The War against Feminism," *Time*, June 24, 2001. Accessed October 24, 2018, http://content.time.com/time/magazine/article/0,9171,159157,00.html.

3. Jenny Lyn Bader, "A Brief History of the Gender Parity Movement in Theater," *HowlRound*, March 4, 2017. Accessed October 24, 2018, https://howlround.com/brief-history-gender-parity-movement-theatre.

4. Elaine Aston, "Daniels in the Lion's Den: Sarah Daniels and the British Backlash," *Theatre Journal* 47, no. 3 (October 1995): 393–403.

5. Jane Milling, *Modern British Playwriting: The 1980s: Voices, Documents, New Interpretations* (London: Bloomsbury Publishing, 2012), 57.

6. Jane Milling, *Modern British Playwriting: The 1980s: Voices, Documents, New Interpretations* (London: Bloomsbury Publishing, 2012), 239.

7. Aston, "Daniels in the Lion's Den."

8. Aston, "Daniels in the Lion's Den," 397.

9. World Bank, "Population, Female (% of Total)," n.d. Accessed October 24, 2018, https://data.worldbank.org/indicator/SP.POP.TOTL.FE.ZS?locations=GB&name_desc=true.

10. Aston, "Daniels in the Lion's Den," 395.

11. Elaine Aston and Janelle Reinelt, eds., *Cambridge Companion to Modern British Women Playwrights* (Cambridge, U.K.: Cambridge University Press, 2000), 195.

12. Deborah Sontag, "Anita Hill and Revitalizing Feminism," *New York Times*, April 26, 1992, p. 31.

13. Aston, "Daniels in the Lion's Den," 394.

14. Irving Wardle, "Reviewing 'Ripen Our Darkness,'" *New York Times*, September 8, 1981, quoted in Aston, "Daniels in the Lion's Den," 395.

15. Lynn Hecht Schafran, "Reagan vs. Women," *New York Times*, October 13, 1981. Accessed October 24, 2018, https://www.nytimes.com/1981/10/13/opinion/reagan-vs-women.html.

16. Jane Velencia, "Americans Didn't Believe Anita Hill. How Will They Respond to Kavanaugh's Accuser?" *FiveThirtyEight*, September 17, 2018.

17. Sarah Daniels, *Head-Rot Holiday* (London: Bloomsbury, 2016), quoted in Gabrielle Griffin, "Violence, Abuse, and Gender Relations in the Plays of Sarah Daniels," in *Cambridge Companion to Modern British Women Playwrights*, ed. Elaine Aston and Janelle Reinelt, pp. 194–212 (Cambridge, U.K.: Cambridge University Press, 2000), 202.

18. Aston and Reinelt, eds., *Cambridge Companion to Modern British Women Playwrights*, 202.

19. Aston and Reinelt, eds., *Cambridge Companion to Modern British Women Playwrights*, 195.

20. Sarah Daniels, *Plays: One* (London: Methuen Drama, 1991), quoted in Aston and Reinelt, eds., *Cambridge Companion to Modern British Women Playwrights*, 202.

21. Paul Taylor, "Pat Hates: Paul Taylor on 'The Madness of Esme and Shaz,'" *Independent*, February 17, 1994. Accessed October 24, 2018, https://www.independent.co.uk/arts-entertainment/theatre-pat-hates-paul-taylor-on-the-madness-of-esme-and-shaz-1394672.html.

22. Aston, "Daniels in the Lion's Den," 396.

23. Luc Gilleman, "Drama and Pornography: Sarah Daniels's Masterpieces and Anthony Neilson's *The Censor*," *Journal of Dramatic Theory and Criticism* 25, no. 1 (2010): 79, 92.

24. Sarah Daniels, *Masterpieces* (London: Bloomsbury, 2016), 1.

25. Daniels, *Masterpieces*, 11.

26. Carolyn Bronstein, "The Origins of Anti-Pornography Feminism," *Fifteen Eighty Four*, August 10, 2011. Accessed October 24, 2018, http://www.cambridgeblog.org/2011/08/the-origins-of-anti-pornography-feminism-by-carolyn-bronstein/.

27. Andrea Dworkin and Catharine A. MacKinnon, *Civil Rights: A New Day for Women's Equality* (Organizing against Pornography, 1988), 24.

28. Aston, "Daniels in the Lion's Den," 400.

29. Sarah Daniels, *Rage and Reason: Women Playwrights on Playwrighting* (London: Bloomsbury, 1997), quoted in Gilleman, "Drama and Pornography," 79.

30. Aston, "Daniels in the Lion's Den," 400.

31. Aston, "Daniels in the Lion's Den," 401.

32. Mary Remnant, *Plays by Women: Volume 6* (London: Methuen, 1988), quoted in Aston, "Daniels in the Lion's Den," 399.

33. Sarah Daniels, "There Are 52 Percent of Us," *Journal of National Drama* 152 (1984): 23–24, quoted in Aston, "Daniels in the Lion's Den," 401.

34. Sarah Hemming, "New Stages in Writing the Wrongs: Hush—Don't Tell Anyone, but April De Angelis No Longer Sees Women as the Big Issue, Sarah Hemming Reports," *Independent*, July 29, 1992. Accessed October 24, 2018, https://www.independent.co.uk/arts-entertainment/theatre-new-stages-in-writing-the-wrongs-hush-dont-tell-anyone-but-april-de-angelis-no-longer-sees-1536207.html .

35. Hemming, "New Stages in Writing the Wrongs," https://www. independent.co.uk/arts-entertainment/theatre-new-stages-in-writing-the-wrongs-hush-dont-tell-anyone-but-april-de-angelis-no-longer-sees-1536207.html.

36. Lyn Gardner, "April De Angelis: 'Being a Feminist in the Real World Is Tough,'" *Guardian*, March 11, 2015. Accessed October 24, 2018, https://www. theguardian.com/stage/2015/mar/11/april-de-angelis-after-electra-motherhood-older-women .

37. Gardner, "April De Angelis," https://www.theguardian.com/stage/2015/mar/11/april-de-angelis-after-electra-motherhood-older-women.

38. Megan Garber, "When Newsweek 'Struck Terror in the Hearts of Single Women,'" *Atlantic*, June 2, 2016. Accessed October 24, 2018, https://www. theatlantic.com/entertainment/archive/2016/06/more-likely-to-be-killed-by-a-terrorist-than-to-get-married/485171/.

39. Carey Purcell, "The 'A' Word: Plays about Not Having the Baby," *American Theatre*, August 23, 2016. Accessed October 24, 2018, https://www. americantheatre.org/2016/08/23/the-a-word-plays-about-not-having-the-baby/.

40. Robert Brustein, *Reimagining American Theatre* (New York: Hill and Wang, 1991), 80.

41. Dorothy Chansky, *Kitchen Sink Realisms: Domestic Labor, Dining, and Drama in American Theater* (Iowa City: University of Iowa Press, 2015), 199.

42. Marsha Norman, *'night, Mother* (New York: Dramatists Play Service, 1983), 13.

43. Norman, *'night, Mother*, 18.

44. Frank Rich, "Theater: Suicide Talk in '''night, Mother,'" *New York Times*, April 1, 1983. Accessed October 24, 2018, https://www.nytimes.com/1983/04/01/theater/theater-suicide-talk-in-night-mother.html.

45. Marsha Norman, interview by Carey Purcell, April 2, 2019.

46. Richard Eder, "'Getting Out' by Marsha Norman," *New York Times*, May 16, 1979. Accessed October 24, 2018, https://www.nytimes.com/1979/05/16/archives/stage-getting-out-by-marsha-norman-2sided-liberation.html.

47. Norman, interview by Carey Purcell.

48. Norman, interview by Carey Purcell.

49. Alisa Solomon, "Why 'The Heidi Chronicles' Failed to Find a New Audience," *Nation*, April 24, 2015. Accessed October 24, 2018, https://www. thenation.com/article/why-heidi-chronicles-failed-find-new-audience/.

50. Joe Holley, "'Heidi Chronicles' Playwright Wendy Wasserstein," *Washington Post*, January 31, 2006. Accessed October 24, 2018, https://www. washingtonpost.com/archive/local/2006/01/31/heidi-chronicles-playwright-wendy-wasserstein/70b4823e-b91c-4375-9bf5-d2ae6faab7e3/?utm_term=. 72b7378ef6bb.

51. Wendy Wasserstein, *Uncommon Women and Others* (New York: Dramatists Play Service, 1978), 28.

52. Wendy Wasserstein, *Isn't It Romantic* (New York: Dramatists Play Service, 1984), 11.

53. Wasserstein, *Isn't It Romantic*, 22.

54. Wasserstein, *Isn't It Romantic*, 45.

55. Wasserstein, *Isn't It Romantic*, 30.

56. Kathleen Betsko and Rachel Koenig, *Interviews with Contemporary Women Playwrights* (New York: Beech Tree Books, 1987), quoted in Heather Baggot, "I Am Woman, Hear Me Gasp for Air: An Analysis of Wendy Wasserstein's 'Isn't It Romantic,'" *Aticulate*, volume 3, article 9. Accessed October 24, 2018, https://digitalcommons.denison.edu/articulate/vol3/iss1/9.

57. Richard Christiansen, "'Isn't It Romantic' Offers a Sweet Look at Modern Women," *Chicago Tribune*, October 11, 1985. Accessed October 24, 2018, https://www.chicagotribune.com/news/ct-xpm-1985-10-11-8503090555-story.html.

58. Mel Gussow, "Isn't It Romantic," *New York Times*, June 15, 1981. Accessed October 24, 2018, https://www.nytimes.com/1981/06/15/theater/theater-isn-t-it-romantic.html.

59. Jan Balakian, "'The Heidi Chronicles': The Big Chill of Feminism," *South Atlantic Review* 60, no. 2 (1995): 94–101.

60. Balakian, "'The Heidi Chronicles,'" 94.

61. Holley, "'Heidi Chronicles' Playwright Wendy Wasserstein," https://www.washingtonpost.com/archive/local/2006/01/31/heidi-chronicles-playwright-wendy-wasserstein/70b4823e-b91c-4375-9bf5-d2ae6faab7e3/?utm_term=.72b7378ef6bb.

62. Laure Winer, "Wendy Wasserstein, the Art of Theater No. 13," *Paris Review* 142 (Spring 1997). Accessed October 24, 2018, https://www.theparisreview.org/interviews/1284/wendy-wasserstein-the-art-of-theater-no-13-wendy-wasserstein .

63. Balakian, "'The Heidi Chronicles,'" 99.

64. Wendy Wasserstein, *The Heidi Chronicles* (New York: Dramatists Play Service, 1990), 59.

65. Mel Gussow, "A Modern-Day Heffalump in Search of Herself," *New York Times*, December 12, 1988. Accessed September 5, 2018, https://www.nytimes.com/1988/12/12/theater/review-theater-a-modern-day-heffalump-in-search-of-herself.html.

66. Solomon, "Why 'The Heidi Chronicles' Failed to Find a New Audience," https://www.thenation.com/article/why-heidi-chronicles-failed-find-new-audience/.

67. Lisa Low, "Feminism and 'The Heidi Chronicles': Betty Friedan and Gloria Steinem Reflect," *Christian Science Monitor*, October 10, 1989, p. 11.

68. Low, "Feminism and 'The Heidi Chronicles.'"

69. Jill Dolan, "'The Heidi Chronicles' Revived on Broadway," *Feminist Spectator*, April 29, 2015. Accessed September 5, 2018, http://feministspectator.princeton.edu/2015/04/29/the-heidi-chronicles-revived-on-broadway/.

70. Aston and Reinelt, eds., *Cambridge Companion to Modern British Women Playwrights*.

71. Aston and Reinelt, eds., *Cambridge Companion to Modern British Women Playwrights*, 154.

72. Low, "Feminism and 'The Heidi Chronicles.'"

6. WINNING AWARDS FOR DOING A "MAN'S JOB"

1. Ellis Nassour, "Remembering Tony Namesake Antoinette Perry," *Playbill*, June 4, 1998. Accessed November 15, 2018, http://www.playbill.com/article/remembering-tony-namesake-antoinette-perry-com-75756.

2. Ellis Nassour, "Antoinette Perry," *Tony Awards*, n.d. Accessed June 23, 2019, https://www.tonyawards.com/history/antoinette-perry/.

3. Ellis Nassour, "Antoinette Perry Makes a Name," *Theatermania*, May 29, 2000. Accessed November 15, 2018, https://www.theatermania.com/new-york/news/antoinette-perry-makes-a-name_752.html.

4. "Antoinette Perry," *Encyclopedia Britannica*, n.d. Accessed November 15, 2018, https://www.britannica.com/biography/Antoinette-Perry.

5. Anne Fliotsos and Wendy Vierow, *American Women Stage Directors of the Twentieth Century* (Urbana and Chicago: University of Illinois Press, 2008), 351.

6. "Antoinette Perry," https://www.britannica.com/biography/Antoinette-Perry.

7. Nassour, "Antoinette Perry," https://www.tonyawards.com/history/antoinette-perry/.

8. Fliotsos and Vierow, *American Women Stage Directors of the Twentieth Century*, 349.

9. Nassour, "Antoinette Perry Makes a Name," https://www.theatermania.com/new-york/news/antoinette-perry-makes-a-name_752.html .

10. Fliotsos and Vierow, *American Women Stage Directors of the Twentieth Century*, 351.

11. Nassour, "Antoinette Perry," https://www.tonyawards.com/history/antoinette-perry/.

12. Fliotsos and Vierow, *American Women Stage Directors of the Twentieth Century*.

13. Nassour, "Antoinette Perry," https://www.tonyawards.com/history/antoinette-perry/.

14. Anita Gates, "Movies on TV," *New York Times*, November 13, 2005. Accessed June 23, 2019, https://www.nytimes.com/2005/11/13/arts/television/movies-on-tv.html .

15. Nassour, "Antoinette Perry," https://www.tonyawards.com/history/antoinette-perry/.

16. Joseph Gustaitis, "The Woman behind the 'TONY': April '97 American History Feature," *History Net*, August 19, 1997. Accessed May 3, 2019, https://www.historynet.com/the-woman-behind-the-tony-april-97-american-history-feature.htm.

17. Nassour, "Antoinette Perry," https://www.tonyawards.com/history/antoinette-perry/.

18. Fliotsos and Vierow, *American Women Stage Directors of the Twentieth Century*.

19. "Zona Gale," *New York Times*, December 29, 1938. p. 18.

20. "'Miss Lulu Bett,'" *Archive.org*, n.d. Accessed November 16, 2018, https://archive.org/details/misslulubettamer00gale/page/n3.

21. Fliotsos and Vierow, *American Women Stage Directors of the Twentieth Century*.

22. Nassour, "Antoinette Perry Makes a Name," https://www.theatermania.com/new-york/news/antoinette-perry-makes-a-name_752.html.

23. Lily Rothman, "This Is the Woman the Tony Awards Are Named After," *Time*, June 8, 2015. Accessed November 15, 2018, https://time.com/3903886/ton-awards-antoinette-perry-history/.

24. Theresa Agovino, "Female Directors Make Power Plays," *Crain's New York Business*, August 29, 2014. Accessed November 15, 2018, https://www.crainsnewyork.com/article/20140829/ARTS/140829823/female-directors-make-power-plays.

25. Iris Weiner, "Why Broadway Has Too Few Female Directors—and Why It Needs More," *Playbill*, November 1, 2016. Accessed November 15, 2018, http://www.playbill.com/article/why-broadway-has-too-few-female-directorsand-why-it-needs-more.

26. Clive Barnes, "'Don't Bother Me, I Can't Cope,'" *New York Times*, April 20, 1972. Accessed November 15, 2018, https://www.nytimes.com/1972/04/20/archives/stage-dont-bother-me-i-cant-cope-micki-grant-presents-footstomping.html.

27. Emily Mann, interview by Carey Purcell, March 15, 2019.

28. Mann, interview by Carey Purcell.

29. Mann, interview by Carey Purcell.

30. Mel Gussow, "Noticing the Women Out of the Spotlight," *New York Times*, July 19, 1989. Accessed November 15, 2018, https://www.nytimes.com/1989/07/19/theater/critic-s-notebook-noticing-the-women-out-of-the-spotlight.html.

31. "Year of the Woman," *United States Senate*, n.d. Accessed November 25, 2018, https://www.senate.gov/artandhistory/history/minute/year_of_the_woman.htm .

32. Janet Maslin, "The Night Oscar Paid Some Attention to Women," *New York Times*, March 31, 1993. Accessed November 25, 2018, https://www.nytimes.com/1993/03/31/arts/review-television-the-night-oscar-paid-some-attention-to-women.html.

33. Frank Rich, "New 'Sweeney' with a New Message," *New York Times*, September 15, 1989. Accessed November 25, 2018, https://www.nytimes.com/1989/09/15/theater/review-theater-new-sweeney-with-a-new-message.html.

34. Frank Rich, "'Once on This Island,' Fairy Tale Bringing Caribbean to 42d Street," *New York Times*, May 7, 1990. Accessed November 25, 2018, https://www.nytimes.com/1990/05/07/theater/review-theater-once-on-this-island-fairy-tale-bringing-caribbean-to-42d-street.html.

35. Fliotsos and Vierow, *American Women Stage Directors of the Twentieth Century*, 136.

36. "Oprah Talks to Julie Taymor," *Oprah.com*, November 2001. Accessed November 25, 2018, https://www.oprah.com/omagazine/oprah-interviews-julie-taymor/all.

37. "Oprah Talks to Julie Taymor," https://www.oprah.com/omagazine/oprah-interviews-julie-taymor/all.

38. Ben Brantley, "Cub Comes of Age: A Twice-Told Cosmic Tale," *New York Times*, November 14, 1997. Accessed November 25, 2018, https://www.nytimes.com/1997/11/14/movies/theater-review-cub-comes-of-age-a-twice-told-cosmic-tale.html.

39. Ben Brantley, "A Gasp for Breath inside an Airless Life," *New York Times*, February 27, 1998. Accessed November 25, 2018, https://www.nytimes.com/1998/02/27/movies/theater-review-a-gasp-for-breath-inside-an-airless-life.html.

40. Stephen Fay, "How She Broke the Abbey Habit: Garry Hynes Took on a Riotous History and a Hollow Legend When She Became Director of Dublin's Abbey Theatre. She Has Fostered Great New Irish Plays and Won Awards Abroad, but at Home the Knives Are Still Out," *Independent*, September 6, 1992. Accessed November 25, 2018, https://www.independent.co.uk/arts-entertainment/theatre-how-she-broke-the-abbey-habit-garry-hynes-took-on-a-riotous-history-and-a-hollow-legend-when-1549778.html.

41.　Liana Cafolla, "Theater Director Garry Hynes on Rebelling against Irish and Discovering Playwright Martin McDonagh," *Post Magazine*, March 16, 2017. Accessed November 25, 2018, https://www.scmp.com/magazines/post-magazine/arts-music/article/2079520/theatre-director-garry-hynes-rebelling-against.

42.　Martina Fitzgerald, "Irish Women in Politics: 'Now, Now, Girlie. There's No Place for Women Here,'" *Irish Times*, October 13, 2018. Accessed November 25, 2018, https://www.irishtimes.com/culture/books/irish-women-in-politics-now-now-girlie-there-s-no-place-for-women-here-1.3658442.

43.　Fay, "How She Broke the Abbey Habit," https://www.independent.co.uk/arts-entertainment/theatre-how-she-broke-the-abbey-habit-garry-hynes-took-on-a-riotous-history-and-a-hollow-legend-when-1549778.html.

44.　Fay, "How She Broke the Abbey Habit," https://www.independent.co.uk/arts-entertainment/theatre-how-she-broke-the-abbey-habit-garry-hynes-took-on-a-riotous-history-and-a-hollow-legend-when-1549778.html.

45.　Fay, "How She Broke the Abbey Habit," https://www.independent.co.uk/arts-entertainment/theatre-how-she-broke-the-abbey-habit-garry-hynes-took-on-a-riotous-history-and-a-hollow-legend-when-1549778.html.

46.　Celia McGee, "Garry Hynes, an Irish Director, Arrives with 8½ Hours of Her Countryman," *New York Times*, July 2, 2006. Accessed November 25, 2018, https://www.nytimes.com/2006/07/02/theater/02mcge.html.

47.　Ben Brantley, "How Ovid Helps Deal with Loss and Suffering," *New York Times*, October 10, 2001. Accessed November 25, 2018, https://www.nytimes.com/2001/10/10/theater/theater-review-how-ovid-helps-deal-with-loss-and-suffering.html .

48.　Chris Jones, *Rise Up! Broadway and American Society from "Angels in America" to "Hamilton"* (New York: Bloomsbury, 2019), 90.

49.　"August: Osage County - Anna D. Shapiro's Tony Award Speech," *YouTube*, July 15, 2008. Accessed November 25, 2018, https://www.youtube.com/watch?v=MLteI3Pnt68.

50.　Gordon Cox, "'Fish in the Dark' Director Anna D. Shapiro on Why She Talks Just Like Larry David," *Variety*, February 26, 2015. Accessed November 25, 2018, https://variety.com/2015/legit/features/fish-in-the-dark-director-anna-d-shapiro-on-why-she-talks-just-like-larry-david-1201440594/.

51.　Christopher Borrelli, "Anna D. Shapiro at Steppenwolf Theatre: Work in Progress," *Chicago Tribune*, August 21, 2015. Accessed November 25, 2018, https://www.chicagotribune.com/entertainment/theater/ct-anna-shapiro-steppenwolf-theatre-column.html.

52.　Scott Brown, "'Who's Afraid of Virginia Woolf?'" *Vulture*, October 15, 2012. Accessed November 25, 2018, https://www.vulture.com/2012/10/theater-review-whos-afraid-of-virginia-woolf.html.

53. Meredith Blake, "Tony Awards: Big Year for Women as Lauper, MacKinnon, Paulus Win," *Los Angeles Times*, June 10, 2013. Accessed November 25, 2018, https://www.latimes.com/entertainment/arts/la-xpm-2013-jun-10-la-et-cm-women-win-best-director-tonys-20130609-story.html.

54. Blake, "Tony Awards," https://www.latimes.com/entertainment/arts/la-xpm-2013-jun-10-la-et-cm-women-win-best-director-tonys-20130609-story.html.

55. Matt Wolf, "Marianne Elliott: An Expansive London Director in Love with Subtle Truths," *New York Times*, December 5, 2006. Accessed November 25, 2018, https://www.nytimes.com/2006/12/05/arts/05iht-lon6.html.

56. Kelly J. Nestruck, "Tony Award–Winning Director Marianne Elliott: 'I Quite Like to Be in the Driver's Seat,'" *Globe and Mail*, October 13, 2017. Accessed November 25, 2018, https://www.theglobeandmail.com/arts/theatre-and-performance/tony-award-winning-director-marianne-elliott-i-quite-like-to-be-in-the-drivers-seat/article36587954/.

57. Wolf, "Marianne Elliott," https://www.nytimes.com/2006/12/05/arts/05iht-lon6.html.

58. Nestruck, "Tony Award–Winning Director Marianne Elliott," https://www.theglobeandmail.com/arts/theatre-and-performance/tony-award-winning-director-marianne-elliott-i-quite-like-to-be-in-the-drivers-seat/article36587954/.

59. Ben Brantley, "A Pedophile Even Mother Could Love," *New York Times*, March 17, 1997. Accessed November 25, 2018, https://www.nytimes.com/1997/03/17/theater/a-pedophile-even-mother-could-love.html.

60. Kathy Henderson, "Paula Vogel Gives Some Valuable Driving Lessons," *Playbill*, May 23, 1997. Accessed November 25, 2018, http://www.playbill.com/article/paula-vogel-gives-some-valuable-driving-lessons-com-100951.

61. "The Top 10 Most-Produced Plays: 1994–2014," *American Theatre*, September 23, 2014. Accessed November 25, 2018, https://www.americantheatre.org/2014/09/23/top-10-most-plays-1994-2014/.

62. J. Wynn Rousuck, "'Baltimore Waltz' Is a Funny, Moving Drama about AIDS," *Baltimore Sun*, April 9, 1992. Accessed November 25, 2018, https://www.baltimoresun.com/news/bs-xpm-1992-04-09-1992100211-story.html.

63. Malcolm Johnson, "Vogel's Stylized 'Waltz' is a Moving, Powerful Triumph," *Hartford Courant*, February 16, 1992.

64. Mel Gussow, "Parents-to-Be Regress to Childhood," *New York Times*, May 7, 1993. Accessed November 25, 2018, https://www.nytimes.com/1993/05/07/theater/review-theater-parents-to-be-regress-to-childhood.html.

65. Maura Troester, "'And Baby Makes Seven,'" *Chicago Reader*, February 17, 1994. Accessed November 25, 2018, https://www.chicagoreader.com/chicago/and-baby-makes-seven/Content?oid=883800.

66. Markland Taylor, "'Hot 'N' Throbbing,'" *Variety*, May 2, 1994. Accessed November 25, 2018, https://variety.com/1994/film/reviews/resident-hot-n-throbbing-1200437376/.

67. Taylor, "Hot 'N' Throbbing,'" https://variety.com/1994/film/reviews/resident-hot-n-throbbing-1200437376/.

68. Laurie Winer, "Vogel's 'Hot' Mixes Reality and Fantasy with a Passion," *Los Angeles Times*, January 31, 1996. Accessed November 25, 2018, https://www.latimes.com/archives/la-xpm-1996-01-31-ca-30475-story.html.

69. Megan Rosenfeld, "One 'Hot' Property," *Washington Post*, September 12, 1999. Accessed June 23, 2019, https://www.washingtonpost.com/archive/lifestyle/style/1999/09/12/one-hot-property/cb2d4e37-5b22-4aae-badf-438b7ebe255d/?utm_term=.22d5dc058c38.

70. Rosenfeld, "One 'Hot' Property," https://www.washingtonpost.com/archive/lifestyle/style/1999/09/12/one-hot-property/cb2d4e37-5b22-4aae-badf-438b7ebe255d/?utm_term=.22d5dc058c38.

71. David Lefkowitz, "Paula Vogel: How She Keeps Driving," *Playbill*, April 7, 1997. Accessed November 25, 2018, http://www.playbill.com/article/paula-vogel-how-she-keeps-driving-com-100927.

72. Michael Paulson, "Two Female Playwrights Arrive on Broadway. What Took So Long?" *New York Times*, March 22, 2017. Accessed November 25, 2018, https://www.nytimes.com/2017/03/22/theater/lynn-nottage-paula-vogel-broadway.html.

73. Ben Brantley, "'Indecent' Pays Heartfelt Tribute to a Stage Scandal," *New York Times*, April 18, 2017. Accessed November 25, 2018, https://www.nytimes.com/2017/04/18/theater/indecent-review-paula-vogel-broadway.html.

74. Jeremy Gerard, "Audience Member Shouts 'Let's Hear It For Women Producers!' as Broadway's Tony-Winning 'Indecent' Extends Run," *Deadline*, June 23, 2017. Accessed November 25, 2018, https://www.yahoo.com/news/audience-member-shouts-let-hear-180534806.html.

75. Paulson, "Two Female Playwrights Arrive on Broadway," https://www.nytimes.com/2017/03/22/theater/lynn-nottage-paula-vogel-broadway.html.

76. Ben Brantley, "'Sweat' Imagines the Local Bar as a Caldron," *New York Times*, March 26, 2017. Accessed November 25, 2018, https://www.nytimes.com/2017/03/26/theater/sweat-review-broadway.html.

77. Jesse Green, "Lynn Nottage's 'Sweat' Tells but Doesn't Show," *New York Magazine*, March 26, 2017. Accessed November 25, 2018, https://www.vulture.com/2017/03/theater-lynn-nottages-sweat-tells-but-doesnt-show.html.

78. Rosenfeld, "One 'Hot' Property," https://www.washingtonpost.com/archive/lifestyle/style/1999/09/12/one-hot-property/cb2d4e37-5b22-4aae-badf-438b7ebe255d/?utm_term=.22d5dc058c38.

79. Sarah Crompton, "Playwright Lynn Nottage: 'We Are a Country That Has Lost Our Narrative,'" *Guardian*, December 2, 2018. Accessed November 25, 2018, https://www.theguardian.com/stage/2018/dec/02/lynn-nottage-interview-play-sweat-america.

7. A WICKED WAVE OF FEMINIST THEATER

1. Rebecca Walker, "Becoming the Third Wave," *Ms*, 1992. Accessed December 22, 2018, http://www.msmagazine.com/spring2002/BecomingThirdWaveRebeccaWalker.pdf.

2. Ginia Bellafante, "Feminism. It's All about Me," *Time*, June 29, 1998. Accessed December 22, 2018, http://content.time.com/time/magazine/article/0,9171,988616,00.html.

3. Ken Tucker, "'Ally McBeal' and 'Buffy the Vampire Slayer,'" *Entertainment Weekly*, October 10, 1997. Accessed December 22, 2018, https://ew.com/article/1997/10/10/tv-show-reviews-ally-mcbeal-and-buffy-vampire-slayer/.

4. Laura Brunell, "The Third Wave of Feminism," *Encyclopedia Britannica*, n.d. Accessed December 15, 2018, https://www.britannica.com/topic/feminism/The-third-wave-of-feminism.

5. Laura Ruttum, "Is Feminism Dead?" *New York Public Library*, March 25, 2009. Accessed December 15, 2018, https://www.nypl.org/blog/2009/03/25/feminism-dead.

6. Stacy Wolf, *Changed for Good: A Feminist History of the Broadway Musical* (Oxford, U.K.: Oxford University Press, 2011), 162.

7. Kimberlé Williams Crenshaw, Kimberle, "Demarginalizing the Intersection of Race and Sex: A Black Feminist Critique of Antidiscrimination Doctrine, Feminist Theory and Antiracist Politics," *University of Chicago Legal Forum*, volume 1989, article 8. Accessed December 15, 2018, https://chicagounbound.uchicago.edu/uclf/vol1989/iss1/8.

8. Ben Brantley and Jesse Green, "The Great Work Continues: The Twenty-Five Best American Plays since 'Angels in America,'" *New York Times*, June 1, 2018. Accessed December 15, 2018, https://www.nytimes.com/interactive/2018/05/31/theater/best-25-plays.html.

9. Eve Ensler, *The Vagina Monologues: The Official Script for the 2008 V-Day Campaigns* (New York: Dramatists Play Service, n.d.), 22.

10. Laura Barnett, "How We Made: 'The Vagina Monologues,'" *Guardian*, February 4, 2013. Accessed December 15, 2018, https://www.theguardian.com/culture/2013/feb/04/how-we-made-vagina-monologues.

11. Charles Isherwood, "'The Vagina Monologues,'" *Variety*, October 11, 1999. Accessed December 15, 2018, https://variety.com/1999/legit/reviews/the-vagina-monologues-1200459522/.

12. Anita Gates, "A Body Part Returns as the Leading Lady," *New York Times*, October 4, 1999. Accessed December 15, 2018, https://www.nytimes.com/1999/10/04/theater/theater-review-a-body-part-returns-as-the-leading-lady.html.

13. Charles Isherwood, "The Culture Project and Plays That Make a Difference," *New York Times*, September 3, 2006. Accessed December 15, 2018, https://www.nytimes.com/2006/09/03/theater/the-culture-project-and-plays-that-make-a-difference.html.

14. Brantley and Green, "The Great Work Continues," https://www.nytimes.com/interactive/2018/05/31/theater/best-25-plays.html.

15. Anthony Gockowski, "AU revamps Vagina Monologues to Avoid 'Gender Binary,'" *Campus Reform*, October 21, 2016. Accessed December 15, 2018, https://www.campusreform.org/?ID=8290.

16. Steven Winn, "'Wicked' Blesses Schwartz/Composer Jumped at Staging Quirky 'Oz' Spin-Off," *SF Gate*, May 11, 2003. Accessed December 15, 2018, https://www.sfgate.com/entertainment/article/Wicked-blesses-Schwartz-Composer-jumped-at-2649112.php.

17. Bruce Weber, "The Wicked Young Witches," *New York Times*, October 26, 2003. Accessed December 15, 2018, https://www.nytimes.com/2003/10/26/theater/theater-the-wicked-young-witches.html.

18. Brooks Barnes, "How 'Wicked' Cast Its Spell," *Wall Street Journal*, October 22, 2005. Accessed December 15, 2018, https://www.wsj.com/articles/SB112994038461876413.

19. Ben Brantley, "There's Trouble in Emerald City," *New York Times*, October 23, 2003. Accessed December 15, 2018, https://www.nytimes.com/2003/10/31/movies/theater-review-there-s-trouble-in-emerald-city.html .

20. "Bitches and Witches," *New Yorker*, November 10, 2003. Accessed December 15, 2018, https://www.newyorker.com/magazine/2003/11/10/bitches-and-witches.

21. Linda Winer, "Bewitched and Bothered, Too/Bewildering 'Wicked' Tries to Be Both Dark and Cute; So Witch Is It?" *Newsday*, October 30, 2003. Accessed December 15, 2018, https://www.newsday.com/lifestyle/bewitched-and-bothered-too-bewildering-wicked-tries-to-be-both-dark-and-cute-so-witch-is-it-1.338904.

22. Brantley, "There's Trouble In Emerald City," https://www.nytimes.com/2003/10/31/movies/theater-review-there-s-trouble-in-emerald-city.html.

23. Ben Brantley, "One Woman's Awakening, in Double Time," *New York Times*, December 2, 2005. Accessed December 15, 2018, https://www.nytimes.com/2005/12/02/theater/reviews/one-womans-awakening-in-double-time.html.

24. Michael Feingold, "Prosaically 'Purple,'" *Village Voice*, November 29, 2005. Accessed December 15, 2018, https://www.villagevoice.com/2005/11/29/prosaically-purple/.

25. David Rooney, "'The Color Purple,'" *Variety*, December 1, 2005. Accessed December 15, 2018, https://variety.com/2005/legit/reviews/the-color-purple-2-1200519919/.

26. Wolf, *Changed for Good*, 162.

27. Walker, "Becoming the Third Wave," http://www.msmagazine.com/spring2002/BecomingThirdWaveRebeccaWalker.pdf.

28. Gina Gionfriddo, *Rapture, Blister, Burn* (New York: Dramatists Play Service, 2013), 21.

29. Gionfriddo, *Rapture, Blister, Burn*, 86.

30. Gionfriddo, *Rapture, Blister, Burn*, 88.

31. Lori Gottlieb, *Marry Him! The Case for Settling for Mr. Good Enough* (New York: Penguin, 2010).

32. Alice G. Walton, "The Marriage Problem: Why Many Are Choosing Cohabitation Instead," *Atlantic*, February 7, 2012. Accessed December 15, 2018, https://www.theatlantic.com/health/archive/2012/02/the-marriage-problem-why-many-are-choosing-cohabitation-instead/252505/.

33. Gina Gionfriddo, "All Hail 'Heidi': Beyond Feminism but Still a Dream," *New York Times*, June 7, 2012. Accessed December 15, 2018, https://www.nytimes.com/2012/06/10/theater/gina-gionfriddo-on-rapture-blister-burn-and-wasserstein.html /.

34. Gionfriddo, *Rapture, Blister, Burn*, 22.

35. Joe Dziemianowicz, "'Rapture, Blister, Burn' with Amy Brenneman at Playwrights Horizons," *New York Daily News*, June 12, 2013. Accessed December 15, 2018, https://www.nydailynews.com/entertainment/music-arts/theater-review-rapture-blister-burn-amy-brenneman-playwrights-horizons-article-1.1094205.

36. Alexis Soloski, "Playwright Gina Gionfriddo Asks, in Her New Play, 'Rapture, Blister, Burn,' and Her Life: What Do Women Want?" *Politico*, May 29, 2012. Accessed December 15, 2018, https://www.politico.com/states/new-york/city-hall/story/2012/05/playwright-gina-gionfriddo-asks-in-her-new-play-rapture-blister-burn-and-her-life-what-do-women-want-067223.

37. Charles Isherwood, "Hard Choices, Same as They Ever Were: 'Rapture, Blister, Burn' at Playwrights Horizons," *New York Times*, June 12, 2012. Accessed December 15, 2018, https://www.nytimes.com/2012/06/13/theater/

reviews/rapture-blister-burn-at-playwrights-horizons.html?mtrref=www.google.
com&gwh=16A766BA63E5023FB185903640A75A92&gwt=pay .

38. Jill Dolan, "'Rapture, Blister, Burn,'" *Feminist Spectator*, June 2, 2012.
Accessed December 15, 2018, http://feministspectator.princeton.edu/2012/06/
02/rapture-blister-burn/.

39. Gionfriddo, "All Hail 'Heidi,'" https://www.nytimes.com/2012/06/10/
theater/gina-gionfriddo-on-rapture-blister-burn-and-wasserstein.html /.

40. Linda Parsons, "Ella Evolving: Cinderella Stories and the Construction of
Gender-Appropriate Behavior," *Children's Literature in Education* 35, no. 2
(June 2004): 144.

41. Stephanie Hayes, "A Modern 'Rodgers and Hammerstein's Cinderella'
Comes to the Straz," *Tampa Bay Times*, October 14, 2014. Accessed December
15, 2018, https://www.tampabay.com/things-to-do/stage/a-modern-rodgers-and-
hammersteins-cinderella-comes-to-the-straz/2202108.

42. Parsons, "Ella Evolving," 136.

43. Parsons, "Ella Evolving," 139.

44. Douglas Carter Beane, Richard Rodgers, and Oscar Hammerstein II,
"Cinderella," final Broadway performance draft, 37.

45. Beane, Rodgers, and Hammerstein II, "Cinderella," 54.

46. Beane, Rodgers, and Hammerstein II, "Cinderella," 15.

47. Beane, Rodgers, and Hammerstein II, "Cinderella," 99.

48. Peter Slevin, "How Michelle Obama Became a Singular American
Voice," *Washington Post*, December 12, 2016. Accessed December 15, 2018,
https://www.washingtonpost.com/graphics/national/obama-legacy/michelle-
obama-biography.html.

49. Michelle Cottle, "Leaning Out: How Michelle Obama Became a Feminist
Nightmare," *Politico*, November 21, 2013. Accessed December 15, 2018, https://
www.politico.com/magazine/story/2013/11/leaning-out-michelle-obama-
100244.

50. Cottle, "Leaning Out," https://www.politico.com/magazine/story/2013/
11/leaning-out-michelle-obama-100244.

51. Abigail Pesta, "The 2012 Election Brings Stunning Array of Firsts for
Women in Congress," *Daily Beast*, November 8, 2012. Accessed December 15,
2018, https://www.thedailybeast.com/2012-election-brings-stunning-array-of-
firsts-for-women-in-congress.

52. Tom Kitt and Brian Yorkey, "'If/Then' Rehearsal Script," January 31,
2014, 54.

53. Kitt and Yorkey, "'If/Then' Rehearsal Script," 56–57.

54. Kitt and Yorkey, "'If/Then' Rehearsal Script," 58.

55. Seija Rankin, "The Psychology of Romantic Comedies: What Are These
Movies Doing to Our Love Lives?" *E Online*, February 12, 2016. Accessed

December 15, 2018, https://www.eonline.com/news/739226/the-psychology-of-romantic-comedies-what-are-these-movies-doing-to-our-love-lives.

56. Kitt and Yorkey, "'If/Then' Rehearsal Script," 84.

57. Kitt and Yorkey, "'If/Then' Rehearsal Script," 4.

58. Kitt and Yorkey, "'If/Then' Rehearsal Script," 83.

59. David Rooney, "'If/Then': Theater Review,'" *Hollywood Reporter*, March 30, 2014. Accessed December 15, 2018, https://www.hollywoodreporter.com/review/idina-menzel-theater-review-692175.

60. Kitt and Yorkey, "'If/Then' Rehearsal Script," 18.

61. Kitt and Yorkey, "'If/Then' Rehearsal Script," 6.

62. Kitt and Yorkey, "'If/Then' Rehearsal Script," 67.

63. Parsons, "Ella Evolving," 140.

64. Marsha Norman, interview by Carey Purcell, April 2, 2019.

65. Norman, interview by Carey Purcell.

66. Marsha Norman, "Why 'The Count' Matters," *Dramatist*, November 2015. Accessed August 21, 2019, http://www.thelillyawards.org/media/2016/06/The-Count-by-The-Lilly-Awards-Dramatists-Guild.pdf.

67. Jason Zinoman, "Theater: The Season of the Female Playwright," New York Times, December 21, 2003, p. 3.

68. Suzy Evans, "The Gender Parity Count Ticks Up: Slightly," American Theatre, July 20, 2015. Accessed August 21, 2019, https://www.americantheatre.org/2015/07/20/the-gender-parity-count-ticks-up-slightly/.

69. "'The Count': Some Progress, but White Male Playwrights Still Manspread on U.S. Stages," *American Theatre*, October 28, 2018. Accessed December 15, 2018, https://www.americantheatre.org/2018/10/18/the-count-some-progress-but-white-male-playwrights-still-manspread-on-u-s-stages/.

70. Catherine Porter, e-mail to Carey Purcell, April 5, 2019.

71. Norman, "Why 'The Count' Matters."

72. Carey Purcell, "Career or Children? Why Theater Parents Feel Forced to Choose," *Playbill*, August 11, 2015. Accessed December 15, 2018, http://www.playbill.com/article/career-or-children-why-theatre-parents-feel-forced-to-choose-com-356866 .

73. Rachel Spencer-Hewitt, interview by Carey Purcell, March 19, 2019.

74. Purcell, "Career or Children?" http://www.playbill.com/article/career-or-children-why-theatre-parents-feel-forced-to-choose-com-356866 .

75. Spencer-Hewitt, interview by Carey Purcell.

76. Spencer-Hewitt, interview by Carey Purcell.

77. "Broadway by the Numbers," *ProductionPro*, June 4, 2018. Accessed January 6, 2019, https://production.pro/broadway-by-the-numbers-2018.

8. BROADWAY COMES TO THE *FUN HOME*

1. June Thomas, "Alison Bechdel on a Very Special Performance of the 'Fun Home' Musical," *Slate*, April 22, 2014. Accessed January 19, 2019, https://slate.com/human-interest/2014/04/alison-bechdel-and-the-cast-of-the-fun-home-musical-descend-on-south-carolina-to-protest-homophobic-cuts.html.

2. Adam Hetrick, "An Author's Life Comes to Life: Alison Bechdel on 'Fun Home,'" *Playbill*, November 9, 2013. Accessed January 19, 2019, http://www.playbill.com/article/an-authors-life-comes-to-life-alison-bechdel-on-fun-home-com-211586.

3. Alysia Abbott, "'We Just Sat and Held Each Other': How It Feels to Watch Your Life Story Onstage," *Atlantic*, November 12, 2013. Accessed January 19, 2019, https://www.theatlantic.com/entertainment/archive/2013/11/we-just-sat-and-held-each-other-how-it-feels-to-watch-your-life-story-onstage/281369/.

4. Carey Purcell, "A Woman's World: 'Ambition, Adventure, and Exploration' Brings 'Fun Home' to Broadway . . . and Defies the Odds," *Playbill*, March 29, 2015. Accessed January 19, 2019, http://www.playbill.com/article/a-womans-world-ambition-adventure-and-exploration-brings-fun-home-to-broadway-and-defies-the-odds-com-345075.

5. Ben Brantley, "Laughter and Horror in a Journey of the Heart," *New York Times*, March 29, 1999. Accessed January 19, 2019, https://www.nytimes.com/1999/03/29/theater/theater-review-laughter-and-horror-in-a-journey-of-the-heart.html.

6. Lisa Kron, *2.5 Minute Ride and 101 Humiliating Stories* (New York: Theatre Communications Group, 2001), xiv.

7. Lisa Kron, *Well* (New York: Theatre Communications Group, 2006), 12.

8. Ben Brantley, "Lisa Kron's 'Well' Opens on Broadway, with Mom Keeping Watch," *New York Times*, March 31, 2006. Accessed January 19, 2019, https://www.nytimes.com/2006/03/31/theater/reviews/lisa-krons-well-opens-on-broadway-with-mom-keeping-watch.html.

9. Greg Evans, "Violet," *Variety*, March 22, 1997. Accessed January 19, 2019, https://variety.com/1997/legit/reviews/violet-1200449123/.

10. Ben Brantley, "Lessons about Life in a Quest for Beauty," *New York Times*, March 12, 1997. Accessed January 19, 2019, https://www.nytimes.com/1997/03/12/theater/lessons-about-life-in-a-quest-for-beauty.html?mtrref=www.google.com&gwh=90F69821583B0BDBCF0A20B23DDE854E&gwt=pay.

11. Adam Feldman, "Change Is Good," *Time Out New York*, May 6, 2004. Accessed January 19, 2019, https://www.timeout.com/newyork/theater/change-is-good.

12. Ben Brantley, "Outsiders Bond in a South of Roiling Change," *New York Times*, December 1, 2003. Accessed January 19, 2019, https://www.nytimes.com/2003/12/01/theater/theater-review-outsiders-bond-in-a-south-of-roiling-change.html.

13. Feldman, "Change Is Good," https://www.timeout.com/newyork/theater/change-is-good.

14. Patrick Healy, "'Shrek' to End Broadway Run on Jan. 3," *New York Times*, October 21, 2009. Accessed January 19, 2019, https://www.nytimes.com/2009/10/22/theater/22shrek.html.

15. Daryl H. Miller, "'Fun Home' Composer Jeanine Tesori Hears the Music in Everyday Life," *Los Angeles Times*, February 23, 2017. Accessed January 19, 2019, https://www.latimes.com/entertainment/arts/la-ca-cm-jeanine-tesori-fun-home-20170226-story.html.

16. Dana Piccoli, "From the AE Archives: Alison Bechdel on the Bechdel Test and 'Fun Home' the Musical," *After Ellen*, n.d. Accessed January 19, 2019, https://www.afterellen.com/people/202574-from-the-ae-archives-alison-bechdel-on-the-bechdel-test-and-fun-home-the-musical.

17. "1,000 Novels Everyone Must Read: The Definitive List," *Guardian*, n.d. Accessed January 19, 2019, https://www.theguardian.com/books/2009/jan/23/bestbooks-fiction.

18. Jeanine Tesori and Lisa Kron, "Fun Home Broadway Rehearsal Draft," April 9, 2015, 1.

19. Purcell, "A Woman's World," http://www.playbill.com/article/a-womans-world-ambition-adventure-and-exploration-brings-fun-home-to-broadway-and-defies-the-odds-com-345075.

20. Ben Brantley, "Family as a Hall of Mirrors," *New York Times*, October 22, 2013. Accessed January 19, 2019, https://www.nytimes.com/2013/10/23/theater/reviews/fun-home-a-new-musical-at-the-public-theater.html.

21. Tesori and Kron, "Fun Home Broadway Rehearsal Draft," 50.

22. Tesori and Kron, "Fun Home Broadway Rehearsal Draft," 43–44.

23. Tesori and Kron, "Fun Home Broadway Rehearsal Draft," 58.

24. Terry Gross, "Lesbian Cartoonist Alison Bechdel Countered Dad's Secrecy by Being Out and Open," *NPR*, August 17, 2015. Accessed January 19, 2019, https://www.npr.org/2015/08/17/432569415/lesbian-cartoonist-alison-bechdel-countered-dads-secrecy-by-being-out-and-open.

25. Tesori and Kron, "Fun Home Broadway Rehearsal Draft," 58–59.

26. Tesori and Kron, "Fun Home Broadway Rehearsal Draft," 3–4.

27. Feldman, "Change Is Good," https://www.timeout.com/newyork/theater/change-is-good.

28. Charles McNulty, "Awkwardness Adds to 'Fun Home' Charm," *Los Angeles Times*, October 21, 2013. Accessed January 19, 2019, https://www.latimes.

com/entertainment/arts/la-xpm-2013-oct-22-la-et-cm-fun-home-review-story.
html.

29. Jill Dolan, "'Fun Home,'" *Feminist Spectator*, October 22, 2013. Accessed January 5, 2019, http://feministspectator.princeton.edu/2013/10/22/fun-home/.

30. Lisa Kron, "Breaking New Ground: Writing about Our Lives, Winning Big on Broadway," *Equality Magazine*, August 23, 2015, pp. 28–29.

31. June Thomas, "'Fun Home' Won Five Tonys. How Did a Graphic Memoir Become a Musical?" *Slate*, June 8, 2015. Accessed January 5, 2019, https://slate.com/human-interest/2015/06/fun-home-2015-tony-winner-how-did-a-graphic-novel-become-a-musical.html.

32. Jesse Green, "The Miraculous 'Fun Home,'" *Vulture*, October 22, 2013. Accessed January 5, 2019, https://www.vulture.com/2013/10/theater-review-fun-home.html.

33. Linda Winer, "'Fun Home' Review: Brilliant, Emotional," *Newsday*, October 22, 2013. Accessed January 5, 2019, https://www.newsday.com/entertainment/theater/fun-home-review-brilliant-emotional-1.6295643.

34. Tesori and Kron, "Fun Home Broadway Rehearsal Draft," 60.

35. Tesori and Kron, "Fun Home Broadway Rehearsal Draft," 67.

36. Tesori and Kron, "Fun Home Broadway Rehearsal Draft," 67.

37. Tesori and Kron, "Fun Home Broadway Rehearsal Draft," 68.

38. Rob Weinert-Kendt, "In 'Fun Home,' a Wife's Late, Desperate Outcry," *New York Times*, May 28, 2015. Accessed January 5, 2019, https://www.nytimes.com/2015/05/31/theater/in-fun-home-a-wifes-late-desperate-outcry.html.

39. Tesori and Kron, "Fun Home Broadway Rehearsal Draft," 8.

40. Tesori and Kron, "Fun Home Broadway Rehearsal Draft," 68.

41. Tesori and Kron, "Fun Home Broadway Rehearsal Draft," 74.

42. Tesori and Kron, "Fun Home Broadway Rehearsal Draft," 40.

43. Tesori and Kron, "Fun Home Broadway Rehearsal Draft," 77.

44. Jon Magaril, "Summer of Sam: An Interview with 'Fun Home' and 'The Flick' Director Sam Gold," *Slant*, June 5, 2015. Accessed January 5, 2019, https://www.slantmagazine.com/theater/summer-of-sam-an-interview-with-fun-home-and-the-flick-director-sam-gold/.

45. Emma Margolin, "South Carolina Lawmakers Advance College Cuts for Promoting Gay-Themed Books," *MSNBC*, March 11, 2014. Accessed January 5, 2019, http://www.msnbc.com/msnbc/south-carolina-college-gay-books.

46. Margolin, "South Carolina Lawmakers Advance College Cuts for Promoting Gay-Themed Books," http://www.msnbc.com/msnbc/south-carolina-college-gay-books.

47. Patrick Healy, "Cast of 'Fun Home' Heading to South Carolina amid Dispute over Book," *New York Times*, April 17, 2014. Accessed January 5, 2019, https://artsbeat.blogs.nytimes.com/2014/04/17/cast-of-fun-home-heading-to-south-carolina-amid-dispute-over-book/.

48. Ashley Sprouse, "Rep. Garry Smith Takes on CofC Student on Twitter," *Charleston City Paper*, April 2, 2014. Accessed January 5, 2019, https://www.charlestoncitypaper.com/charleston/rep-garry-smith-takes-on-cofc-student-on-twitter/Content?oid=4894670.

49. Thomas, "Alison Bechdel on a Very Special Performance of the 'Fun Home' Musical," https://slate.com/human-interest/2014/04/alison-bechdel-and-the-cast-of-the-fun-home-musical-descend-on-south-carolina-to-protest-homophobic-cuts.html.

50. Purcell, "A Woman's World," http://www.playbill.com/article/a-womans-world-ambition-adventure-and-exploration-brings-fun-home-to-broadway-and-defies-the-odds-com-345075.

51. Purcell, "A Woman's World," http://www.playbill.com/article/a-womans-world-ambition-adventure-and-exploration-brings-fun-home-to-broadway-and-defies-the-odds-com-345075.

52. Ben Brantley, "'Fun Home' at the Circle in the Square Theatre," *New York Times*, April 19, 2015. Accessed January 5, 2019, https://www.nytimes.com/2015/04/20/theater/review-fun-home-at-the-circle-in-the-square-theater.html.

53. Marilyn Stasio, "'Fun Home,'" *Variety*, April 19, 2015. Accessed January 5, 2019, https://variety.com/2015/legit/reviews/broadway-review-fun-home-1201475487/.

54. Sean T. Collins, "Alison Bechdel on 'Fun Home's' Tony-Award Triumph," *Rolling Stone*, June 18, 2015. Accessed January 5, 2019, https://www.rollingstone.com/culture/culture-news/alison-bechdel-on-fun-homes-tony-award-triumph-74091/.

55. Kalle Oskari Mattila, "Selling Queerness: The Curious Case of 'Fun Home,'" *Atlantic*, April 25, 2016. Accessed January 5, 2019, https://www.theatlantic.com/entertainment/archive/2016/04/branding-queerness-the-curious-case-of-fun-home/479532/.

56. "'Fun Home' Breaks Box Office Record after Five Tony Wins," *Playbill*, June 8, 2015. Accessed January 5, 2019, http://www.playbill.com/article/fun-home-breaks-box-office-record-after-five-tony-wins-com-350886.

57. Ben Brantley, "'An American in Paris,' a Romance of Song and Step," *New York Times*, April 12, 2015. Accessed January 5, 2019, www.nytimes.com/2015/04/13/theater/review-an-american-in-paris-a-romance-of-song-and-step.html.

58. Elysa Gardner, "'American in Paris' Has Rhythm, Rapture," *USA Today*, April 12, 2015. Accessed January 5, 2019, https://www.usatoday.com/story/life/theater/2015/04/12/an-american-in-paris-broadway-review/25518893/.

59. Gordon Cox, "'An American in Paris' Musical Brings Ballet to Broadway with French Flair," *Variety*, April 9, 2015. Accessed January 5, 2019, https://variety.com/2015/legit/news/american-in-paris-musical-broadway-ballet-1201468786/.

60. Alexandra Samuels, "Duke University Freshmen Refuse to Read 'Fun Home' for Moral Reasons," *USA Today*, August 24, 2015. Accessed January 5, 2019, https://www.usatoday.com/story/news/nation-now/2015/08/24/incoming-freshman-duke-university-fun-home-alison-bechdel/32290321/.

61. "Broadcast the Tony Awards for Best Book and Score to Show Women Being Represented," *Change.org*, n.d. Accessed January 19, 2019, https://www.change.org/p/members-of-the-tony-awards-management-committee-broadcast-the-tony-awards-for-best-book-and-score-to-show-women-succeeding.

62. Adam Hetrick, "'For Girls, You Have to See It to Be It'—the Historic and Powerful 'Fun Home' Tony Acceptance Speeches You Didn't See on TV," *Playbill*, June 8, 2015. Accessed January 19, 2019, http://www.playbill.com/article/for-girls-you-have-to-see-it-to-be-it-the-historic-and-powerful-fun-home-tony-acceptance-speeches-you-didnt-see-on-tv-com-350817.

63. Hetrick, "'For Girls, You Have to See It to Be It,'" http://www.playbill.com/article/for-girls-you-have-to-see-it-to-be-it-the-historic-and-powerful-fun-home-tony-acceptance-speeches-you-didnt-see-on-tv-com-350817.

64. Jesse Green, "Surprises and Disappointments at Last Night's Tony Awards," *Vulture*, June 8, 2015. Accessed January 19, 2019, https://www.vulture.com/2015/06/surprises-and-disappointments-at-the-tony-awards.html.

65. David Sims, "'Fun Home's' Success Defines the 2015 Tony Awards," *Atlantic*, June 8, 2015. Accessed January 19, 2019, https://www.theatlantic.com/entertainment/archive/2015/06/fun-home-caps-a-triumphantly-diverse-tony-awards/395153/.

66. Carey Purcell, "Cast and Creators of 'Fun Home' on How They Built a Broadway Game-Changer," *Playbill*, June 12, 2015. Accessed January 19, 2019, http://www.playbill.com/article/cast-and-creators-of-fun-home-on-how-they-built-a-broadway-game-changer-com-351012.

67. Adam Hetrick, "Broadway Erupts with Joy and Tears for Marriage Equality—Audra McDonald, Jonathan Groff, Harvey Fierstein, Lea DeLaria, Lin-Manuel Miranda, 'Fun Home' Stars, and More React!" *Playbill*, June 26, 2015. Accessed January 19, 2019, https://www.playbill.com/article/broadway-erupts-with-joy-and-tears-for-marriage-equality.

68. Hetrick, "Broadway Erupts with Joy and Tears for Marriage Equality," https://www.playbill.com/article/broadway-erupts-with-joy-and-tears-for-marriage-equality.

69. "'Fun Home': First Performance after Marriage Equality Ruling, June 26, 2015," *YouTube*, June 26, 2015. Accessed January 19, 2019, https://www.youtube.com/watch?v=mDyjv1uFvoE.

70. Carey Purcell, "The Life of 'Fun Home's' 12-Year-Old Understudy—Covering Two Boys, One Girl, and Going on at a Moment's Notice," *Playbill*, July 10, 2015. Accessed January 19, 2019, http://www.playbill.com/article/the-life-of-fun-homes-12-year-old-understudy-covering-two-boys-one-girl-and-going-on-at-a-moments-notice-com-352859.

71. John Moore, "Beth Malone on 'Fun Home': 'It's about Anyone Born of a Mother,'" *Denver Center for the Performing Arts News Center*, December 14, 2016. Accessed January 19, 2019, https://www.denvercenter.org/news-center/beth-malone-on-fun-home-its-about-anyone-born-of-a-mother-2/.

72. Moore, "Beth Malone on 'Fun Home,'" https://www.denvercenter.org/news-center/beth-malone-on-fun-home-its-about-anyone-born-of-a-mother-2/.

73. "'Fun Home' Breaks Box Office Record after Five Tony Wins," http://www.playbill.com/article/fun-home-breaks-box-office-record-after-five-tony-wins-com-350886.

74. Robert Viagas, "Tony-Winning Musical 'Fun Home' Closes on Broadway Today," *Playbill*, September 10, 2016. Accessed January 19, 2019, http://www.playbill.com/article/tony-winning-musical-fun-home-closes-on-broadway-today.

75. Shoshana Greenberg, "The Revolutionary 'Fun Home' Ends Its Broadway Run," *Women and Hollywood*, September 7, 2016. Accessed January 19, 2019, https://womenandhollywood.com/the-revolutionary-fun-home-ends-its-broadway-run-34b5b84b474/.

9. REVIVALS ECLIPSED BY MILESTONES

1. Joanna Kao, "The Tonys Have Never Been So Dominated by Women," *FiveThirtyEight*, June 8, 2015. Accessed April 25, 2018, https://fivethirtyeight.com/features/the-tonys-have-never-been-so-dominated-by-women/.

2. Carey Purcell, "A Woman's World: Pam MacKinnon on the Decision to Restore Wasserstein's Cut Dialogue to *The Heidi Chronicles*," *Playbill*, February 28, 2015. Accessed August 27, 2019, http://www.playbill.com/article/a-womans-world-pam-mackinnon-on-the-decision-to-restore-wassersteins-cut-dialogue-to-the-heidi-chronicles-com-342388.

3. Jennfer Szalai, "The Complicated Origins of 'Having It All,'" *New York Times*, January 2, 2015. Accessed April 25, 2018, https://www.nytimes.com/2015/01/04/magazine/the-complicated-origins-of-having-it-all.html.

4. Charlotte Alter, "Kirsten Gillibrand on Why She Hates the Phrase 'Having It All,'" *Time*, October 2, 2014. Accessed April 25, 2018, https://time.com/3453839/kirsten-gillibrand-have-it-all/.

5. George Guilder, "Women in the Work Force," *Atlantic*, September 1986. Accessed August 21, 2019, https://www.theatlantic.com/magazine/archive/1986/09/women-in-the-work-force/304924/.

6. Claire Cain Miller and Liz Alderman, "Why U.S. Women Are Leaving Jobs Behind," *New York Times*, December 12, 2014. Accessed April 25, 2018, https://www.nytimes.com/2014/12/14/upshot/us-employment-women-not-working.html.

7. Anne-Marie Slaughter, "Why Women Still Can't Have It All," *Atlantic*, July/August 2012. Accessed April 25, 2018, https://www.theatlantic.com/magazine/archive/2012/07/why-women-still-cant-have-it-all/309020/.

8. Tina Rodia, "How the Idea of 'Having It All' Makes Women Feel Terrible about Themselves," *Washington Post*, January 15, 2015. Accessed April 25, 2018, https://www.washingtonpost.com/?utm_term=.b0db12780f61.

9. Wendy Wasserstein, *The Heidi Chronicles* (New York: Dramatists Play Service, 1990), 62.

10. Betsey Stevenson and Justin Wolfers, "The Paradox of Declining Female Happiness," *American Economic Journal: Economic Policy* 1, no. 2 (August 2009): 190–225.

11. Charles Isherwood, "'The Heidi Chronicles,' with Elisabeth Moss, Opens on Broadway," *New York Times*, March 19, 2015. Accessed April 25, 2018, https://www.nytimes.com/2015/03/20/theater/review-the-heidi-chronicles-with-elisabeth-moss-opens-on-broadway.html.

12. David Rooney, "'The Heidi Chronicles': Theater Review," *Hollywood Reporter*, March 19, 2015. Accessed April 25, 2018, https://www.hollywoodreporter.com/review/elisabeth-moss-heidi-chronicles-theater-783123.

13. Jennifer Schuessler and Michael Paulson, "'The Heidi Chronicles' Is Trailed by Questions of Feminism and Legacy," *New York Times*, April 22, 2015. Accessed April 25, 2018, https://www.nytimes.com/2015/04/23/theater/the-heidi-chronicles-is-trailed-by-questions-of-feminism-and-legacy.html.

14. Alisa Solomon, "Why 'The Heidi Chronicles" Failed to Find a New Audience," *Nation*, April 24, 2015. Accessed April 25, 2018, https://www.thenation.com/article/why-heidi-chronicles-failed-find-new-audience/.

15. Joy Meads, "The Kilroys Were Here," *HowlRound*, June 22, 2014. Accessed April 25, 2018, https://howlround.com/kilroys-were-here.

16. Julia Jordan and Sheri Wilner, "Discrimination and the Female Playwright," *Dramatist*, September/October 2009. Accessed April 25, 2018, https://www.giarts.org/article/discrimination-and-female-playwright.

17. Emily Mann, interview by Carey Purcell, March 15, 2019.

18. Peter Marks, "For Forty-Four D.C. Area Theater Companies, New Plays by Women Will Take Center Stage in Fall of 2015," *Washington Post*, January 23, 2014. Accessed April 25, 2018, https://www.washingtonpost.com/?utm_term=.d4a03f089393.

19. Laura Collins-Hughes, "Women's Voices Theater Festival Celebrates Female Playwrights," *New York Times*, September 8, 2015. Accessed August 27, 2019, https://www.nytimes.com/2015/09/09/theater/womens-voices-theater-festival-celebrates-female-playwrights.html.

20. Carey Purcell, "'We Want to Start a National Movement,' Say the Founders of the Women's Voices Theater Festival," *Playbill*, September 8, 2015. Accessed April 25, 2018, http://www.playbill.com/article/we-want-to-start-a-national-movement-say-the-founders-of-the-womens-voices-theater-festival-com-361006.

21. Nelson Pressley, "The Women's Voices Theater Festival Is a Winner. But It Could Use Some Work," *New York Times*, February 23, 2018. Accessed April 25, 2018, https://www.washingtonpost.com/?utm_term=.94aa2535e145.

22. Collins-Hughes, "Internet Outcry Over Diversity Leads Manhattan Theatre Club to Announce Season Details Early," https://www.nytimes.com/2015/08/22/theater/after-outcry-over-diversity-manhattan-theater-club-is-making-a-change.html.

23. Anna Winter, "Therese Raquin by Emile Zola," *Guardian*, July 31, 2010. Accessed April 25, 2018, https://www.theguardian.com/books/2010/aug/01/therese-raquin-emile-zola-review.

24. Ashley Lee, "Keira Knightley on the Lack of Women Playwrights on Broadway: 'There Are Very, Very Few' Interesting Roles," *Hollywood Reporter*, October 30, 2015. Accessed April 25, 2018, https://www.hollywoodreporter.com/news/keira-knightley-lack-women-playwrights-835633.

25. Helen Edmundson, *Therese Raquin* (London: Nick Hern Books, 2014), 10, 40.

26. Terry Teachout, "'Therese Raquin' Review: Lethal Leading Lady," *Wall Street Journal*, October 29, 2015. Accessed April 25, 2018, https://www.wsj.com/articles/therese-raquin-review-lethal-leading-lady-1446165000.

27. Joe Dziemianowicz, "'Therese Raquin' Review: Keira Knightley Washes Up in Soggy Broadway Drama," *New York Daily News*, October 29, 2015. Accessed April 25, 2018, https://www.nydailynews.com/entertainment/theater-arts/keira-knightley-adrift-soggy-therese-raquin-article-1.2416140.

28. Jeremy Gerard, "Keira Knightley's Broadway Debut as 'Therese Raquin' Is a Lust Cause," *Deadline*, October 29, 2015. Accessed April 25, 2018, https://deadline.com/2015/10/keira-knightley-therese-raquin-broadway-debut-1201597527/.

29. Ben Brantley, "Review: In 'Therese Raquin,' Keira Knightley as a Baleful Adulteress," *New York Times*, October 29, 2015. Accessed April 25, 2018, https://www.nytimes.com/2015/10/30/theater/review-in-therese-raquin-keira-knightley-as-a-baleful-adulteress.html.

30. "Danai Gurira Gets Why We Live for the Living Dead," *YouTube*, February 26, 2016. Accessed April 25, 2018, https://www.youtube.com/watch?v=3bvhC44tp10.

31. "Danai Gurira Gets Why We Live for the Living Dead," https://www.youtube.com/watch?v=3bvhC44tp10.

32. Bennett Marcus, "The Shocking Thing about Lupita Nyong'o's Broadway Show," *Cut*, March 8, 2016. Accessed April 25, 2018, https://www.thecut.com/2016/03/lupita-nyongo-eclipsed-broadway.html.

33. Jeremy Gerard, "With Her Broadway Debut, Lupita Nyong'o Lights Up 'Eclipsed,' Danai Gurira's Savagely Funny War Drama," *Deadline*, March 6, 2016. Accessed April 25, 2018, https://deadline.com/2016/03/lupine-nyongo-eclipsed-danai-gurira-review-1201715447/.

34. Charles Isherwood, "Review: In *Eclipsed*, a Captive Lupita Nyong'o Is Captivating," *New York Times*, March 6, 2016, p. C1.

35. Jesse Green, "The Power of 'Eclipsed'; a Watery Gin Game," *Intelligencer*, October 14, 2015. Accessed April 25, 2018, http://nymag.com/intelligencer/2015/10/theater-reviews-the-gin-game.html.

36. Marcus, "The Shocking Thing about Lupita Nyong'o's Broadway Show," https://www.thecut.com/2016/03/lupita-nyongo-eclipsed-broadway.html.

37. Michelle Ruiz, "'Eclipsed' Playwright Danai Gurira on Bringing Activism to Broadway," *Vogue*, June 10, 2016. Accessed April 25, 2018, https://www.vogue.com/article/danai-gurira-eclipsed-interview.

38. Green, "The Power of 'Eclipsed,'" http://nymag.com/intelligencer/2015/10/theater-reviews-the-gin-game.html.

39. Jennifer Schuessler, "Lupita Nyong'o Shines a Light on Africa," *New York Times*, September 26, 2015. Accessed April 25, 2018, https://www.nytimes.com/2015/09/27/theater/lupita-nyongo-shines-a-light-on-africa.html.

40. Green, "The Power of 'Eclipsed,'" http://nymag.com/intelligencer/2015/10/theater-reviews-the-gin-game.html .

41. Diep Tran, "From 'The Walking Dead' to 'Eclipsed,' Danai Gurira Is Killing It," *American Theatre*, January 26, 2016. Accessed April 25, 2018, https://www.americantheatre.org/2016/01/26/between-the-walking-dead-and-eclipsed-danai-gurira-is-killing-it/.

42. Joanna Kao, "'Waitress' Is Making Broadway History with Its All-Female Creative Team," *FiveThirtyEight*, March 26, 2016. Accessed April 25, 2018, https://fivethirtyeight.com/features/waitress-is-making-broadway-history-with-its-all-female-creative-team/.

43. Ashley Ross, "How the Women of 'Waitress' Are Changing Broadway behind the Scenes," *Time*, April 19, 2016. Accessed April 25, 2018, https://time.com/4285668/waitress-broadway-sara-bareilles/.

44. Chris Jones, "'Waitress' Is an Intimate Broadway Musical of the Highest Order," *Chicago Tribune*, April 24, 2016. Accessed April 25, 2018, https://www.chicagotribune.com/entertainment/theater/sc-waitress-broadway-musical-review-0424-20160424-column.html.

45. Peter Marks, "Ingredients of 'Waitress': Sara Bareilles, Jessie Mueller—and Lots of Syrup," *Washington Post*, April 24, 2016. Accessed April 25, 2018, https://www.washingtonpost.com/news/arts-and-entertainment/wp/2016/04/24/ingredients-of-waitress-sara-bareilles-show-tunes-and-syrup/.

46. Danielle Feder, "Feminism and Femininity in Broadway's 'Waitress,'" *HowlRound*, August 2, 2016. Accessed April 25, 2018, https://howlround.com/feminism-and-femininity-broadways-waitress.

47. Marilyn Stasio, "'Waitress,' the Musical," *Variety*, April 24, 2016. Accessed April 25, 2018, https://variety.com/2016/legit/reviews/waitress-review-broadway-musical-1201759570/.

48. Michael Riedel, "A Feminist War Is Being Waged at Broadway's 'Waitress,'" *New York Post*, February 4, 2016. Accessed April 25, 2018, https://nypost.com/2016/02/04/a-feminist-war-is-being-waged-at-broadways-waitress/.

49. Benjamin Sutton, "Art by Women Sells for 47.6 Percent Less Than Works by Men, Study Finds," *Hyperallergic*, December 14, 2017. Accessed April 25, 2018, https://hyperallergic.com/417356/art-by-women-gender-study-sexism/.

50. Diana Tourjée, "Women Are Punished More for Being Assholes at Work," *Vice*, June 3, 2016. Accessed April 25, 2018, https://www.vice.com/en_us/article/qvdd35/women-are-punished-more-for-being-assholes-at-work.

51. Feder, "Feminism and Femininity in Broadway's 'Waitress,'" https://howlround.com/feminism-and-femininity-broadways-waitress.

52. Kao, "'Waitress' Is Making Broadway History with Its All-Female Creative Team," https://fivethirtyeight.com/features/waitress-is-making-broadway-history-with-its-all-female-creative-team/.

53. Mimi Onuoha, "Broadway Won't Document Its Dramatic Race Problem, So a Group of Actors Spent Five Years Quietly Gathering This Data Themselves," *Quartz*, December 4, 2016. Accessed April 25, 2018, https://qz.com/842610/broadways-race-problem-is-unmasked-by-data-but-the-theater-industry-is-still-stuck-in-neutral/.

54. Ben Brantley, "'Hamilton,' Young Rebels Changing History and Theater," *New York Times*, August 6, 2015. Accessed April 25, 2018, https://www.nytimes.com/2015/08/07/theater/review-hamilton-young-rebels-changing-history-and-theater.html.

55. Jesse Green, "Is 'Hamilton' Even Better Than It Was?" *Vulture*, August 6, 2015. Accessed April 25, 2018, https://www.vulture.com/2015/08/theater-review-hamilton.html.

56. Leah Greenblatt, "'Hamilton': *EW* Stage Review," *Entertainment Weekly*, August 6, 2015. Accessed April 25, 2018, https://ew.com/article/2015/08/06/hamilton-ew-stage-review/.

57. Green, "Is 'Hamilton' Even Better Than It Was?" https://www.vulture.com/2015/08/theater-review-hamilton.html .

58. Kelsey Klotz, "Hamilton Is Innovative, but Not Quite Revolutionary," *Common Reader*, February 28, 2017. Accessed April 25, 2018, https://commonreader.wustl.edu/c/hamilton-innovative-not-quite-revolutionary/.

59. Carey Purcell, "A Woman's World: Hamilton's Leading Ladies, the Schuyler Sisters, on Being the Kardashians of the 1700s," *Playbill*, September 3, 2015. Accessed April 25, 2018, http://www.playbill.com/article/a-womans-world-hamiltons-leading-ladies-the-schuyler-sisters-on-being-the-kardashians-of-the-1700s-com-360665.

60. Purcell, "A Woman's World," http://www.playbill.com/article/a-womans-world-hamiltons-leading-ladies-the-schuyler-sisters-on-being-the-kardashians-of-the-1700s-com-360665.

61. Hilton Als, "Boys in the Band: A Musical about the Founding Fathers," *New Yorker*, March 2, 2015. Accessed April 25, 2018, https://www.newyorker.com/magazine/2015/03/09/boys-in-the-band.

62. Kate Keller, "The Issue on the Table: Is 'Hamilton' Good For History?" *Smithsonian.com*, May 30, 2018. Accessed April 25, 2018, https://www.smithsonianmag.com/history/issue-table-hamilton-good-history-180969192/.

63. Schuessler and Paulson, "'The Heidi Chronicles' Is Trailed by Questions of Feminism and Legacy," https://www.nytimes.com/2015/04/23/theater/the-heidi-chronicles-is-trailed-by-questions-of-feminism-and-legacy.html.

64. Klotz, "'Hamilton' Is Innovative, but Not Quite Revolutionary," https://commonreader.wustl.edu/c/hamilton-innovative-not-quite-revolutionary/.

65. James McMaster, "Why Hamilton Is Not the Revolution You Think It Is," *HowlRound*, February 23, 2016. Accessed April 25, 2018, https://howlround.com/why-hamilton-not-revolution-you-think-it.

10. CRITICAL PROGRESS?

1. Jeremy Gerard, "*New York Times* Culture Desk Sees More Upheaval as Layoffs Loom," *Deadline*, February 7, 2017. Accessed February 12, 2019, https://deadline.com/2017/02/new-york-times-culture-desk-charles-isherwood-leaves-as-layoffs-loom-1201903894/.

2. Winter Miller, "Hi *NY Times*! Time to Hire a POC Who Is Female &/or Transgender for 2nd Theater Critic," *Change.org*, February 11, 2017. Accessed February 12, 2019, https://www.change.org/p/the-new-york-times-masthead-and-culture-desk-hi-ny-times-time-to-hire-a-poc-female-and-or-transperson-for-2nd-string-theater-critic.

3. Rob Weinert-Kendt, "Linda Winer: I'm a Critic, Not a Click-Chaser," *American Theater*, April 24, 2017. Accessed February 12, 2019, https://www.americantheatre.org/2017/04/24/linda-winer-im-a-critic-not-a-click-chaser/.

4. "Roundtable: Is Jesse Green the Right Choice for the *New York Times*?" *Exeunt*, April 10, 2017. Accessed February 12, 2019, http://exeuntnyc.com/features/not-new-day-new-york-times/.

5. "Roundtable," http://exeuntnyc.com/features/not-new-day-new-york-times/.

6. Weinert-Kendt, "Linda Winer," https://www.americantheatre.org/2017/04/24/linda-winer-im-a-critic-not-a-click-chaser/ .

7. Ben Brantley, "Review: Ye Olde Go-Go's Songs Hit the Renaissance in 'Head over Heels,'"*New York Times*, July 26, 2018.

8. Emily Mann, interview by Carey Purcell, March 15, 2019.

9. Gerard Raymond, "Interview: Kate Bornstein on Their Broadway Debut in 'Straight White Men,'" Slant, July 11, 2018. Accessed February 12, 2019, https://www.slantmagazine.com/interviews/pretty-damn-bowie-kate-bornstein-on-their-broadway-debut-in-straight-white-men/.

10. Adam Kampe, "Actor Ty Defoe on Performing in 'Straight White Men,'" Arts Work Blog, *National Endowment for the Arts*, December 12, 2018. Accessed February 12, 2019, https://www.arts.gov/art-works/2018/actor-ty-defoe-performing-straight-white-men.

11. Brennan Carley, "Peppermint Is Turning Broadway on Its Head," *GQ*, September 6, 2018. Accessed February 12, 2019, https://www.gq.com/story/peppermint-is-turning-broadway-on-its-head.

12. Michael Schulman, "'Head over Heels' Reviewed: A Trans-Positive Spin on a Sixteenth-Century Romance, with Help from the Go Go's," *New Yorker*, July 27, 2018. Accessed February 12, 2019, https://www.newyorker.com/culture/culture-desk/head-over-heels-reviewed-a-trans-positive-spin-on-a-sixteenth-century-romance-with-help-from-the-go-gos.

13. Louis Peitzman, "'Head over Heels' Is the Most Radically Queer Show on Broadway," *Buzzfeed*, July 27, 2018. Accessed February 12, 2019, https://www.buzzfeednews.com/article/louispeitzman/head-over-heels-is-the-most-radically-queer-show-on-broadway.

14. Carley, "Peppermint Is Turning Broadway on Its Head," https://www.gq.com/story/peppermint-is-turning-broadway-on-its-head.

15. Pooya Mohseni, interview by Carey Purcell, April 9, 2019.

16. Alexis Soloski, "Transgender Playwrights: 'We Should Get to Tell Our Own Stories First,'" *New York Times*, November 9, 2016. Accessed February 12, 2019, https://www.nytimes.com/2016/11/13/theater/transgender-playwrights-we-should-get-to-tell-our-own-stories-first.html.

17. Jim Sullivan, "John Cameron Mitchell Reflects on 'Hedwig and the Angry Inch' Years Later," *Wbur*, February 26, 2019. Accessed February 28, 2019, https://www.wbur.org/artery/2019/02/26/john-cameron-mitchell-hedwig-and-the-angry-inch.

18. Soloski, "Transgender Playwrights," https://www.nytimes.com/2016/11/13/theater/transgender-playwrights-we-should-get-to-tell-our-own-stories-first.html.

19. Mohseni, interview by Carey Purcell.

20. Dan Cairns, "Patti LuPone Interview: Why I'm Coming Back to London for 'Company,'" *Times*, September 23, 2018. Accessed February 28, 2019, https://www.thetimes.co.uk/article/patti-lupone-interview-why-im-coming-back-to-london-for-company-0jgzkprhn.

21. Henry Hitchings, "'Company' Review: Marianne Elliott's Glorious Show Savors Sondheim's Subtleties," *Evening Standard*, October 17, 2018. Accessed February 28, 2019, https://www.standard.co.uk/go/london/theatre/company-review-theatre-marianne-elliott-sondheim-a3964531.html.

22. Sophie Gilbert, "A Classic Sondheim Musical Gets a Thrilling Twist," *Atlantic*, October 19, 2018. Accessed February 28, 2019, https://www.theatlantic.com/entertainment/archive/2018/10/rosalie-craig-and-patti-lupone-shine-in-a-gender-flipped-company/573262/.

23. "Token Theater Friends: Dominique Morisseau Wants More Diverse Audiences," *American Theatre*, April 4, 2019. Accessed April 28, 2019, https://www.americantheatre.org/2019/04/04/token-theatre-friends-dominique-morisseau-wants-more-diverse-audiences/.

24. John Moore, "American Theater's Leadership Vacuum: Who Will Fill It?" *American Theatre*, August 31, 2017. Accessed April 28, 2019, https://www.americantheatre.org/2017/08/31/american-theatres-leadership-vacuum-who-will-fill-it/.

25. Sarah Greenman, "Leading Women: Four Theaters Name Women to Top Posts," *Women Arts*, February 14, 2019. Accessed April 10, 2019, https://www.womenarts.org/2018/02/14/leading-women-at-four-theaters/.

26. Marsha Norman, interview by Carey Purcell, April 2, 2019.

27. Mann, interview by Carey Purcell.

INDEX

Als, Hilton, 37, 64, 224
American Theatre Wing, 109
ancient Greece: family, 2–3; festivals, 1
Aristophanes, 4, 7, 9
Arts Council (Great Britain), 54, 55, 56, 57, 58, 59

Baby, 91–94
backlash: to feminism, 84–85, 88, 89, 93, 97; to women writing, 16, 18, 28, 30
Backlash (Susan Faludi), 81, 84
Baker, Elizabeth, 22–23
Beane, Douglas Carter, 153, 155
Bechdel, Alison, 171, 172, 176, 181–182, 188, 190. *See also Fun Home* (book)
Behn, Aphra, 15, 19–21, 22
Bornstein, Kate, 231–232
Brantley, Ben, 40, 122, 125, 128, 133, 135, 142, 145, 147, 173, 180, 190, 191, 209, 220, 228, 229, 231

Camille, 74
Caroline, or Change, 175
Carroll, Vinette, 115
Case, Sue-Ellen, 83
Centlivre, Susanna, 17
Chains, 22
child care, 167–169
The Children's Hour, 33–36, 37–38
Churchill, Caryl, 57, 77–78

Cinderella, 153–157; 2013 Broadway production, 155–157, 158; *Cendrillon*, 153; Grimms fairy tale, 153
The Color Purple, 145, 146–148, 207. *See also* Walker, Alice
Comden, Betty, 112, 113
Company, 2018 revival, 235–236
"The Count," 165–166, 239
Cryer, Nancy, 66, 67. *See also* Ford, Gretchen; *I'm Getting My Act Together and Taking It on the Road*
Cunning Stunts, 54–55

Damashek, Barbara, 113, 117, 214
Daniels, Sarah, 84–89
De Angelis, April, 89–90
Defoe, Ty, 231–232
divorce: law, 2, 29, 30; in plays, 18, 29–30
Dolan, Jill, 104, 153, 183, 203
Dworkin, Andrea, 86–88

Eclipsed, 207, 209–214. *See also* Gurira, Danai; Tommy, Liesl
Elliott, Marianne, 127–128, 194, 235, 236
employment of women, 170, 239
Ensler, Eve, 140–143

Faludi, Susan, 81, 84
The Feminine Mystique, 85, 103, 150
feminism: 1970s, 51–78; 1980s, 81–89, 93; 1990s, 138–143; 2010, 158–159;

backlash to, 84, 85, 88, 89, 92, 97
*for colored girls who have considered
    suicide when the rainbow is enuf*,
    62–66, 112. *See also* Shange, Ntozake
Ford, Gretchen, 66, 67. *See also* Cryer,
    Nancy; *I'm Getting My Act Together
    and Taking It on the Road*
Friedan, Betty, 85, 103
Fun Home (book), 178; College of
    Charleston controversy, 187–188. *See
    also* Bechdel, Alison
Fun Home (musical), 171–172, 176,
    179–182; Tony Awards, 191–194. *See
    also* Kron, Lisa; Tesori, Jeanine

gay marriage, 189, 195
Gay Sweatshop, 59–61
Gems, Pam, 55, 71–75
Getting Out, 95
Gionfriddo, Gina, 150, 151–152, 153
Gold, Sam, 179, 187, 193
Goldsberry, Renee Elise, 222–223
Green, Jesse, 135, 142, 184, 194, 212, 213,
    214, 220, 221, 229
Gurira, Danai, 209–210, 213, 214
Gussow, Mel, 64, 75, 96, 101, 103, 117,
    228

Hamilton (musical), 207, 220–225
Hamilton, Cicely, 24, 26–28
Hansberry, Lorraine, 40–49, 111. *See also
    A Raisin in the Sun*
"Having It All," 81–82, 91, 94, 99, 151,
    200, 201, 203
Head over Heels, 231, 232–233
The Heidi Chronicles (2015 Broadway
    revival), 199–203
The Heidi Chronicles (original Broadway
    production), 96–97, 102–105, 111, 117,
    150, 151–152
Hellman, Lillian, 33–40, 111
Hill, Anita, 81, 83, 85
Holzman, Winnie, 143–144, 145. *See also
    Wicked*
hormone imbalance, 61
How I Learned to Drive, 128–129
Hrotsvitha, xv, 9–13
Hynes, Gary, 119, 122–124

If/Then, 160–165
*I'm Getting My Act Together and Taking It
    on the Road*, 66–69; 2013 performance,
    68–69. *See also* Cryer, Nancy; Ford,
    Gretchen
Indecent, 111, 133–134. *See also*
    Taichman, Rebecca; Vogel, Paula
intersectionality, 139–140
Isherwood, Charles, 68, 126, 141, 142,
    152–153, 202, 212, 228
Isn't It Romantic, 98–101

Jones, Chris, 46, 125, 215, 228
Jordan, Julia, 165, 167, 168

The Kilroys, 204
Knightley, Keira, 208, 209
Kron, Lisa, 113, 171, 172–173, 183, 185,
    189, 193. *See also Fun Home* (musical)

Landau, Tina, 113
Lauper, Cyndi, 113, 188
Lavery, Bryony, 58, 70–71
League of Professional Theatre Women,
    105, 166, 239
Lee, Young Jean, 231–232
Lilly Awards, 165, 239
The Lion King, 119, 122. *See also* Taymor,
    Julie
The Little Foxes, 36–37
Lysistrata, 7, 9

MacKinnon, Pam, 126–127, 200, 207, 238
Manley, Delarivier, 15
Mann, Emily, 115–117, 204, 231, 237,
    239–240
Marks, Peter, 216, 228
marriage, 18; in plays, 6, 18–19, 22, 27–28,
    29; laws, 2, 7, 18–19, 21. *See also*
    ancient Greece
Masterpieces, 86–89
Meadow, Lynne, 207
Medea, 6
Miranda, Lin-Manuel, 220–225
Mohseni, Pooya, 233, 235
Monstrous Regiment, 56, 57, 58–59
motherhood: character/representation, 61,
    76, 90–94, 103, 173, 184–186, 217;
    working in theater, 167–170. *See also*

Baby; *Parent Artist Advocacy League*
Mrs. Worthington's Daughters, 59
myths, Greek, 3, 4–5

Nelson, Jessie, 113, 214
New York Times theater critic, 228–230;
  female critics, 230–231. *See also*
  Winer, Linda
'night, Mother, 94–95, 96, 112. *See also*
  Norman, Marsha
Norman, Marsha, 94, 95–96, 112, 113,
  146, 165, 239; critical response to, 95.
  See also The Color Purple; Lilly
  Awards; *'night, Mother*; *The Secret
  Garden*
Nottage, Lynn, 63, 134–136, 214

Once on This Island, 119

Parent Artist Advocacy League (PAAL),
  168–170. *See also* Spencer-Hewitt,
  Rachel
Parity Productions, 227
Paulus, Diane, 126, 127, 207, 214,
  214–215, 218
Peppermint, 232–233
Perry, Antoinette, 107–111; childhood,
  107; critical response to, 109; directing,
  108–109, 110; marriage, 108;
  partnership with Brock Pemberton,
  108–109, 110
Piaf, 74
Pix, Mary, 15, 16
pornography, 86–88, 132. *See also*
  Daniels, Sarah; *Masterpieces*; Vogel,
  Paula: *Hot 'N' Throbbing*

Queen Christina, 55, 73
queer representation: in *Fun Home*,
  182–183, 190; lesbian representation,
  237; nonbinary representation, 231,
  231–232; trans representation, 232–235
queer theater: *Any Woman Can*, 60–61;
  Mister X, 60. *See also* Gay Sweatshop

A Raisin in the Sun, 41–45, 46. *See also*
  Lorraine Hansberry
Rapture, Blister, Burn, 150–153; critical
  response to, 152–153

Reza, Yasmina, 111
Rich, Frank, 39, 76, 77, 78, 95, 228
Robins, Elizabeth, 24–25. *See also Votes
  for Women!*
Rutherford and Son, 23, 59

Schulman, Susan, 118–119
Schwartz, Stephen, 143–144. *See also
  Wicked*
The Secret Garden, 112–113
Shange, Ntozake, 62–66. *See also for
  colored girls who have considered
  suicide when the rainbow is enuf*
Shapiro, Anna D., 125–126
The Sign in Sidney Brustein's Window,
  46–47
Sowerby, Githa, 22, 23–24
Spencer-Hewitt, Rachel, 168–169
Stage Door Canteen, 109
Straight White Men, 231–232
Stroman, Susan, 124
suffragettes, 24; in plays, 23, 24, 25–26,
  27, 28. *See also* Baker, Elizabeth;
  Hamilton, Cicely; Robins, Elizabeth
Swados, Elizabeth, 112, 113, 117, 214
Sweat, 111, 134, 135–136

Taichman, Rebecca, 128, 133–134
Taymor, Julie, 119–122
Teaneck Tanzi, 75–76
Tesori, Jeanine, 113, 171, 173–176, 183,
  184, 189, 192, 193, 194. *See also Fun
  Home* (musical)
Thatcher, Margaret, 56, 57, 58
Therese Raquin, 207, 208–209
Third Wave feminism, 137–139, 148. *See
  also* Walker, Rebecca
Tommy, Liesl, 209, 212, 213, 214
Tony Award, 65, 91, 94, 103, 107,
  111–128, 134, 136. *See also Fun Home*
  (musical); Hynes, Gary; Perry,
  Antoinette; Taymor, Julie
Top Girls, 77–78; 2009 Broadway revival,
  78
Trotter, Catharine, 15

Uncommon Women and Others, vii, 97

The Vagina Monologues, 140–143. *See also* Ensler, Eve
Vogel, Paula, 111, 128–134, 136; *And Baby Makes Seven*, 131; *The Baltimore Waltz*, 129–130; *Hot 'N' Throbbing*, 132
Votes for Women!, 24, 25–26

Waitress, 113, 207, 214–219; all-female team, 215, 218–219; critical response to, 215–217, 218–219
Walker, Alice, 146, 147, 148. *See also The Color Purple*
Walker, Rebecca, 137, 148
Wandor, Michelene, 53, 57, 60, 61, 104

Wasserstein, Wendy, vii, 93, 96–105, 111, 117, 152, 153. *See also The Heidi Chronicles*; *Isn't It Romantic*; *Uncommon Women and Others*
Wicked, 143–145. *See also* Holzman, Winnie; Schwartz, Stephen
Winer, Linda, 145, 184, 230
Wolf, Stacy, 138–139, 148
Women's Project Theater, 70, 234, 239
Women's Street Theatre Group, 52–53
Women's Theatre Group, 55, 56, 70
Women's Voices Theater Festival, 205–206

Zimmerman, Mary, 111, 124–125

ABOUT THE AUTHOR

Carey Purcell is a New York City–based journalist, theater critic, and author. For more than a decade, she has contributed writing on culture and current events to such publications as the *New York Times*, the *Guardian*, *Vanity Fair*, the *Nation*, the *Village Voice*, and *American Theatre Magazine*. She worked as the features editor at Playbill.com, incorporating issue-based reporting and gender parity into its arts coverage. A member of the League of Professional Theatre Women, the Drama Desk, and the Outer Critics Circle, Carey has a BS in print and multimedia journalism and a BA in writing, literature, and publishing from Emerson College. This is her debut nonfiction book.